A Study of Concepts

C000151507

Representation and Mind
Hilary Putnam and Ned Block, editors

Representation and Reality
Hilary Putnam

Explaining Behavior: Reasons in a World of Causes
Fred Dretske

The Metaphysics of Meaning
Jerrold J. Katz

A Theory of Content and Other Essays
Jerry A. Fodor

The Realistic Spirit: Wittgenstein, Philosophy, and the Mind
Cora Diamond

The Unity of the Self
Stephen L. White

The Imagery Debate
Michael Tye

The Rediscovery of the Mind
John R. Searle

A Study of Concepts
Christopher Peacocke

A Study of Concepts

Christopher Peacocke

A Bradford Book
The MIT Press
Cambridge, Massachusetts
London, England

© 1992 Massachusetts Institute of Technology
All rights reserved. No part of this book may be reproduced in any form by any electronic or mechanical means (including photocopying, recording, or information storage and retrieval) without permission in writing from the publisher.

This book was set in Times Roman by DEKR Corporation and was printed and bound in the United States of America.

Second MIT Press paperback edition, 1999

Library of Congress Cataloging-in-Publication Data

Peacocke, Christopher.
 A study of concepts / Christopher Peacocke.
     p.   cm. — (Representation and mind)
 "A Bradford book."
 Includes bibliographical references (p.   ) and index.
 ISBN 978-0-262-16133-6 (hc.: alk. paper)—978-0-262-66097-6 (pb.: alk. paper)
 1. Concepts. I. Title. II. Series.
BD181.P43   1992
121'.4—dc20   91-46487
                                                                          CIP

10 9 8 7 6

For Alexander and Antonia

Contents

Preface

This book is based on material developed in lectures and seminars, first at London University and then at Oxford University, over the years 1988–1990. It was my good fortune to be able to give two of the series of seminars with Martin Davies. As so often before, I learned much from his comments and from his advice on earlier drafts of this book. Of the many other occasions on which parts of this work have been presented, I wish to mention also the valuable discussions after the three lectures I gave to the Princeton Philosophy Colloquium in December 1988.

Much of the material of this book will have appeared, usually in earlier versions, in the articles listed in the bibliography as Peacocke 1988, 1989a, 1989b, 1990a, 1990b, 1991a, and 1992. Rather than simply collect these papers together, with annotations and additional essays, I have aimed here to give an integrated and continuous treatment of the subject matter. This is not least because the order in which the ideas in the articles occurred to me is very far from a rational order of presentation. Indeed, the treatment of concepts presented in the first chapter of this book is arguably an explicit statement of a framework presupposed in my previous book, *Thoughts: An Essay on Content* (Peacocke 1986b). (I have, though, resisted any temptation to rewrite that book too.)

Concept possession is such a fundamental subject in philosophy and the ramifications of any theory of the matter are so extensive that no one book can hope to do justice to all its aspects. I have not found it easy to decide on which ramifications should be included and which omitted. Any drawing of the line inevitably excludes highly relevant adjacent territory. In the end, I have been guided by a desire not to overstretch the reader's goodwill and by the thought that the later pages of even the most significant works of philosophy tend to receive less attention when they number well above three hundred. Two topics in particular for which the account presented here has immediate consequences, and which I have not included, are the theory of the acquisition of concepts and the theory of the relations between concept possession and linguistic understanding. Indeed, as the reader proceeds, it will become clear that my goal in trying to provide a theory of concepts is a natural analogue of the goal, in the philosophy of language, of providing what Michael Dummett (1975) calls a full-blooded theory of meaning. I intend to write more elsewhere on the relations between my theory of concepts and the theory of linguistic meaning.

Conversations over the years with Stephen Schiffer have been invaluable to me. As I was developing this treatment of concepts, his formidable *Remnants of Meaning* appeared (1987). As will rapidly become apparent, we are in disagreement on almost all the major issues in the theory of conceptual content. Attempting to provide an account that meets his objections has been a great stimulus. Even where the present text is not explicitly considering his views, the desire to develop an approach that meets those of his constraints I accept has been a driving force. Where I disagree with his constraints, I have tried to give explicit arguments.

The comments of many other philosophers have helped me very substantially. I thank Akeel Bilgrami, Simon Blackburn, John Campbell, Bill Child, Paul Churchland, Adrian Cussins, Michael Dummett, Dorothy Edgington, Graeme Forbes, Elizabeth Fricker, Gilbert Harman, James Higginbotham, Mark Johnston, David Lewis, Saul Kripke, Michael Martin, John McDowell, Ruth Millikan, Michael Morris, Philip Pettit, Leah Savion, Michael Smith, John Skorupski, David Wiggins, Timothy Williamson, and Crispin Wright. I am also grateful for the outstanding copyediting skills of Alan Thwaits and for the use of the excellent research facilities of Indiana University, Bloomington, where this book was completed. I also thank the editor of *Mind* and Oxford University Press, the owners of the copyright of my 1991a article, for permission to draw on that material here; Stephen Palmer and the Academic Press for permission to reproduce figure 3.2 of chapter 3; and Nigel Shardlow for preparing the index.

Introduction

This work is primarily a philosophical investigation of concepts. It has an aim that has long been part of philosophy. It aims to derive consequences about thought from positive and negative theses about the nature of concepts. Hume, Kant, Wittgenstein early and late, Quine, and recent realists and antirealists have all carried through projects of that general description. While agreeing on little else, all these thinkers are committed to holding that without a general treatment of concepts one will not have a satisfying philosophy.

Though this project is primarily philosophical, the particular way in which it is carried out does have consequences for those branches of the cognitive sciences concerned with concepts. At various points I try to say what it is to possess certain concepts. Until we have an account of what it is, as a constitutive matter, to possess a given concept, we cannot give full, or fully justified, answers to such empirical questions as What is the subpersonal, computational basis of the subject's possession of the concept? or How is this concept acquired?

The opening chapter of this book proposes a general form that should be instantiated by an account of any concept and elaborates various aspects of the proposal. Developing such a proposal is a pivotal task for a philosophical theory of concepts. The general form sets a standard to which accounts of particular concepts must conform. Insofar as certain alleged concepts are declared to be spurious, as beyond the limits of genuine thought, it must also be by appeal to properties of this general form that such claims are justified. I further argue in this first chapter that recognition of the appropriate general form allows us to steer a middle course between more extreme views about concepts canvassed in recent years.

The second chapter seeks to explain some quite general properties of thought by tracing them back to the nature of this general form. The properties to be explained include the recombinability of elements of the contents of attitudes, what Fodor calls the systematicity of thought. I argue that this and related phenomena are neither stipulative nor merely empirical but are rather consequences of the referential properties of concepts. The chapter notes certain affinities with, and also differences from, the position Wittgenstein developed in the *Tractatus*. I think that the remarkable power that certain parts of the *Tractatus* can still exercise over us, even when we have been steeped in more recent philosophy, is explained by the fact that many of the insights captured there are fundamental truths at the level of thought, sometimes misformulated as points at the level of reference.

Many concepts are individuated in part by their relations to perceptual concepts that refer to objects and properties in the thinker's immediate environment. The proper treatment of perceptual concepts themselves is thus a central issue for a general theory of concepts. I make a start on the topic in chapter 3. According to the view adopted in this chapter, conceptual content rests ultimately on several kinds of nonconceptual but nevertheless representational contents. I sketch an outline of these kinds, their relations to one another and to conceptual contents, and their role in psychological explanation. This chapter is only a brief overview of a territory that seems to me highly structured and worthy of much further investigation.

The next two chapters address general questions that must be faced by any theory of concepts, whatever its shape. Chapter 4 is concerned with the ontology of concepts taken for granted in the earlier chapters. I treat the problem of the legitimacy of an ontology of concepts as a special case of the general problem of the application to the empirical world of discourse apparently mentioning abstract objects. Parallels are developed with other forms of discourse in which abstract objects are mentioned in the description of the empirical world. These parallels suggest a positive account of the practice of mentioning concepts in the description of the empirical mental states of thinkers, a positive account that also supports the claim of legitimacy for the practice.

The other general challenge for a theory of concepts is that of accounting for and elucidating their normative dimension. Chapter 5 attempts to characterize the normative aspects of concepts and to account for their presence within the framework of the theory of concepts developed so far. Unlike many recent writers, I do not believe that natural-teleological approaches give a full or even a correct account of the normative dimension of concepts and content. I do, though, attempt to give a theory that is broadly naturalistic and to say what is involved in a naturalistic approach.

Chapter 6 is on the concept of belief. This chapter can be regarded to an extent as a case study, a partial treatment of a particular concept in accordance with the forms proposed in the earlier chapters. But there are other reasons for taking a theoretical interest in this particular concept. Suppose you sincerely attribute to Ralph the belief that whales are mammals. It is plausible that the truth of this attribution depends in part upon Ralph's satisfying the possession condition for an appropriate concept of whales and for a similar concept of the property of being a mammal. It is also plausible that your sincere attribution of the belief must be sensitive, in a way to be elucidated, to this dependence upon Ralph's satisfying those possession conditions. In the chapter on belief, I elaborate and defend these intuitively plausible claims in a way that draws upon the treatment of concepts in the preceding chapters.

A second reason for attending to the concept of belief is that epistemological and cognitive phenomena that ought to be explained by a theory of a particular concept are vividly present for the concept of belief. I propose some explanations of these phenomena. The explanations appeal to general principles relating the theory of concepts to epistemology. A third reason for considering the concept of belief is that it leads one to reflect on certain structural constraints on the coherence of putative accounts of a particular concept. I attempt to formulate one of these constraints and also to consider its application to accounts of other concepts.

The penultimate chapter discusses briefly the large question of the proper relation between philosophical and psychological theories of concepts. It disputes the claim that such theories can be relatively independent of one another. It also discusses ways in which the present approach to concepts endorses the claim that there can be an empirical, psychological explanation of a thinker's proceeding in one way rather than another when applying a concept to a new case. The chapter argues that this aspect of the theory supports the thesis that the correctness of a thought is an objective matter.

In the final chapter I make some regulative use of the theory of concepts developed in this book. I argue that certain putative hypotheses and concepts, widely regarded as spurious, can indeed be shown not to meet the requirements upon genuine concepts that emerge from the treatment in this book. The principles that rule out the spurious conceptions are free of commitment to any kind of verificationism. A conception of thought emerges that is genuinely realistic but on which it is not true that anything goes.

Conventions

For clarity I have adopted the following conventions. I use *italics* for terms that denote concepts and variables that range over concepts. For variables that range over entities of other types, I use **bold sans serif** type. Script $\mathcal{A}$ in $\mathcal{A}(C)$ is a schematic letter indicating a condition on concepts.

A Study of Concepts

1 Individuating Concepts

1.1 The Aims of a Philosophical Theory of Concepts

There can be few areas of philosophy where the issues do not at some point turn on the nature of a particular concept. Anyone who has reflected philosophically on first-person thought, the exercise of a perceptual concept, our grasp of some psychological notion, or our use of an arithmetic concept will rapidly come to ask the question, What is distinctive of mastery of this concept? and he will attempt to put his answer to work. Anyone engaged in such reflection has reason to be concerned with the philosophical study of concepts.

A theory of concepts is also of philosophical interest in its own right, and the motivation for developing it does not have to start from some specific problematic concept. The motivation may rather be the desire to explain some phenomenon exhibited by a more or less broad class of concepts. Some concepts have the property that they can combine with others to form complete propositional contents that can be true though unverifiable. What is common to all these concepts that allows for this possibility? Again, it has often been noted that all indexical or demonstrative concepts have distinctive epistemological and psychological properties. If we are convinced that the properties are genuine, we should ideally aim for an explanation of these properties that flows from a substantive theory of what is common to all demonstrative concepts. At the most general level, we may have principles that hold for all concepts whatsoever. One candidate for such a principle is Gareth Evans's "Generality Constraint" (1982, chap. 4, sec. 3). To oversimplify a little, this constraint entails that if a thinker is capable of attitudes to the content Fa and possesses the singular concept b, then he is capable of having attitudes to the content Fb. If this principle is an entirely general truth, there must be something about the nature of concepts in general which explains its truth. A good theory of concepts must say what it is.

We need to be clear about the subject matter of a theory of concepts. The term "concept" has by now come to be something of a term of art. The word does not have in English a unique sense that is theoretically important. Those who think it does should consider the contribution made to our subject by Woody Allen, when in his film *Annie Hall* he has one of his characters in the entertainment industry say, "Right now it's only a notion, but I think I can get money to make it into a concept, and later turn it into an idea." This quotation suggests that we would not make progress by undertaking an analysis of the word "concept" in the style of 1950s linguistic philosophy. I will be using the term "concept" stipulatively as follows:

Distinctness of Concepts   Concepts C and D are distinct if and only if there are two complete propositional contents that differ at most in that one contains C substituted in one or more places for D, and one of which is potentially informative while the other is not.

This use of the notion corresponds to one strand, but only one strand, in the everyday notion of a concept. By the standard of the criterion I am adopting, the conceptual constituent *12 noon* and the conceptual constituent *now* in your judgement *It is now 12 noon* are distinct. The content of that judgement is informative, whereas *It is now now* is not. (Note my use of italics for concepts.) Similarly, *I* as used in thought by Descartes is distinct from *the author of the "Meditations";* provably equivalent logical or mathematical concepts may be distinct; and one and the same empirical property, such as a shape property, may be presented by different concepts (see chap. 3, sec. 3). As I use the notion, concepts may be of any category: singular, predicative, or of higher levels.

My concepts, even in the case of a first-level predicative concept, are thus distinct from what are called "concepts" in English translations of Frege, i.e., functions from objects to truth values. My concepts are also to be clearly distinguished from properties.[1] There can be many different concepts of the same property. To mistake the requirements on a theory of a concept for requirements on a theory of a property, and vice versa, can lead to errors and spurious problems. The results of such a mistake are comparable to those that result in the singular case from confusing theories of modes of presentation with theories about the objects so presented. Several illustrations of such a state of affairs will emerge in this work. The point still holds for theorists who think that to believe in a tripartite classification into concepts, properties, and extensions is to believe in one level too many. Even if the roles of the property are severally absorbed into those of the concept or those of the extension, the theory of this book is still a theory of the level of concepts or modes of presentation.

The concepts that concern us are at the level of Frege's senses, since they are individuated by considerations of cognitive significance. You can, though, still have a theoretical interest in these concepts even if you are quite unhappy with some uses of the notion of sense in the semantics of natural language. In particular, there is no commitment in my enterprise to assuming that for every significant expression of English, there is such a thing as the concept expressed by it. It is sufficient for significance in the language that the expression has a reference: an object, property or suitable function. It is not required that it be associated with a concept in the present sense. More generally, the theory developed here is neutral on the question of whether meaning in the public language always, sometimes, or never cuts finer than reference.

In the literature of the cognitive sciences, the term "concept" is often assigned a different sense from that chosen here. Sometimes it is used to mean *mental representation*. Thus, for instance, Jackendoff 1989, 73. Sometimes it is used to capture what I would call central but inessential beliefs involving the concept. This use is found in both artificial intelligence (Hayes 1979) and psychology (Keil 1989). Yet again, it was once frequently used to mean *prototype*. All these notions are of great interest and importance, but they each are to be distinguished from concepts in my sense. It is possible for one and the same concept to receive different mental representations in different individuals. Again, what is in fact a relatively central belief for us, such as the belief that rain is water, can be informative to someone from a desert country who already possesses the concept *water*. And it is well known that it need not even be true, let alone uninformative, that all and only grandmothers fall under the prototype (small, old, fragile, etc.) associated in some cultures with the concept *grandmother*. I do not mean to devalue any of these other notions.[2] I will be relying only on the point that concepts as I am delineating them form a subject of proper philosophical interest. Recognition of the level of concepts in the present sense is also needed for a proper description of cases in which there is a change of prototype or of relatively central beliefs associated with a concept. Indeed, as elsewhere, describing a case as one of change, rather than as one of replacement, is correct only if there is something that persists through the change, and it is the concept in my sense that so persists.

With this preliminary clarification of subject matter, we can consider the tasks of a philosophical account of concepts. These tasks fall into at least five very broad areas. First, a theory must be given of the general form to be taken by a philosophical account of a particular concept. This general form must be motivated and shown to be appropriate for concepts as they are understood here.

Second, there is the task of tracing out the philosophical consequences of this general form. Any plausible general form will restrict the range of legitimate accounts of particular concepts. Insofar as there persists a philosophical ambition to derive interesting philosophical results from the idea of a concept in general, as Kant might say, it is in this part of the theory of concepts that the ambition would have to be realized.

Third, there is the development of accounts of particular concepts, where the accounts meet the general form that emerges when the first task is carried out. Obviously, these first and third tasks cannot rationally be carried out independently of one another. On the one hand, if we have a manifestly acceptable account of a particular concept, we had better have a general form that includes that account. On the other, if we have good reasons for accepting a general form, that will constrain the acceptable accounts of particular concepts.

Fourth, we have to elaborate the consequences of the accounts we accept of various particular concepts. Indeed, all the phenomena that depend only upon the identity of a particular concept ought to be explained by reference to an account of that concept. The same applies to phenomena dependent only upon the identity of a certain class of concepts. The phenomena to be explained may be semantic, epistemological, psychological, metaphysical, or of any other kind, provided that their source is the nature of the concept or concepts in question. It is for this reason that a full theory of concepts would include a substantial part of philosophy.

Finally, there are questions to be addressed that are in one way or another metatheoretical issues about the philosophical theory of concepts developed in carrying out the first four tasks. There are questions about how the philosophical theory relates to other theories about the application of concepts. The other theories may be of any kind, from empirical, psychological theories to metaphysical (or antimetaphysical) theories about the application of concepts. There are also questions about whether the philosophical theory of concepts satisfies various constraints whose satisfaction we would demand of any acceptable theory. Many, for instance, would today insist that the theory fit properly into a naturalistic world view. Also, many would have questions to raise about the ontology of a theory of concepts.

This list of tasks is by no means exhaustive. Among other things, it omits the very important issue of the acquisition of concepts. I will also not be giving anything like a complete treatment of the topics that are on this list. But I will try to say something about each of the five areas. The structure of this book does not in fact correspond at all closely to the divisions between the areas on this list. That is mainly because certain concepts, in particular perceptual concepts, are so fundamental that their treatment affects one's treatment of other concepts, one's view of the general structure of a theory of concepts, and one's view of the ways in which the metatheoretical issues might be resolved. In the remainder of this chapter I make a start on some issues in the first of the areas.

1.2 Possession and Individuation

Throughout this book I will try to respect the following principle:

Principle of Dependence There can be nothing more to the nature of a concept than is determined by a correct account of the capacity of a thinker who has mastered the concept to have propositional attitudes to contents containing that concept (a correct account of "grasping the concept").

Suppose that someone suggests there are concepts that do not conform to this principle. Then the respects in which these alleged concepts slice more finely than concepts that do conform to it must be nothing to us. The extra properties of these alleged concepts will play no role in propositional-attitude psychology. The Principle of Dependence is the concept-theoretic analogue of one of Dummett's principles about language (Dummett 1975). As a theory of meaning should be a theory of understanding, so a theory of concepts should be a theory of concept possession.

Accepting the Principle of Dependence opens up the possibility that we can simultaneously say in a single account what individuates a particular concept and also what it is to possess that concept. The general form that could be taken by such an account is this:

Simple Formulation   Concept F is that unique concept C to possess which a thinker must meet condition $\mathcal{A}(C)$.

For the enthusiasts, "C" is a genuine variable over concepts, and $\mathcal{A}$ is a schematic letter. The Principle of Dependence claims not merely that suitable instances of the displayed general form are true. The claim is stronger. The claim is that a suitably chosen true instance of the form individuates the concept it treats: it says what it is about the concept F that makes it the concept it is.

A simple example of the general form is the following treatment of the concept of conjunction.

Conjunction is that concept C to possess which a thinker must find transitions that are instances of the following forms primitively compelling, and must do so because they are of these forms:

$$
\frac{\begin{array}{c} p \\ q \end{array}}{p\,C\,q} \qquad \frac{p\,C\,q}{p} \qquad \frac{p\,C\,q}{q}
$$

To say that the thinker finds such transitions primitively compelling is to say this: (1) he finds them compelling; (2) he does not find them compelling because he has inferred them from other premises and/or principles; and (3) for possession of the concept C in question (here conjunction) he does not need to take the correctness of the transitions as answerable to anything else. (The thinker may in fact take them as answerable to something else. If he is a philosophical theorist himself, he may take them as ultimately answerable to requirements drawn from his theory of concepts. But neither having such theories nor even having some thought of them can be required for possession of the concept of conjunction.) In chapter 7, section 1, I will return to what is required for the form of a transition to be explanatory. What matters for present purposes is that there is nothing circular about this account of conjunction.

Another example of an account of the general form is the following treatment of universal quantification over the natural numbers. Such a quantifier is the unique second-level concept $Cx \ldots x \ldots$ to possess which a thinker must find certain inferences of the form

$$\frac{CxFx}{Fn}$$

primitively compelling. The inferences that he has to find primitively compelling are those involving a concept n for which the content n *is a natural number* is uninformative. It will be uninformative when n is a canonical concept of a natural number (a sense of a canonical numeral). It will also be uninformative when n is, for instance, the sense of a complex arithmetical expression. It is also required for possession of the concept of universal quantification over the natural numbers that the thinker find these inferences compelling because they are of the given form. The thinker is not required to find any other inferences essentially involving $Cx \ldots x \ldots$ primitively compelling.[3]

Logical constants are peculiarly simple cases, and conjunction is probably the simplest among them. Later I will be developing accounts of concepts that cannot be handled so easily. Meanwhile, here is a third example, for those acquainted with, and well-disposed to, the idea of such a sensational property of experience as the visual-field property red' (Peacocke 1983). (The prime indicates a sensational property.) According to the theory of *Sense and Content,* the perceptual concept *red* can be individualized as follows. The concept *red* is that concept C to possess which a thinker must meet these conditions:

1. He must be disposed to believe a content that consists of a singular perceptual-demonstrative mode of presentation m in predicational combination with C when the perceptual experience that makes m available presents its object in a red' region of the subject's visual field and does so in conditions he takes to be normal, and when in addition he takes his perceptual mechanisms to be working properly. The thinker must also be disposed to form the belief for the reason that the object is so presented.

2. The thinker must be disposed to believe a content consisting of any singular mode of presentation k not meeting all the conditions on m in (1) when he takes its object to have the primary quality ground

(if any) of the disposition of objects to cause experiences of the sort mentioned in (1).[4]

Again, this is hardly uncontroversial. But it is not circular; it does not presume that the thinker already possesses the concept *red*.[5] This account does tacitly use "red" in specifying a sensational property red' of the thinker's visual field. This is so because red' is fixed as that property characteristically instantiated in regions of the visual field in which red objects are properly perceived. But the sensational property red' is one that can be instantiated without the subject of the experience possessing the concept *red*. The account does not use "red" within the "that" clauses attributing propositional attitudes to the thinker.

Since my intent is purely illustrative at this point, I should emphasize that even if you think there are no sensational properties, you can still use techniques similar to those used in these possession conditions to avoid circularity in the account of possession of the concept *red*. Suppose that the concept *red* is regarded as not explicable in terms of sensational properties and is regarded as covering a range of more finely sliced shades of surfaces and volumes. A theorist who accepts that can adapt the above possession condition by removing from it the clause in (1) "presents its object in a red' region of the subject's visual field." That theorist should replace these words with "represents its object as having a shade that is in fact a shade of red." In the resulting possession condition, the concept *red* is used in classifying shades. It does not occur within the scope of the thinker's psychological attitudes.

The last point to be noted about the example of the possession condition for the concept *red* is that it attributes neither the concept of predicational structure nor the concept of predicational combination to the thinker himself. We as theorists of thought use those categories in picking out certain contents, beliefs in which have to have the specified sensitivities to perceptual experience. Nor should this be regarded as the imposition of categories on previously unstructured material. In formulating a possession condition, we are aiming at a correct constitutive characterization of a structure already and pre-philosophically employed in our ordinary attribution of content-involving mental states.

In a good account of a particular concept of the suggested general form, the condition $\mathscr{A}(C)$ may itself use the concept F outside the scope of the description of the thinker's psychological attitudes. The concept of conjunction does so occur in the above account of conjunction. More generally, it must be legitimate for an account of mastery of a concept to require that the thinker have some kind of sensitivity to instances of that concept in the world around him. In general, a formulation of the required sensitivity will have to make use of the very concept in question. What a good account must avoid is ineliminable mention of the concept F as the concept F within the scope of psychological attitudes of the thinker. If the account does mention the concept in *that* way, it will not have eludicated what it sets out to elucidate. Any ineliminable use of an expression for the concept F inside the scope of a psychological attitude context will just take for granted what we wanted to explain, possession of the concept. To avoid various kinds of trivialization, we should also require that it be a substantive claim in the theory of content that a concept C meeting the condition $\mathscr{A}(C)$ can only be the concept F. This identity must not follow simply by logic or by considerations independent of the theory of content.[6] When an account of this form for a given concept F is correct, I will say that it gives the *possession condition* for the concept F. Sometimes acceptance of certain patterns of reasons for judging a given content or for judging other contents on the basis of that content are internal to the identity of a content. In such cases the possession condition will mention them. I call the general form here outlined "the $\mathscr{A}(C)$ form."

A statement that individuates a concept by giving its possession condition is an identity statement. The above statement of the possession condition for conjunction, for instance, is of the following logical form:

Conjunction = the unique concept C such that for a thinker to possess C is for . . . C . . . .

This identity does not imply that the concept of conjunction is identical with the *concept* of being the unique concept C such that for a thinker to possess C is for . . . C . . . . On the contrary, those concepts are evidently distinct by Frege's criterion of informativeness. Quite generally, a definite description of the form "the unique concept C such that for a thinker to possess it is for . . . C . . ." always has a sense if its constituents have sense and are properly combined. But not all such definite descriptions refer. Even some of the descriptions of this form that superficially may seem to refer to a concept may fail to do so. I will give examples below. The moral is that we should be as careful in this area as we would elsewhere in distinguishing the following two things: the identity of the entities referred to, here concepts, and the identity of sense of the descriptions used in making the references.

Some relaxations consistent with the underlying motivation of the form $\mathscr{A}(C)$ make that general form less demanding. One relaxation is motivated by the fact that in a wide range of cases a set of concepts has the property that one can give an account of possession of any one of its members only by mentioning what is involved in possession of the other members of the set. In such cases we have a local holism. The pair of concepts *mass* and *force* constitute one such local holism. It is in the spirit of the $\mathscr{A}(C)$ form to accommodate several concepts simultaneously:

Formulation for Local Holisms   Concepts $F_1, \ldots, F_n$ are those concepts $C_1, \ldots, C_n$ to possess which a thinker must meet the condition $\mathscr{A}(C_1, \ldots, C_n)$.

On my understanding of "concept," the claim that a particular concept is involved in a local holism is much stronger than it would be if I followed one of the uses mentioned earlier, on which "concept" means something determined by a subject's central beliefs involving a concept in my sense. On that less strict notion, the account for almost any concept will mention other concepts.

Another modification of the $\mathscr{A}(C)$ form is needed to accommodate concepts that have an indexical or demonstrative character. Thinkers who at different times each think something of the form "It's so-and-so now" think thoughts with different truth conditions. But each of their thoughts contains a conceptual constituent of a common indexical type, the present-tense type. The same applies to the first-person thoughts of different thinkers, which each contain a constituent of a common first-person type. Each such indexical type of concept is individuated by the condition that has to be met for a thinker to possess an instance of that type. If the indexical or demonstrative type is H, then the schematic form appropriate for this case is this:

Formulation for Indexicals Indexical type H is that type T such that for any thinker and any time, for that thinker to possess a concept h of type T is for the thinker to meet condition $\mathcal{A}$ in relation to h at that time.

For different indexical types, it may be necessary to introduce other parameters besides the thinker and the time. To illustrate the general indexical form, let us concern ourselves with perceptual demonstratives, such as "that cup" or "that apple," of the sort made available to the thinker by his perceiving a cup or an apple in a particular way. Here I should give a general account of the individuation of concepts of the type fixed by the pair of an individuative concept F, such as *cup* or *apple,* and a way **W** of perceiving an object. I call the type in question "[F, **W**]." Gareth Evans argued that what is distinctive of a particular concept of this type is that the thinker's evaluation of thoughts containing it is controlled by perceptual information from the object perceived in way **W** (1982, 121–122). The details and the terms of art do not matter for present purposes. What matters is the structural point that such an account can be recast so that a perceptual-demonstrative type is individuated in a way conforming to the schema of the formulation for indexicals. When written out, the recast version is this:

Formulation for Perceptual Demonstratives [F, **W**] is that type T of singular concept such that for any thinker and time, if an object is the F perceived by the thinker at that time in way **W**, then for the thinker to possess a concept m of type T is for the thinker's evaluation of thoughts containing m to be controlled as thoughts about an F by perceptual information about the object, information acquired by his then perceiving it in way **W**.

A further relaxation of the $\mathcal{A}(C)$ form as first formulated starts from the observation that there may be an ordering of the "occurrences" of a given concept. When there is, it does not matter if the account of higher-level occurrences can be given in terms that presuppose the thinker's possession of the concept, provided what is presupposed involves only occurrences earlier in the ordering. This is an intuitively motivated refinement of the noncircularity requirement. Allowing such cases is actually implicit even in admitting as legitimate so humble a possession condition as that given above for conjunction. That possession condition individuates the concept of conjunction as it occurs in *p and q* containing **n** "occurrences" of conjunction, in terms of the contents *p* and *q,* which will both contain fewer than **n** occurrences of conjunction.

More generally, we will expect a hierarchy, a partial ordering, of concepts and families of concepts. The proposed possession conditions for one concept cannot presuppose the thinker's possession of a second concept if in turn the possession condition for the second presupposes the thinker's possession of the first. In such a case we could not claim to have individuated both concepts in terms of what it is to possess them. Similar reasoning excludes finite circles of dependence in possession conditions. In cases where we are tempted by such circular formulations, we are probably mischaracterizing something of a different and legitimate sort, a local holism.[7]

Where mastery of a concept requires grasp of a certain theory or type of theory, that fact will be incorporated in the possession condition. The point applies equally to a family of concepts that form a local holism. In fact, a common explanation of the existence of a local holism is that the concepts therein can be grasped only by their role in a certain kind of theory that contains all the other concepts in the family too. This certainly applies to the concepts *mass* and *force.* The "commonsense-framework theories" discussed by developmental psychologists arguably fall within this case too (Wellman 1990, chap. 5).[8]

Though in general I distinguish prototypes from concepts, in some special cases prototypes may enter the possession conditions for a particular concept. Mastery of a concept—particularly a perceptual, vague, and relatively observational concept—may involve knowledge of a prototype, a similarity relation, and a means of classifying objects in respect of such similarity to the prototype.[9] When a concept is genuinely like this, there will be a reflection of the fact in epistemic possibilities and impossibilities. It will not, for instance, be epistemically possible that something fails to fall under the concept when it is very close in the similarity space to the prototype mentioned in the possession condition.

Offering an account that instantiates the $\mathcal{A}(C)$ form is also consistent with acknowledging a major insight of the later Wittgenstein. This is the insight that an account of what is involved in employing one concept rather than another, following one rule rather than another, has at some point to mention what thinkers employing the concept find it natural to believe. This is the point Wittgenstein emphasizes when discussing the sense in which someone who has grasped a particular rule, possesses a particular concept, has already settled how to apply it in some future case. He characterized the claim he opposed thus:

"All the steps are really already taken" means: I no longer have any choice. The rule, once stamped with a particular meaning, traces the lines along which it is to be followed through the whole of space.

His reply was as follows:

But if something of this sort really were the case, how would it help?
  No; my description only made sense if it was to be understood symbolically.—I should have said: *This is how it strikes me.*
  When I obey a rule, I do not choose.
  I obey the rule *blindly*. (Wittgenstein 1958, sec. 219)

The consistency of both accepting this insight and endorsing the $\mathcal{A}(C)$ form can be illustrated by the possession condition for conjunction. Its mention of what is found primitively compelling respects the Wittgensteinian insight. A thinker who meets the possession condition for conjunction does not need examples of an impossible kind that somehow determines a unique correct application in a new case. Nor does he need to have surveyed in advance all the correct applications.[10] He just has to find certain transitions compelling in a certain way, and his finding them so has to have a particular explanation.

The fact that the possession condition for a concept makes reference to certain of the thinker's reactions does not make the concept anthropocentric. It is indeed true that if we possess the concept, we will find certain contents compelling in the circumstances specified in the possession condition. But the possession condition by which the concept is individuated need not be making reference to a peculiarly human reaction. Rather, the possession condition specifies outright a judgemental reaction, which an arbitrary thinker must be capable of if he is to have the concept.

This is one of the points at which it is also crucial to distinguish, in whatever vocabulary, between concepts and properties. Consider a theorist who sees that the Wittgensteinian insight discussed two paragraphs back can be incorporated into a possession condition, or an account of following a particular rule, but who also equates concepts and properties. He will then be led into making such claims as that the individuation of any property whatever (including, of course, mathematical and physical properties) depends ultimately on how certain thinkers find it natural to go on. But as long as we distinguish properties from concepts, no such entirely general claims about properties follow from an acknowledgment of Wittgensteinian insight. All that follows is that which concepts a thinker is capable of possessing depends on the ways in which he is capable of finding it natural to go on, and there is nothing implausible or metaphysically revisionary in that. The general topic of the different relations that different families of concepts bear to the properties they pick out is indeed a fascinating and important one. But no unrestricted conclusions about the subjectivity or relativity of all properties can be drawn from the present framework. Such conclusions can be reached only with additional premises about particular concepts and properties.[11]

The possession condition for conjunction plausibly specifies an intrinsic property of the thinker.[12] There is, however, nothing in these constraints to exclude the possibility that the possession condition for a given concept makes reference to the thinker's social and physical environment, nor indeed to exclude the possibility that it requires him to have a language. On the present approach, whether these possibilities are realized must depend upon further argument, and perhaps upon particular features of the concept in question. Consider, for example, the case of a possession condition for a relatively observational concept. It is plausible that such a possession condition will link mastery of the concept in question to the representational contents of the thinker's perceptual experience. Anyone who holds that the perceptual contents of experience are not fixed by the thinker's intrinsic properties will then be equally committed to saying that such a possession condition for an observational concept does not specify an intrinsic property of the thinker either.

I have already endorsed Frege's intuitive identity condition for concepts: (to speak in a multiply un-Fregean fashion) concept F is identical with concept G if and only if propositional contents differing only in that one has G where the other has F do not differ in potential informativeness. In the present framework, it is a condition of adequacy on proposed possession conditions for a pair of concepts that they be in *concord* with Frege's intuitive identity condition as applied to those concepts. What I mean by being "in concord" is this. Suppose we have proposed possession conditions $\mathcal{A}(C)$ for F and $\mathcal{B}(D)$ for G. Concord with Frege's condition then requires two things. First, if content ____ C ____ containing a concept individuated by the possession condition $\mathcal{A}(\ )$ can be informative when the counterpart content ____ D ____ containing the concept individuated by $\mathcal{B}(\ )$ is not, then ____ F ____ really can be informative when ____ G ____ is not. This requirement bites when, for example, F and G are logical concepts and the proposed possession conditions for each mention two different sets of introduction rules. Suppose that instances of the premises of one of the proposed introduction rules for F may rationally be accepted when no instances of the premises of the rules proposed for G are accepted. Then according to these proposals, the thinker may be in a position rationally to move to a conclusion containing F but not to the corresponding conclusion containing G. This must indeed be a real possibility if the proposals are to be acceptable.

The second requirement for concord is that if the possession conditions $\mathcal{A}(\ )$ and $\mathcal{B}(\ )$ are actually identical, then there are no circumstances in which thought ____ F ____ is informative while thought ____ G ____ is not. On the present approach, there can be no "bare truths" about differences in informativeness. To fail on that requirement would be to allow that the possession condition for a concept does not uniquely individuate it.

Neither the Principle of Dependence nor the $\mathcal{A}(C)$ form leads to an elimination or a reduction of the ontology of concepts or senses. You no more eliminate or reduce a concept by saying that it is determined by its possession condition than you eliminate or reduce a number by saying that the number is determined by the condition for it to number the things having a given property. Ontological issues about concepts are of great interest, both in themselves and for the theory of abstract objects more generally. I will defer further discussion of this issue until chapter 4 because it is not possible to discuss it fruitfully until we have more of the theory of concepts before us. I do note briefly, though, that substitutional quantification provides no rapid way of avoiding these ontological issues. If, as a possession condition, we formulate something that requires the truth of a sentence with a certain *expression* substituted for the variable "C" (previously taken as a variable over concepts), then the only suitable expressions are ones that express the concept in question. So, for instance, in the possession condition for conjunction, the only expressions that, when substituted for the variable "C," yield a truth (with the first "C" also deleted) are "and" and its synonyms. This gives a circular account of possession of the concept, for "and" then occurs within the scope of the thinker's propositional attitudes. The effect is general and inevitable for any corresponding replacement in any possession condition. A substitutional reading of the quantification would thus undermine the attraction of the $\mathcal{A}(C)$ form.

1.3   Concepts and Reference

The concepts I am discussing occur as constituents of complete propositional contents that are potentially evaluable as true or false. The truth value of a complete propositional content depends on properties of the semantic values of its constituent concepts. A concept, together with the world, determines a semantic value. In the present context, these platitudes impose an obligation on us. If a concept is individuated by its possession condition and a concept (together with the world) determines a semantic value, then we had better be able to establish that a possession condition, together with the world, determines a semantic value. If we cannot, then the claim that concepts are individuated by their possession conditions will not have been substantiated. The obligation exists whatever one's favored theory of references and semantic values for concepts other than singular concepts. As I have hinted, I agree with many other philosophers in supporting, for the predicative case, a threefold partition into the concept itself, the property to which it refers, and the extension of the property. If we say that the property itself together with the world determines an extension, we still have an obligation to say how the possession condition for the concept determines such a property. The situation can be diagrammed as below.

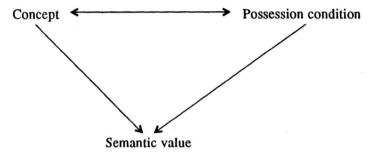

The need, on the present approach to concepts, for a theory of the determination of semantic value does not result merely from reverence for the classical doctrine that sense, together with the world, determines reference. As a matter of principle, the level of reference is inextricably involved with concepts, as understood here. Concepts are individuated by their possession conditions; the possession conditions mention judgements of certain contents containing the concepts; judgement necessarily has truth as one of its aims; and the truth of a content depends on the references of its conceptual constituents. It would be wrong, then, to regard the referential relations in which concepts stand as grafted onto a structure of concepts that can be elucidated without any reference to reference. Referential relations are implicated in the very nature of judgement and belief.

We need, then, for each concept a theory of how the semantic value of the concept is determined from its possession conditions (together with the world). I call this part of the theory of content "determination theory." Often we take a particular concept and its determination of a semantic value for granted and ask what it is to possess that concept. Sometimes what are called theories of manifestation can be regarded as aiming to address, among other things, that question. At other times, by contrast, it is better understood what possession of a sense or concept consists in; what is less clear is how it can fix an appropriate semantic value. In that case we need a determination theory. A determination theory takes for granted what a theory of possession tries to elucidate; a theory of possession takes for granted what a determination theory tries to elucidate. The construction of theories of both kinds should be on our agenda because it is in some cases one part, and in other cases another part, of the system of relations between concept, possession, and reference that are obscure to us.

A simple example of a determination theory can be given for the proposed possession condition for conjunction displayed above. The theory would state that the truth function that is the semantic value of conjunction is the function that makes transitions of the forms mentioned in the possession condition truth-preserving under all assignments to their constituents p and q. That function is the classical truth function for conjunction.[13]

Similarly, for the above possession condition for universal quantification over the natural numbers we can offer the following determination theory. The semantic value of this quantifier is the function from extensions of concepts (true or false of natural numbers) to truth values that makes elimination inferences of the form mentioned in the possession condition always truth-preserving. This is the classical, realistic semantic value for the universal quantifier. This is one of the simplest examples that shows how the theorist of possession conditions can also acknowledge contents whose truth may transcend verification.

This is a natural point at which to note the divergence between the approach I am developing here and Wilfrid Sellars's thoughts on meaning and content. Indeed, the theory of possession conditions has some Sellarsian features. The theory of possession conditions certainly treats a classification of mental states by their conceptual contents as a form of functional classification in some very broad sense. The idea of meaning as functional classification was one of Sellars's central themes (1974). But Sellars was also inclined to identify truth with a certain form of assertibility. He wrote, "'True', then, means *semantically* assertible ('S-assertible') and the varieties of truth correspond to the varieties of semantical rule" (1968, 101). Thus in the case of logical and mathematical propositions he held that "*S-assertibility means provability*" (1968, 115; Sellars's italics), and he rejected bivalence for such propositions. Hilary Putnam (1974, 454) objected that under such an identification it is not clear that any room is provided for propositions that are unverifiable, and this objection is well taken. But when we reject any such general identification of truth with assertibility, the requirement that a determination theory exist is especially challenging. Indeed, for concepts of conscious psychological states, I think we do not at present know how to give a theory which meets the requirement. In any case, the difference between the theory of possession conditions and Sellars's account is already shown by the simple determination theory for universal quantification over the natural numbers, which does allow such a quantification to be true though unprovable in any given system.

The two examples of determination theories I have given so far are, of course, formulated in a way congenial to a broadly realistic point of view. Developing acceptable realistic determination theories for concepts is an important part of the defence of a realist's task. But it should not be supposed that the need for determination theories for particular concepts is something peculiar to the realist (though it is particularly challenging for the realist). For the verificationist or any other theorist who in one way or another claims there are epistemic constraints on truth, it is still a requirement that the possession conditions he accepts can be given determination theories that fix the appropriate epistemically constrained semantic values that he does recognize. I will continue to formulate the issues from a realistic point of view, but the reader with antirealistic inclinations can note that at many points there are corresponding antirealistic versions of the constraint in question.

We would expect there to be a general form common to the relation between the determination theory for each concept and its possession condition. The cases of conjunction and universal quantification just considered suggest that the common form is as follows. The determination theory for a given concept (together with the world in empirical cases) assigns semantic values in such a way that the belief-forming practices mentioned in the concept's possession condition are correct. That is, in the case of belief formation, the practices result in true beliefs, and in the case of principles of inference, they result in truth-preserving inferences, when semantic values are assigned in accordance with the determination theory. If this is right, it identifies a link between semantic value, possession conditions, and correctness. I will return to the significance of this link later in this section and in chapter 5.

The requirement that for each concept there be a determination theory also plays a regulative role in the theory of conceptual content. The requirement may operate in one of at least three ways. In one type of case we know what semantic value a concept should receive and some proposed possession condition for the concept fails to give it that semantic value. A relatively uncontroversial example would be the proposed possession condition for *red* that results from that displayed in section 2 by omitting clause (2), so the possession condition speaks only of a disposition to form beliefs in response to presumed perceptions of an object as red. Such an account would fail to explain how unperceived objects can fall under the concept *red*. This is a special instance of the more general case in which we know that the semantic value of a certain concept has a property and we use this fact to rule out all accounts in which the semantic value fixed in accordance with determination theory does not have this property.

A second regulative use of the requirement that a determination theory exist applies particularly to certain proposed possession conditions with multiple clauses. Sometimes a plausible possession condition for a concept *F*, in particular, an observational or a psychological concept, takes the following general form. It states that for an object thought about in way *t*—for example, in the first-person way in the psychological case or in a perceptual-demonstrative way in the observational case—a thinker must be prepared to judge (or reject) *Ft* in such and such circumstances, while for an object thought about in some other way *s*—for example, a third-person way or again a nonperceptual way—the thinker must be prepared to judge (or reject) *Fs* in such and such circumstances. But, of course, it is possible that the singular concepts *t* and *s* refer to the same object. In such a case it had better be that the semantic value of the concept *F* is fixed from the possession condition in such a way that it ensures that *Fs* is true iff *Ft* is true. This nontrivial requirement provides a substantial constraint upon the possession conditions and determination theories for some observational and psychological concepts. I discuss it in more detail under the heading of "Referential Coherence" in chapter 6.

A third, more radical, regulative use of determination theory is one where an alleged concept is declared spurious because no account is possible of what has to be the case for something to be its semantic value. This is to be distinguished, of course, from ruling out partially defined concepts. A singular concept, for instance, is partial if, to-gether with the world, it does not always determine a referent. But a partial concept is still a genuine concept because there is an account to be given of how the world has to be for it to have a referent. It is just that, for one reason or another, no object fulfills the requirements of that account. For a spurious concept, by contrast, there is no such account to be given: it has not been settled how the world has to be for something to be its semantic value. Corresponding remarks apply *pari passu* for other categories of concepts.

Spurious cases commonly result from the following combination of circumstances: The spurious concept purports to be of a general kind for which there *does* exist a uniform determination theory for members of that kind. But applying that uniform account to the particular fea-tures of the alleged concept determines no semantic value. Prior's famous nonconnective *tonk* arguably falls into this category.[14] The rules given for *tonk* are (1) that from p, it can be inferred that p *tonk* q (2) and that from p *tonk* q it can be inferred that q. It is impossible to assign a binary truth function to *tonk* that makes these rules truth-preserving under every valuation. In the case in which p is true but q is false, the first rule requires p *tonk* q to be true, while the second rule requires it to be false. It would be wrong to assimilate the failure of an (alleged) thought of the form "p *tonk* q" to have a truth value to the failure of a complex term such as "the greatest prime number" to have a referent. In the latter case, the term has components with determinate senses and references: we know for arithmetic reasons that nothing can meet the condition for being the referent of the whole phrase. In the case of *tonk*, by contrast, we have not settled *which* function is to be its semantic value. In chapter 8, I will argue that some conceptions of absolute space and of subjective experience also arguably permit this kind of radical regulative use of determination theory.[15] On these conceptions, no account of possession of concepts of them can be given that determines semantic values of the sorts they ought to possess on those conceptions. Where *tonk* suffers from a surfeit of conditions for something to be its semantic value, a combi-nation of mutually inconsistent conditions, these alleged concepts of space and experience suffer from insufficiency. No amount of material in the account of possession suffices to determine the desired reference.

Meeting the possession condition for a concept can be identified with knowing what it is for something to be the concept's semantic value (its reference). Dummett has forcefully argued that grasping a sense should be identified with knowing the condition for something to be its semantic value.[16] The apparatus introduced so far helps to underwrite these identifications. For these identifications can be sustained only if the possession condition for a concept, together with the world, determines its reference. Without this, it would be unjustifiable to describe meeting the possession condition as knowing what it is for something to be the reference of a concept. The required justification is provided once we give, for any possession condition, the appropriate determination theory.

The form "knowing what it is for something to be the semantic value of a concept" does not presuppose that someone can first grasp a concept and then go on to raise the question of what it is for something to be its semantic value. On the present theory, grasp consists in knowing the answer to that question, so such a state of ignorance is not possible. It is important, then, that in the form "knows what it is for something to be the semantic value of concept so-and-so," the concept in question either is not thought of by the subject under a mode of presentation at all or is thought of under a mode of presentation available only to those who already possess the concept.

One can conceive of a theorist who agrees that meeting the possession condition is part of knowing what it is for something to be the reference of a concept but who asserts that it is not the whole story. That is not my position. If meeting the possession condition were not enough, then there would have to be something insufficient for the required knowledge in the case of the earlier possession condition for conjunction. But it is hard to see what the extra could be: it seems that meeting that possession condition is enough for grasping conjunction. If it is enough, then any stronger notion should not be made a requirement for concept possession.

The notion of knowing what it is for something to be the reference of a concept has application far beyond the case of unstructured concepts. It applies to arbitrarily complex concepts, and in particular to complete propositional concepts, the case of knowing what it is for a complete thought to have a certain semantic value. Knowledge of what it is for something to be the semantic value of a complex rests upon knowledge of the conditions for entities of the appropriate categories to be the semantic values of its constituents. Take a complex content $[s_1, \ldots, s_n]$, where the s_i are concepts and $[\ ]$ is a particular mode of combining them. To grasp this complex content is to know the condition for something to be its semantic value solely as a result of applying one piece of knowledge to certain other pieces of knowledge. The piece of knowledge applied is knowledge of the way the semantic values of a content of the form $[\ ]$ is determined from those of its constituents; it is applied to one's knowledge, for each component sense s_i, of what it is for something to be the semantic value of s_i. In all cases, whether complex or not, I will refer to the following as simply "the Identification":

The Identification   Possessing a concept is knowing what it is for something to be its semantic value.

It is, of course, a theoretical issue what the semantic value of a complete thought should be. On a classical Fregean view, it is a truth value. On what I call the "Stanford view" (Barwise and Perry 1983), it will be something built up from the semantic value of its constituents. This will, together with the world, determine a truth value. The Stanford view will sit better with the claim that it is important to recognize properties, as distinct from extensions or functions from objects to truth values or anything else extensional, as the semantic values of predicative concepts. For the motivation for such recognition of properties is likely to be that there are complex constructions, such as "is explained by the fact that **x** is F" that are not properly treated unless a property is the semantic value of F. This suggested advantage would be annulled if the theorist took the relevant semantic value of "that **x** is F" as a truth value. If the approach of this book is developed in combination with the Stanford treatment of the semantic value of complexes, rather than the Fregean treatment, it becomes important to acknowledge how much is involved in the Identification of grasp of a concept with knowledge of what it is for something to be its semantic value. If the semantic value of a concept is a property, then under the Identification, grasp of a concept, meeting its possession condition, is knowledge of what it is for a property to be the semantic value of the concept. This may make it sound as if such knowledge falls short of knowledge of what it is for something to fall under the concept. But it does not. Included in knowledge of what it is for a property to be the semantic value of a concept F is knowledge that for an object to be F is for it to exemplify the property that is its semantic value. This is just an expansion of what is involved in a property being the semantic value of a concept.

I have so far not addressed the question, With what, in the present framework, are we to identify knowledge of the semantic significance of a mode of combination, and derivatively, with what are we to identify knowledge of what it is for something to be the semantic value of a complex content? It seems, though, that an implicit semantic role for the combination of concepts in the thinker's thoughts has already been assumed throughout. Taking for simplicity the semantic values of complexes to be Fregean, I said earlier that the truth function referred to by "*and*" is what makes the transitions in the possession condition for conjunction always truth-preserving. I was making an assumption: that the function in question takes as arguments the (Fregean) semantic values of the thoughts p and q on which conjunction operates, and has as its value the truth value of the complete thought p and q. Without this assumption, the question, What assignment to "*and*" makes the transitions always truth-preserving? has no determinate meaning. But with the assumption, we are taking for granted an implicit semantic role for combination.

Suppose, then, that we have a possession condition for a monadic concept F and a possession condition for a singular concept b and that these conditions determine references for their respective concepts. I conjecture that these possession conditions together implicitly determine the conditions under which the complete thought Fb is true. By parity of reasoning with the case of unstructured concepts, this determination allows us to say that a thinker who possesses F and b knows what it is for the thought Fb to be true and does so on the basis of his knowledge of what it is for its components to have particular references. On such a treatment, the role of a first-level concept in predicational combination is essential to it and is given automatically in its individuating possession condition. This is only to be expected if, as is plausible, there is no such thing as possessing a concept while failing to grasp its significance in predicational combination.

Much of the discussion of this section has presupposed that judgement or belief has truth as one of its aims. Reference has had a role
to play in the present theory of concepts because of this link between
belief and truth and because the truth of a content depends upon the
references of its constituent concepts. Stich (1990) questions whether
there really is any link of fundamental importance between belief and
truth. The chapter in which he addresses the issues is entitled "Do We
Really Care Whether Our Beliefs Are True?" A full discussion of the
differences between my position and Stich's view would need to be
very wide-ranging, for some of Stich's arguments are committed to
general claims about the possibility of content-involving psychological
explanation. But I can indicate the nature of the issues between Stich's
position and my own without straying too far from the theory of
concepts.

Stich gives two kinds of arguments for his views. First, he says that
if mental states involve relations to syntactically structured mental
representations, there will be many syntactically characterizable patterns of interaction among representations that have no plausible semantic interpretation at all (1990, 113). The interpretation function, in
effect, has a limited domain. To value truth in our beliefs may well
result from "a profoundly conservative normative stand" that cuts us
off from a space of mental states where there is neither truth nor falsity
(1990, 119). Second, Stich notes that truth conditions result from
particular reference relations, and he doubts that there are good reasons for valuing reference and truth in preference to various variants:
REFERENCE* and TRUTH*, REFERENCE** and TRUTH**, etc. Stich
writes, "Let REFERENCE* be a word-world relation just like reference
save for the fact that if the majority of the (nontrivial) descriptions a
speaker associates with the name actually apply to no one, then the
name is empty" (1990, 116). "REFERENCE*** might be designed so
that 'water' includes in its EXTENSION*** not only H_2O but also the
famous stuff that looks and tastes just like it, XYZ" (1990, 116). Stich
does not doubt that current theories of reference are correct in saying
that these asterisk-labeled relations are not genuine reference. But
this, he holds, is just a fact about our linguistic intuitions: we could
bring up our children to have intuitions based on the REFERENCE*
relation, say, and "there is no reason, or at least no obvious reason,

to think that people whose intuitions diverged from ours in these ways would be any worse off" (1990, 117).

On the treatment of concepts I am advocating, the reference of a concept is something that, given the way the world is, makes correct the belief-forming practices described in the concept's possession condition. Suppose we hold constant the way the world is. If we try to assign a nonstandard reference relation to a concept, then either some of the belief-forming practices mentioned in the possession condition will not be correct for that nonstandard relation, or else some of the resulting nonstandard "truth" conditions will not be justifiable on the basis of any features of our belief-forming practices. The point can be illustrated for Stich's examples. A plausible possession condition for one sort of natural-kind concept, a sort that includes the way we think of water, will include a clause stating, roughly, that from the premise that something falls under the concept, the thinker is willing to infer that it is of the same underlying kind as certain samples he has encountered. But a relation of REFERENCE*** under which "water" refers to both H_2O and XYZ will not make this inference TRUTH***-preserving. If we really were indifferent to whether it is truth or TRUTH*** at which we aim in our beliefs, then we would not be making the inference mentioned in the possession condition. Similarly, if we came to care about Stich's relation of REFERENCE* for proper names, some of our belief-forming practices would differ from our actual practices. Someone aiming at REFERENCE* and TRUTH* will be willing to assert "Jonah never existed" when he discovers that there is nothing satisfying most of the nontrivial descriptions he associates with the name "Jonah." This is certainly not our actual practice with proper names: for us it is a substantive question whether there really was such a person as Jonah and whether we have perhaps inherited misinformation about him.

In sum, on the view for which I am arguing, if we did not care about truth, we would not have the (canonical) belief-forming practices we do have. So the theorist of possession conditions will be skeptical about the claim that the importance to us of reference and truth rests on nothing more than some easily retrainable linguistic intuitions. According to the theorist of possession conditions, reference and truth are inextricably involved with the concepts we possess and the belief-forming practices that individuate them. Changing the semantic property at which we aim must involve changing much else too. It should, of course, be no part of the theory of possession conditions that we should not change our concepts, perhaps very radically. The theory of possession conditions is committed only to the view that if we do change them, and still have a recognizable concept of belief, then the new concepts will determine a corresponding reference relation under which the new concept-individuating practices are correct, given the way the world is.

Stich's first class of arguments emphasized the limited domain of the semantically interpretable. I would argue that if there is a distinctive kind of content-involving explanation possible only when a state has an intentional content, then it is unobjectionable for states with content to be treated differently, when such explanations are in question, from states that lack intentional content. Stich (1983) is skeptical in various ways about the notion of content itself, let alone the explanatory powers of states that have intentional content. Whether Stich's first class of arguments is sound depends, then, on the wider issue of the defensibility of a suitable notion of content. To answer all doubts, if they can be answered, would take a different book. Naturally, I hope the remainder of this book at least contributes to the case. In any case, even with a robust notion of content and a distinctive kind of explanation for content-involving states, we can still agree that explanatory principles whose application depends only on the nonsemantical properties of a mental representation will apply uniformly across the interpretable and the uninterpretable.

1.4 Possession Conditions and Attribution Conditions

I now turn to an issue whose resolution affects the conditions of adequacy for any theory of concepts and that has widespread ramifications for the appropriate defence of a theory. It can be introduced by the following four propositions. They are all superficially plausible, but they are jointly inconsistent. To fix ideas, I take the concept *red* as an illustration. Many other concepts, with appropriate alterations, could be made to serve in its place.

1. The above possession condition for *red* (section 1.2) is correct.

2.   The construction "x believes that ____ red ____ expresses a prop-ositional-attitude relation to a structured thought containing the con-cept *red* as a constituent.

3.   A thinker who has attitudes to thoughts containing the concept *red* must fulfill its possession condition.

4.   A thinker who has false beliefs about the boundaries of the color spectrum covered by the word "red" and who sincerely says of an object "It's red" or "It's not red" is correctly described as believing the object in question to be red, or not red, respectively.

Consider a thinker of the sort described in (4). Suppose that he believes that the word "red" does not cover some shades that are in fact dark red. Suppose too that he is properly perceiving a book of a dark red color and is taking his perceptual experiences at face value. If asked, he will sincerely say of the book, "It's not red." If (4) is true, he believes that it is not red. From (2) it follows that he stands in a propositional-attitude relation to a thought containing the concept *red*. So by (3), he should meet the possession condition for *red*. Surely my description of the case does not make our thinker clearly inconsistent. If he is to be consistent, then he does not believe that the book is red. But then he is violating the possession condition given earlier for the concept *red*. The book is presented in a red' region of his visual field. In the circumstances described, he should be willing to judge that the book is red were he to meet the possession condition. Since (1) through (4) require him both to meet the given possession condition and also to violate it, they are inconsistent.

It is not plausible that the contradiction should be blamed on the particular possession condition offered for the concept *red*. That con-dition is no doubt controversial. But whatever the correct condition, this problem can be made to arise. Even if some other possession condition is correct, a word expressing the concept *red* could still be misunderstood as a result of failure to appreciate the range of the spectrum it covers. That would still be a possibility under the other possession condition for *red* mentioned in section 1.2, the possession condition that does not mention sensational properties. We would still be able to derive a contradiction from suitably altered premises.

A radical approach would be to deny premise (2). But simply to reject it is not by itself to give an intellectually satisfying treatment of the problem. Certain possession conditions that have been offered for concepts do seem highly plausible. If we rejected (2), we would still have to address the question of the relation between such possession conditions and true attributions that apparently place such concepts as *red* in oblique occurrences.

I will not reject premise (4) either. The view that a thinker's incomplete understanding of a word does not prevent true ascriptions of propositional attitudes using that word in oblique occurrences has been extensively defended by Tyler Burge (1979).[17] I take his arguments as compelling.

You will not be surprised to learn that it is premise (3) that I reject. Premise (3) is false because possession conditions are different from attribution conditions. A possession condition states what is required for full mastery of a particular concept. The attribution conditions for *red*, the conditions under which something of the form "x believes that _____ red _____" is true, are much weaker than the possession condition. The following are jointly sufficient for such an attribution to be true.

a.   The subject is willing sincerely to assert some sentence of the form "_____ red _____" containing the word "red" (or some translation of it).

b.   He has some minimal knowledge of the kind of reference it has (e.g., that it is a color word).

c.   He defers in his use of the word to members of his linguistic community.

(I take his understanding of the other expressions in _____   _____ for granted.) When an attribution of an attitude with a content containing the concept *red* is correct only because sufficient conditions of this sort obtain, I will call it "deference-dependent." In these attribution conditions, requirement (c) of deference is essential. It is what distinguishes the case we are interested in, partial understanding (and partial misunderstanding) of a word in a communal language, from the quite different case of an individual's taking over a word from his community and using it in his own individual, different sense. Requirement (b) is also essential if the case is not to be one in which only a metalinguistic attribution of belief is correct, such as the belief that whatever property is expressed by the word "red," it is thus and so. I should also note that while possession conditions are given for concepts, attribution conditions and deference-dependence primarily concern words and sentences.

The crucial point in explaining why (3) is false is thus that, with these sufficient conditions for a deference-dependent attribution, a statement of the form "x believes that ____ red ____" can be true without the thinker meeting the possession condition for the concept *red*. Hilary Putnam confesses that he knows nothing which distinguishes elms from beeches.[18] He can nevertheless still believe that no elm is a beech. In these circumstances the attribution of this belief is another example of one that is deference-dependent: it meets conditions (a) to (c).

The importance of acknowledging deference-dependent attributions goes well beyond the need to resolve the contradiction in (1) through (4). I will mention just three points particularly relevant to concepts.[19]

First, presented with any philosophical argument that turns on properties of a belief attribution, we must always consider whether recognizing the existence of deference-dependent attributions may affect our estimate of its soundness. In the chapter entitled "The Real Trouble with Propositions" in *Remnants of Meaning* (1987, 67 ff.), Stephen Schiffer considers the belief attribution "Tanya believes that Gustav is a dog." He wonders how any theory that admits senses can adequately say what the objects of belief are when we turn to examine the predicate "is a dog." For classical reasons of cognitive significance, the sense should not be identified with the property of being a dog, since that can be thought about in many different ways. The least implausible candidate that Schiffer says he can find for being the sense of the predicative phrase "is a dog" is the concept of having the same internal explanatory properties that account for the observable characteristics of certain sample creatures that have been encountered by Tanya or her community. But nothing of this sort can be correct, Schiffer emphasizes, because Tanya may be a nine-year-old who is in no position to think about explanatory underlying properties. I do not say that Schiffer's rejected candidate explication is successful, but the validity of this type of reasoning is questionable if we acknowledge deference-dependent attributions. Nine-year-old Tanya can certainly defer in her use of the word "dog" (or some translation of it). If she does, the truth of the attribution is unproblematic.

Second, the existence of deference-dependent attributions ought to alert us to the danger of hasty, invalid reasoning to a conclusion of the language dependence of certain concepts. As I said, the general framework of possession conditions is itself neutral on the issue of whether some, all, or no concepts require language mastery for their possession. The whole issue is to be settled by arguments additional to the framework given so far. If some concepts can be possessed without having a linguistic means of expressing them, it is plausible that the concept *red* is one of them. Now, is the following paragraph a sound argument for the language dependence of the concept *red*?

We can conceive of someone who, in the actual world, misunderstands the word "red" in the way mentioned earlier: as concerning a range of the color spectrum shifted toward orange. His sincere utterances containing the word "red" express beliefs whose content involves the concept *red*. Now consider the counterfactual circumstance in which that individual's history is held constant, molecule for molecule, while the word "red" in his communal language does indeed cover a different range of shades shifted toward orange. Let us say that it then expresses the concept *o-red*. In these counterfactual circumstances, the beliefs he expresses using the word "red" have a content involving the concept *o-red*; this claim is supported by the same Burgean considerations that support (4) above. But since the individual's history has been held constant between the actual and the counterfactual cases and only the relevant properties of his linguistic community have been altered, the concept *red* must be individuated in part by linguistic facts.

On my view, the last clause of this argument is a non sequitur. What can be soundly concluded from the argument is this: the *relations* in which a thinker stands to concepts may depend upon facts about his linguistic community. If there are deference-dependent attributions, we should expect that which attributions are true will depend on the communal meaning of the subject's words. A deference-dependent attribution involving a given concept is true in part because the subject has some minimal understanding of the word and defers to a community use in which it expresses the given concept. If we counterfactually vary which concept the word expresses in the community, it is only to be expected that there will be a corresponding variation in which attributions are true. This is entirely consistent with the concept *red* itself being individuated by a possession condition for full mastery that does not make reference to language at all.

Third, acknowledging deference-dependent attributions should make me sharpen the formulation of the conditions of adequacy of the account of concepts at which I have been aiming. I said that facts about epistemic possibilities and impossibilities specific to a given concept or set of concepts should be grounded in properties of the possession conditions of that concept or those concepts. But if we react to the inconsistency of (1) to (4) in the way I have suggested, we will be committed to counting it as informative that a certain perceptually presented shade, which is in fact definitely a shade of red, is a shade of red. This can be informative for someone who has misunderstood the range of shades covered by the word "red" but who can still be properly said to express beliefs involving the concept red when using the word. But it would be desperate to hope that any plausible possession condition for the concept *red*, aiming to characterize full mastery, could explain that epistemic possibility! On the contrary, it seems uninformative for someone who has fully mastered the concept.

In this particular example, it suffices for a theory of concepts to aim to explain those patterns of epistemic possibility that exist only for one who fully understands the word (and any synonyms of it he may acquire). But in general, it should not be supposed that the possibility of a state of full understanding of an expression entails that there is a concept it expresses, in the sense of "concept" in question here. As I noted, there are expressions, of which most proper names are arguably examples, for which there is such a thing as full understanding but where understanding involves no more than knowing of the expression's referent that it is the referent. The correct restriction on the range of facts about epistemic possibility or impossibility that a theory of possession conditions is required to explain is rather as follows. A theory of possession conditions is required to explain the fact that in such and such circumstances it is informative (uninformative) to a subject that ____ **A** ____ only if there is a concept expressed in the language by the expression replacing "**A**" and the thinker in question fully understands the expression.

I have several times emphasized that on my position one cannot assume that for every meaningful expression **A**, the definite description "the concept expressed by **A**" denotes something. It may or may not, depending on the details of the case. Two consequences follow. First, my use of "concept" is not pleonastic in Schiffer's sense, the sense in which "*a* falls under the concept *F*" is a trivial stylistic variant of "*a* is *F*."[20] Second, the question "What is the possession condition for **A**?" does not always have an answer, even when "**A**" is replaced by a meaningful English expression. The fact that it does not always have an answer would show that concepts do not always have possession conditions if I were to use "concept" pleonastically. But I am not doing so.

I should not leave the impression that deference-dependent attributions are somehow a curiosity or dispensable. Quite the contrary. An individual for whom only deference-dependent attributions involving a certain expression are true may nevertheless be a reliable gatherer and transmitter of information about the referent of the expression. If we want to report the mental state of such an individual, we will often have to resort to a deference-dependent attribution, for we will often not know in what idiosyncratic and partial way he is thinking of the referent of the expression. (Ordinary members of a linguistic community will not themselves use the concept of a deference-dependent attribution.) If the practice of making deference-dependent attributions did not initially exist in a linguistic community, we would for the same reasons expect it to emerge. New members will join or be born into the community. Their understanding of some expressions will initially, and perhaps always, be merely partial, and they will defer in their uses of the community's expressions. Their attitudes will need to be reported, again by persons who are in no position to make an equally informative attribution that is not deference-dependent. The transmission of information, both about others' attitudes and about the nonmental world, would be impoverished without deference-dependent attributions.[21]

1.5   The $\mathcal{A}(C)$ Form: Modesty, Interpretation, and Intelligibility

I now begin to put the outlined account of concepts and possession conditions to work by considering its bearing upon two issues at the center of recent philosophical discussions of conceptual content.

First, requiring an account of a concept to meet the $\mathcal{A}(C)$ form points to a middle way between two more extreme positions. The two more extreme positions are those of John McDowell and a possible philosopher I will call "Michael Dummett*." (See Dummett 1975, McDowell 1987, and Dummett 1987.) Whether Michael Dummett* is identical with any real philosopher, and in particular, with Michael Dummett, is a question I defer for a few paragraphs. In any case, Dummett* agrees with the real Dummett when the real Dummett offers this sketch of grasp of the concept *square*: "At the very least, [to grasp the concept] is to be able to discriminate between things that are square and those that are not. Such an ability can be ascribed only to one who will, on occasion, treat square things differently from things that are not square; one way, among many other possible ways, of doing this is to apply the word 'square' to square things and not to others" (Dummett 1978a, 7; quoted in McDowell 1987, 62). This sketch of an account uses the concept *square* as applied to things in the world; the legitimacy of using the concept in such an account is not in question. What the sketch does not do is to use the word "square" within attributions of propositional attitudes to the subject. Furthermore, the sketch does not quantify over or mention the concept *square*, as opposed to using it. According to the hypothetical Michael Dummett*'s position, these negative features of the account are mandatory; that is, an account of possession of a concept must not, according to him, quantify over or mention (as opposed to making use of) that concept. A fortiori, then, such an account does not make any requirements on the role of the concept in question within complete propositional contents the thinker may judge.

John McDowell (1987, 68) reasonably objected to any such account, saying that no account can be correct that purports to say what it is to possess a concept without mentioning its role in complete propositional contents. McDowell concluded that theories of meaning should be modest; that is, they should not aim to give accounts of the primitive concepts of a language. Indeed, he stated that "the possibility of avoiding both behaviourism and psychologism depends precisely on the embracing of modesty" (1987, 69).

Both parties to this dispute, McDowell and Dummett*, seem to me to overlook the possibilities implicit in requiring an account of a concept to meet the $\mathcal{A}(C)$ form. As a result, each party overshoots in moving to a position that avoids the bad features of his opponent's position. Consider an account of a concept of the $\mathcal{A}(C)$ form. This account need not attempt to characterize possession of the concept "as from outside" its role as a determinant of complete propositional contents, in McDowell's phrase (1987, 61). On the contrary, for a given concept we would always expect its possession condition to concern in part the conditions under which the thinker judges or rejects certain complete propositional contents containing that very concept. All the possession conditions given above do just that.

Yet equally, there is nothing in the general $\mathcal{A}(C)$ form to suggest that we can go any further in Dummett*'s direction. There is nothing to suggest that some account of possession of a concept is possible that does not explicitly mention its role in contents to which the thinker has propositional attitudes. Accounts of the $\mathcal{A}(C)$ form need not be free of intentional notions. The instances of the $\mathcal{A}(C)$ form that I just gave for conjunction and for *red* contain intentional notions. So do Gareth Evans's accounts of particular kinds of singular modes of presentation, which can be cast in the $\mathcal{A}(C)$ form. Indeed, endorsing the $\mathcal{A}(C)$ form is consistent with holding McDowell's views on the relations between language and thought. The desire for a noncircular account should not motivate a nonintentional, and certainly not a behaviorist, requirement. I have already avoided circularity by requiring that if $\mathcal{A}(C)$ is the possession condition for a concept F, then F must not be mentioned *as F* within the scope of the thinker's propositional attitudes within the condition $\mathcal{A}(C)$. To demand more cannot be forced by a noncircularity requirement.

On the present suggestion, then, avoiding both behaviorism and psychologism does not depend on embracing modesty. We have a form of account that explicitly concerns a concept's role in the determination of complete contents of propositional attitudes but that is also consistent with the knowability of another's propositional attitudes. We need not lower our sights as far as modesty to preserve these crucial properties.[22]

If the positions of Dummett* and McDowell were the only options, we would indeed have a painful choice. Theories are developing in the literature of what it is to possess certain specific concepts: the first person, logical notions, and many others. While there is much that is still not understood and not all of what has been said is right, it is hard to accept that the goal of this work is completely misconceived. On the contrary, there are often phenomena specific to the concept treated that are explained by these accounts. McDowell would not let us say that these accounts are theories of what it is to possess these concepts. But I cannot see what else they can be, and we can hardly just dismiss them. If Dummett* were right, on the other hand, we can accept these theories at face value only if they are taken as way stations on the road to accounts that do not mention the role of these concepts in propositional attitudes at all. We have no reason to believe this destination exists. If we endorse the $\mathcal{A}(C)$ form, though, we can take the accounts at face value without prejudice as to the existence of that destination.

It is not easy to determine from the published literature whether Michael Dummett* is the real Michael Dummett. The feature of possession conditions that Michael Dummett* says is mandatory is found in some of the real Michael Dummett's examples, but it does not follow that the real Dummett would endorse only possession conditions that have it. On the other hand, the real Michael Dummett does not consider the $\mathcal{A}(C)$ form in his reply to John McDowell, even though doing so would provide a strong response. It is perhaps worth explicitly noting again that the $\mathcal{A}(C)$ form is available both to realists and to antirealists.

Second, what is the relation between my theory of concepts and the view of a theorist like Donald Davidson, whom we would expect to emphasize the role of radical interpretation procedures in an account of the possession of concepts? Such a theorist is likely to propose that to possess the concept F is to be credited with propositional attitudes containing F in their content by application of an adequate radical interpretation procedure (or more generally, radical ascription procedure) to the thinker in question.

This proposal cannot be cast in the $\mathcal{A}(C)$ form. In saying what it is to possess the concept F, it mentions propositional attitudes with that very concept F in the content. In this interpretational approach, it will not help to replace the particular concept-specifying word with a variable "C" over concepts. We lose uniqueness in the most radical possible way. Not only the given concept F, but every other concept too is a concept C to possess which is to be credited with propositional attitudes containing it by an adequate radical ascription procedure.

This very point in fact brings us to the issue I want to address. Even if the interpretationist's proposal cannot be cast in the $\mathcal{A}(C)$ form and made individuating, it is nevertheless highly plausible that it is *true*. Let us grant its truth. Why is it true, and is it in competition with accounts that are cast in the $\mathcal{A}(C)$ form?

A radical ascription procedure must rely in part upon constraints derived from the possession conditions for particular concepts. Suppose, say, we have a candidate assignment of content-involving mental states to a subject that makes attributions to him involving the concept of conjunction, without deference-dependence, but has him failing to accept inferences clearly of the form "*p; q;* therefore, *p and q.*" This would be an assignment of mental states we should reject, *ceteris paribus*, and the possession condition for conjunction makes it clear why we should reject it. When we generalize this reflection, it begins to seem that there could not be any competition between a theory of possession conditions in the $\mathcal{A}(C)$ form and the claim that every case of possessing a concept is one in which an adequate radical ascription procedure ascribes it to the subject. This impression of harmony between the two approaches will certainly be correct if the constraints on intelligibility in the ascription procedure are precisely those given by the possession conditions for concepts.

More precisely, the impression of harmony will be correct if two conditions are met:

1. All constraints deriving from possession conditions are incorporated into the radical ascription procedure.

2. There are no other constraints in that procedure.

Condition (1) will presumably hold of any acceptable radical ascription procedure. Does condition (2) also hold? It is not to the point to mention constraints we apply in attributing attitudes to humans that evidently derive from a species-specific psychology (such as limitations on memory or perceptual powers). We surely do use such constraints all the time, and they will not be reflected in the possession conditions for the concepts ascribed. Nor should they be if possession conditions aim to be an account of what it *is* to have the concepts. An objection to (2) would rather have to be an example of ascriptions of attitudes that result in unintelligibility of the ascribee but in which this unintelligibility could not be accounted for by appeal to accounts of what it is to have the concepts in the contents of the attitudes in question. It is not easy to think of examples of this. It may be in the nature of unintelligibility that there can be none: perhaps an assignment of attitudes makes the subject unintelligible only if there are facts about the component concepts in question that make the assignment unintelligible. If this should prove to be so, those approaching these matters from an interpretational angle and those using my apparatus may be studying the same system of constraints from different perspectives. The point also means that those approaching content from the standpoint of radical ascription procedures do after all have a great deal more to say about the possession of a particular concept than the general remark that it can be correctly attributed if a correct radical ascription procedure says that it can.

A preestablished harmony between the possession-condition approach and an interpretation-theoretic approach can obtain only if we have imposed no substantive restrictions on the nature or circumstances of the radical interpreter. It is much more problematic whether interpretational theories that do impose such restrictions will be in harmony with the results of a theory of possession conditions. It is particularly problematic for interpretation-theoretic approaches, which are motivated by, or are endorsed in the context of, a subjectivism about attributions of content. Subjectivist approaches to interpretation are those that restrict legitimate assignments of contents to those that in one way or another are intelligible by *us*. One kind of subjectivism has been endorsed by John McDowell: "We cannot find any use for a distinction between what makes sense and what could come to make sense to us, if necessary as a result of our learning from those whom we thereby come to find intelligible" (McDowell 1986, 396).

This form of subjectivism seems to be inconsistent with the possibility that there exist concepts, perhaps of the mathematical and physical sciences, that, because of our limited intellectual capacities, we can never grasp. If there are such concepts, we can never find fully intelligible the actions, including the linguistic actions, of mathematically more intelligent beings who do grasp them.[23]

On the natural formulation of the possession-condition approach to concepts, there is no guarantee that every concept is one we could grasp. At one remove from us will be possession conditions we can formulate but cannot, as thinkers, instantiate. At two removes will be concepts individuated by possession conditions we cannot even formulate. For these reasons I doubt that such a subjectivism about content-involving states is consistent with a plausible realism about mathematics, physics, or even the thoughts of beings very different from us in other ways.[24] It should be noted, though, that this point does not rule out a certain subjectivity of the ways in which we think about content-involving states (as opposed to the nature of the states themselves). I will defend such a limited subjectivity in chapter 6 below.

I close this chapter with some disclaimers. One source of unease about the view that concepts are individuated by their possession conditions may be the idea that the view is committed to a reductive account of rationality. But there is no such commitment. There is much more to rationality than is ever captured in the possession conditions for concepts. The possession conditions will capture only what very minimal rationality is required for grasp of the concepts in question.

A second source of unease may be the idea that individuation by possession conditions must fail to capture the open-endedness of some concepts. Perhaps this is best addressed by noting what kinds of open-endedness the present framework does permit. First, I have emphasized that a possession condition for a concept may use that concept itself in describing the requirements for mastery. When it does, the open-endedness of the concept can make for open-endedness of the requirement for mastery. Second, a possession condition may use some concept, such as *theoretical coherence*, that defies reduction to anything less open-ended. A further type of case worth noting is that in which a kind of open-endedness flows from possession conditions that are not themselves open-ended.

Two further illustrations of open-endedness, from the standpoint of possession conditions, should make us agree that in certain senses the structure of the ideal involved in propositional-attitude psychology cannot be fixed once and for all from the outside. A possession condition, possibly together with the world, fixes a semantic value for a concept. Certain principles and inferences will hold for the semantic value thus determined, and in some cases they will hold a priori. We cannot fix once and for all what this class of principles and inferences will be for two reasons. First, we may come to possess new concepts, and new principles and inferences involving the combination of the new with old concepts may be valid. An example would be the introduction of a concept of probability, in combination with concepts of logical constants already possessed. This will generate new a priori principles involving the interaction of probability with the logical constants. Second, even for a fixed family of concepts, we may know that we can never enumerate the set of valid principles involving them, as with the family of concepts of second-order logic. We can specify the ideal as aiming at truth in one's judgements and validity in one's logic. But without in effect using the notions of truth and validity themselves, we cannot even from the standpoint of possession conditions fix once and for all, or in any more specific way, precisely what fulfillment of this ideal involves.

1.6 Conclusion and Challenges

In this chapter I have tried to say quite generally how a concept is individuated by its possession condition and to outline the constraints on genuine possession conditions. Some of these constraints involve the form of the possession condition. Others concern the relation of the possession condition to the level of reference and truth. The claims of this chapter leave us with both a resource and a set of problems, and in both cases with a challenge. The challenge posed by the resources is to employ them to explain other phenomena that are properly the concern of a theory of conceptual content. The challenges posed by the problems they leave include those of elucidating the ontology of concepts, of locating the proper role of a theory of possession conditions in relation to empirical theories of possession conditions, and of explaining how the constraints for which I have been arguing can really be met for some problematic concepts. In the next chapter, I turn to one of the explanatory challenges.

2 Structure and System

The concepts that feature in a given set of thoughts can be recombined to form new thoughts. This recombinability is about as general a phenomenon as one can hope to find in the realm of conceptual content. Any theory of conceptual content that aspires to generality must explain the phenomenon. In this chapter I attempt to discharge this obligation.

Throughout the chapter I will be considering a restricted class of attributions of propositional attitudes. I will consider only attributions of attitudes that meet these three conditions: there are concepts expressed by the words in the "that" clause; those concepts are fully grasped by the subject of the attribution; and the attribution is not deference-dependent, in the sense of section 1.4. The reason for these restrictions is that the phenomena discussed here hold without qualification only for such attributions. It should not be surprising that there should be classes of phenomena for which that is true. When an attribution of the belief that Fa is true and the subject has only a partial grasp of the embedded concepts, there is a sense in which the believer does not know what it is for it to be true that Fa. What that sense involves will emerge, I hope, in more detail below.

I will be using the theory of possession conditions to explain the various phenomena of recombinability. I distinguish generally between two ways in which possession conditions can contribute to the explanation of some state of affairs. In cases of the first type, the possession condition itself is at least partially explanatory of some phenomenon. What is partially explanatory is the general fact that for an arbitrary thinker to possess the concept in question is for certain conditions to be met. In cases of the second type, what is at least partially explanatory of some phenomenon is a particular thinker's meeting the possession condition at some particular time. In cases of this second kind, the facts explained will be particular historical facts relating to the thinker in question. In cases of the first kind, by contrast, what is explained will, characteristically and in the first instance, be general facts about an arbitrary thinker. On the general conception I am advocating, explanations of both kinds are possible. Given the agenda for this chapter, I will be concerned primarily with explanations of the first kind. The discussion will, though, lead into some issues about the possibility of explanations of the second sort.

2.1 Generality, Productivity, and Their Explanations

The recombinability of concepts to form new thoughts has been largely unquestioned in the published literature. There have, though, been a variety of competing views about the explanation of the phenomenon. In fact, the phenomenon itself needs to be characterized with some care. The first datum I will consider is essentially what Evans called the Generality Constraint (1982, sec. 4.4). For the special case of a first-level, monadic predication, the Generality Constraint states this:

Generality Constraint   If a thinker can entertain the thought Fa and also possesses the singular mode of presentation b, which refers to something in the range of objects of which the concept F is true or false, then the thinker has the conceptual capacity for propositional attitudes containing the content Fb.

So it follows from the Generality Constraint that, for instance, if a thinker can entertain the thought that *Mrs. Thatcher is blonde* and possesses the singular mode of presentation *the greatest living soprano*, he has the conceptual capacity for attitudes toward the thought *The greatest living soprano is blonde*. It will be convenient to label the range of objects of which a given concept is true or false its "range of significance." The Generality Constraint also holds for concept vis-à-vis singular modes of presentation. If a thinker is capable of entertaining the thought Fa and possesses a concept G with the same significance range as F, then he is capable of attitudes toward the thought Ga. The constraint applies to relational concepts too.

The constraint applies at every level in the Fregean hierarchy. If, for example, a thinker can have attitudes toward the thought *Every F is G* and he possesses the concept H with the same range of significance as that of G, then he has the conceptual capacity for attitudes toward the thought *Every F is H*.

By speaking of a "conceptual capacity" for attitudes with the content Fb, I do not mean merely that the thinker possesses the conceptual constituents of Fb. Nor by "conceptual capacity" do I mean that the thinker will easily entertain the thought that Fb. For certain contents, such mechanisms as self-deception, repression, and the like may prevent the thought from being so much as entertained. There may also be preventing factors at the level of hardware. A thinker might really have a language of thought, and it might be that attempts to concatenate his Mentalese symbols for the concepts F and b produce strange chemical reactions that prevent him from entertaining the thought Fb. What I do mean by a conceptual capacity for attitudes with the content Fb is rather this: The thinker is in a position to know what it is for the thought Fb to be true. That is, if there is some block to the thinker's attaining states with the content Fb, what is missing is not any knowledge about concepts, nor any conceptual capacity.

I will be endorsing what I will label "the Referential Explanation" of the Generality Constraint, so understood.

Referential Explanation   The Referential Explanation starts from two premises. The first premise is implicit in the whole framework so far. (1) Attitudes are relations to complex contents, composed in a distinctive way from concepts possessed by the thinker. The second premise is the Identification of chapter 1. (2) Possessing a concept is knowing what it is for something to be its semantic value.

We are given that a thinker is capable of entertaining the thought Fa and possesses the singular sense b. What we are required to prove is that he is in a position to know what it is for the thought Fb to be true. I consider the case in which F is an atomic, monadic, first-level predicative concept. I will also be taking it that a thinker is in a position to know what it is for a given thought to be true just in case these two conditions are met: for each constituent of the thought, he knows what it is for something to be its semantic value, and he grasps the semantic significance of the mode of combination of the constituents of the thought. Since the thinker is capable of entertaining the thought Fa, he possesses the concept F. From the Identification together with the thinker's possession of F, we conclude that the thinker knows what it is for an arbitrary object to fall under F. (For conciseness I henceforth drop the qualification about significance ranges. The derivations go through *pari passu* if the qualifications are inserted throughout. Note also that if the discussion of section 1.3 is correct, these points hold whether or not we treat properties as the semantic values of concepts.) Similarly, from the Identification and the thinker's possession of b, we conclude that the thinker knows what it is for an arbitrary object to be the referent of b. The thinker's grasp of the semantic significance of predicational combination is also already presupposed in his fulfillment of the possession conditions for F and b (see section 1.3 again). There could not be a thinker who knows what it is for an arbitrary object to fall under the concept F but does not implicitly grasp the semantic significance of the predicational combination of F with an appropriate first-level sense. Possession of any concept requires the capacity to make judgements whose contents contain it. Judgement necessarily aims at truth, and aiming at truth in judging a content presupposes implicit grasp of the semantic significance of the modes of combination in the content. If all this is correct, then when the antecedents of the Generality Constraint are met, the thinker has all that is required to be in a position to know what it is for the thought Fb to be true. He knows what it is for an arbitrary object to fall under F, he knows what it is for an arbitrary object to be the referent of b, and he grasps the significance of predicational combination. This concludes the Referential Explanation of the constraint for such concepts F, a, and b.[1]

The derivation of the Generality Constraint that I have endorsed can be reapplied recursively to treat the case in which F is first-level but not atomic. It can also be generalized to other levels.

The Referential Explanation of the constraint prompts two observations. The first observation concerns the interplay of the levels of sense and reference in the Referential Explanation. The constraint is an explanandum about concept possession. But if the Referential Explanation is correct, one cannot properly explain this datum without mentioning the role of reference in an account of concepts and their possession. In the first-level case, for instance, the explanation turns on the implicit generality in grasp of a predicative concept. This generality explicitly concerns the level of reference; it is knowledge of what it is for an arbitrary object at the level of reference to fall under the concept that allows the two derivations to go through.

Second, the Referential Explanation is independent of the kind of object referred to by the concepts quantified over in the constraint. It is of equal application to thoughts about material objects, numbers, sets, mental events, or anything else. As far as the explanation of the constraint is concerned, no subject matter has any explanatory priority. As soon as we have a domain of reference and concepts presenting members of the domain, the holding of the constraint is guaranteed by the nature of the relations between concept, possession, and reference.[2]

For any particular concept, its fulfillment of the Generality Constraint may well be trivially establishable from its possession condition. The earlier possession condition for conjunction illustrates the point. That possession condition leaves no room for the possibility that a thinker has the resources for entertaining the thought *p and q* and the thought *r* but lacks the conceptual capacity for attitudes to the content *p and r*. The interest of the Referential Explanation lies not in such particular instances. It lies rather in the fact that it aims to establish that the constraint will hold for any concept whatever. The Referential Explanation is not, of course, a causal explanation. It aims rather to derive a property of all concepts, fulfillment of the constraint, from the Identification, and so ultimately from the requirement that for any possession condition, there exist a determination theory for it in the sense of chapter 1. According to the account I have given, whenever we have genuine concepts with corresponding possession conditions and determination theories, the Generality Constraint will be fulfilled.

The sense in which this gives an explanation of the Generality Constraint is not that the explanans is completely innocent of semantic notions (it is not). It is rather that we have no conception of how something could be a genuine concept without there being a determination theory for it. To lack a determination theory is for there to be no account of how thoughts containing the concept are answerable for their correctness to how things are in the world. When there is such a determination theory, then, I have been arguing, the Generality Constraint is met. The Referential Explanation is explanatory because it derives recombinability from the fundamental requirement of the existence of a determination theory for any genuine concept.

The Generality Constraint is not the only principle that results from facts about an arbitrary concept, its relation to the level of reference, and its possession condition. Suppose a thinker possesses the predicative concept *spherical* and continues to possess it after acquiring a new singular concept, say *the physical particle meeting condition R*. Such a thinker is in a position to know what it is for the thought *the physical particle meeting condition R is spherical* to be true without any further stipulations or determinations about the concept *spherical*. This holds even if the object picked out by the description *the particle meeting condition R* is one that was not, prior to his acquiring the new concepts in *R*, in his ontology. The principle illustrated here I call the "Productivity Principle," by analogy with the phenomenon linguists pick out by that name. A more general statement of the Productivity Principle is this:

Productivity Principle   Suppose that a thinker possesses the first-level concept *F* and acquires a new singular concept *m* that denotes something in the significance range of *F*. If in these circumstances the thinker continues to possess *F*, then he is in a position to know what it is for the thought *Fm* to be true without any further stipulations or determinations about the concept *F*.

The Productivity Principle also holds at all levels of the Fregean hierarchy. It is not strictly entailed by the Generality Constraint, since the principle speaks of new concepts, and the constraint is silent on the thinker's capacities in relation to new concepts. We could, though, formulate a Superprinciple that has both the Generality Constraint and the Productivity Principle as logical consequences. For a monadic concept *F*, the Superprinciple goes as follows:

Superprinciple   If a thinker possesses concept *F*, then necessarily for any suitably lower-level concept *c* that refers to something in the significance range of *F*, if the thinker continues to possess *F* and possesses (or comes to possess) *c*, then he is in a position to know what it is for the thought *Fc* to be true without any further information or stipulation.

In considering potential explanations of the Generality Constraint, one should always check to see whether they carry over to give an explanation of the Productivity Principle too. The Referential Explanation does. Suppose that the antecedents of the Productivity Principle are fulfilled. In possessing the concept *F*, the thinker, we can infer from the Identification, knows what it is for an arbitrary object within its significance range to fall under it. The thinker also grasps the predicational mode of combination, and he knows what it is for an object to be the reference of *m*. So he is in a position to know what it is for the thought *Fm* to be true.

The Referential Explanation takes it for granted that possession conditions have a modal dimension. This can be brought out as follows in connection with the example of conjunction. We would not accept the following as a good objection to what has been said so far: "The possession condition for conjunction speaks only of what inferences a thinker finds compelling involving the actual range of contents he grasps; it cannot commit us to anything about what he would find compelling in relation to any enlarged range of contents that he may come to grasp and that may feature as conjuncts in his thoughts." On the contrary, the possession condition is put forward as having such modal or counterfactual commitments. As always with a possession condition, we can consider the matter either from the aspect of requirements on grasp of a concept or from the aspect of the concept of individuation.

From the aspect of grasp, a concept *C* is intuitively not conjunction if, in relation to some newly acquired content *q,* a thinker does not find inferences from a premise of the form *p C q* to a conclusion of the form *q* primitively compelling (and similarly for the other forms). From the aspect of concept individuation, the corresponding point about the modal dimension is as follows. A possession condition is meant to *individuate* a concept. Even if a possession condition is stated entirely nonmodally, when it is put forward as a possession condition, it should be understood as incurring the commitment that in worlds other than the actual world, there is nothing more to being the concept in question than having the same possession condition as has been stated for the actual world. This is an instance of a general point about the individuation of abstract objects. We can pursue the parallel with the individuation of a natural number by the condition for it to number the instances of some property. We may say, nonmodally, that the number 3 is individuated by the condition for it to be the number of *F*s, a condition familiarly formulable in a first-order schema. If we say that this is all there is to being the number 3, we will endorse the consequence that in other possible worlds too the condition for 3 to be the number of *F*s is the same condition required for it to number them in the actual world.

2.2 Neither Stipulative nor Empirical

I have been offering the Referential Explanation as correct for both the Generality Constraint and the Productivity Principle. My stance contrasts with that of a position that also holds the constraint and the principle are indeed both necessary, but that offers a different reason for their necessity. According to this rival account, the constraint (to concentrate on it) is a trivial definitional truth. This account states as a stipulative matter that we will not count anything as a thought, or as an exercise of concepts, unless it meets the constraint. On this view, the constraint has a status like that of "All sloops have only one mast."

A plausible, rough account of what is involved in a truth being stipulatively restrictive is this: "All sloops have only one mast" is stipulatively restrictive, because (a) sloops are yachts (or vessels); (b) it is not necessary that all yachts (or vessels) have only one mast; and (c) it is a priori that sloops have only one mast, and knowledge that they do is necessary for full mastery of the concept. Generalizing, we can say that a necessary and a priori truth "All Fs are Gs" is stipulatively restrictive just in case there is some underlying sortal kind such that (a) Fs are objects of that sortal kind; (b) it is not necessary that all members of the sortal kind have the property G; and (c) it is a priori that all Fs are Gs, and knowledge that they are is necessary for full mastery of the concept F.[3] The underlying intuition here is that when a truth of the relevant form is stipulatively restrictive, being an F amounts to falling under some more general sortal concept together with the further restriction of being G.

When a necessary, a priori truth of the form "All Fs are Gs" is not stipulatively restrictive, we would expect there to be some explanation of its truth, an explanation that appeals to what is involved in falling under the fundamental sortal kind that has Fs as members. The idea of a deeper explanation is out of place where a truth is stipulatively restrictive. When a necessary, a priori truth of the form "All Fs are Gs" is not stipulatively restrictive, let me say that it is *inextricable*. If the Referential Explanation of the constraint and the principle is correct, those necessary and a priori truths are inextricable, and their explanation traces back to the general nature of concept possession.

So far, this is not an argument, just a further characterization of the Referential Explanation.

A theorist who holds that the principles I have been discussing are stipulatively restrictive has to explain how it is possible that thought conforms to them. Take the Productivity Principle. How is a thinker able to have the capacity it mentions, a capacity that concerns arbitrary new concepts? It is not plausible that the statement that the thinker has the capacity to grasp a new thought *Fm* of the sort mentioned in the Productivity Principle can be a *barely true* statement, in Dummett's sense.[4] If the statement cannot be barely true, we have to address the question of what actual property of the thinker, one that he has prior to his acquisition of the new singular concept *m,* grounds this capacity. If we accept the Identification, we have an answer to this question: in possessing the concept *F,* the thinker already knows what it is for an arbitrary object to fall under it. But if he offers this answer to the question, the theorist begins to shift from the stipulatively restrictive view of the Productivity Principle to the view that it is inextricable.

A defender of the stipulative view of the Generality Constraint and of the Productivity Principle is committed to holding that there can be exercises of what are otherwise just like concepts and a faculty of judgement that do not conform to the constraint or to the principle. At this point, the position of the stipulative defender overlaps with that of a third theorist, one who claims that though the constraint and the principle are true, they are simply contingent. The positions overlap because both are committed to the real possibility of cases in which there is the exercise of an ability that is in all other respects just like judgement involving thoughts and concepts but whose contents differ from those of actual thought solely in failing to conform to the constraint and the principle.

I want lastly in this section to consider the view that the constraint and the principle are simply contingent. It is no easy matter to spell out in detail a hypothetical counterexample to the necessity of the Generality Constraint of the sort that must exist if it is contingent. Attempts to do so all seem to founder on the same general dilemma. Suppose it is suggested that we have a description of a possible case in which a thinker is, for instance, capable of judging something of the form *Rab* but does not have the conceptual capacity to judge that

Rba. Does the thinker know what it is for an arbitrary ordered pair of objects to fall under *R*, or not? If he does, he has the capacity to judge that *Rba* after all. If he does not, how are we to justify the claim that he is capable of judging *Rab*? There is no such state as knowing what it is for the pair ⟨*a, b*⟩ to stand in the relation *R* while not knowing what it is for the pair ⟨*b, a*⟩ to stand in that same relation. In ascribing to a thinker the use of the concept *R*, we are ascribing use of something that has an ineliminable element of generality. The ascription is undermined if the thinker is not capable of doing what, in context, he ought to have the capacity to do in view of the generality involved in grasp of a concept. (This is arguably yet another application of the Tightness Constraint of Peacocke 1983, chapter 3.)

These difficulties in spelling out the details of a counterexample to the Generality Constraint are not just an appeal to a definition of the sort to which we would be reduced if we were queried whether sloops have to have only one mast. They are difficulties in reconciling requirements on the grasp of concepts with failure of the Generality Constraint. The problem is more pressing when the issue is formulated not schematically but instead in terms of particular concepts. Can we make sense of the possibility that someone grasps the thought that 17 is a prime number, but is not capable of grasping the thought that 31 is a prime number, even though he is capable of thinking of the number 31? It seems that if he knows what it is for a number to be prime, he cannot fail to have the capacity for grasping that 31 is prime, and if he does not have that knowledge, he will not have the capacity to judge that 17 is prime either. At one point (1987, 152) Fodor notes that on certain "inferential role" theories of the logical constants, as a matter of what is constitutive of grasping the concept, certain sorts of systematicity are guaranteed. Though I am not defending an inferential-role semantics for all concepts, my position is indeed that what is constitutive of grasping an arbitrary concept ensures the form of systematicity stated in the Generality Constraint.[5]

To clarify my position, I should emphasize that I am not denying that, for instance, it is an empirical and contingent matter that if a creature is making a selective, discriminative response to situations in which the cup is to the left of the box, it is also capable of making the same selective response to situations in which the box is to the left of the cup. The necessity of the Generality Constraint does not contradict the fact that such conditionals are contingent. The Constraint says nothing about such conditionals, since they do concern not the creature's exercise of concepts but only kinds of situation to which the creature responds. What I am committed to claiming is noncontingent is this: if a creature is capable of forming the conditional intention to do so-and-so when the cup is to the left of the box, then there is no conceptual bar to its forming the intention to do so-and-so when the box is to the left of the cup.[6]

2.3 Links with the *Tractatus*

In the *Tractatus* (1961b) Wittgenstein did not operate with a notion of sense as distinct from that of reference. But he was clearly concerned with abstract, general requirements on the meaningfulness of sentences. Many of these general requirements continue to stand after a sense-reference distinction is introduced and after the formulations are reapplied at the level of thought. There are complex interrelations between the framework I am advocating and the *Tractatus*. Some of the connections consist of compelling conditions of adequacy formulated in the *Tractatus*, conditions of adequacy that proposers of other theories must show are equally met by their own efforts. There are also connections resulting from the bearing of my framework on issues and problems in the *Tractatus*. I will give three illustrations.

First, Wittgenstein complained that one of Russell's theories of judgement does not meet the requirement that one can only judge what makes sense. Wittgenstein wrote, "From the proposition '**A** judges that (say) **a** is in relation **R** to **b**', if correctly analyzed, the propositions [*sic*] '**aRb** $\lor$ ~**aRb**' must follow directly *without the use of any other premiss*" (1961a, 121). My theory meets this condition. A thinker can judge only contents that he grasps (remember that we are continuing to prescind from deference-dependent attributions). Grasp consists in knowing the condition for the content to be true (on the basis of his grasp of its components and its mode of composition). If there is such a condition, any sentence expressing the content will make sense. In my neo-Fregean theory, Wittgenstein's requirement is met in a very direct way: grasp of the content consists in knowing the very condition the grasped content imposes on the world.

Second, in his penetrating study of the development of Wittgenstein's philosophy, Pears (1987, 132–133) notes a tension between separatist and holistic elements of Wittgenstein's early thought. The holistic aspects are found in Wittgenstein's comparison of a proposition with a set of coordinates fixing a point in space (1961b, pars. 3.032, 3.41, 3.411, 3.42). As Pears emphasizes, one understands a given set of coordinates only if one has grasped a system of reference to points by coordinates. The separatist element is at the fore in such passages as this: "The reality that corresponds to the sense of the proposition can surely be nothing but its component parts, since we are surely *ignorant* of *everything* else" (1961a, 20 Nov. 1914). With a sense/reference distinction and in the context of my theory, we can resolve this tension. Separatism holds at the level of reference. The reality relevant to the truth of a proposition consists of the semantic values of its component concepts; the truth or falsity of the proposition depends only on the relations of these semantic values to one another, and not on anything else. But holism (in the sense with which Pears is concerned) is correct at the level of concepts. If the considerations of the earlier sections above are correct, what is involved in possessing the concept F necessarily puts someone who grasps it in a position to grasp the contents $Fa, Fb, Fc, \ldots$ for suitable lower-level concepts $a, b, c, \ldots$ drawn from his conceptual repertoire. Similarly, what is involved in possessing the lower-level concept a necessarily places someone who grasps it in a position to grasp the contents $Fa, Ga, Ha, \ldots$ for suitable predicative concepts drawn from his repertoire.

Third, the requirement that an account of a concept meet the $\mathcal{A}(C)$ form also bears on one reading of the elusive doctrine that some things can only be shown and not said. Pears, with some hesitation, expounds part of that doctrine thus: "There is certainly something here which we cannot do: we cannot give a complete account of the sense of any factual sentence" (1987, 144). More particularly, "[if the doctrine of showing is right] we cannot give a complete account of the sense of a factual sentence without reusing that sentence's method of correlation with the possibility presented by it" (p. 148). Pears notes that this means that an explanation of the method of correlation of sentences with the world would be no use to someone who does not already understand it or something equivalent to it (pp. 144–145, 148). This is certainly true of what Pears would label, in the literary rather than truth-functional sense, the "tautological" account that "George is bald" means that George is bald. In reply to someone who says that we know what the sentence means and what we want is an explanation of it having the meaning it does, Pears writes, "The tautological account manifests another deficiency: it cannot explain a fact of this kind, because it has no way of getting past it and finding any further independently specifiable fact to support it" (p. 148).[7]

We need to distinguish here two readings of "independently specifiable." For, once we acknowledge that the $\mathcal{A}(C)$ form is correct, things are not so bleak. If the Principle of Dependence of section 1.2 is right, then a full account of grasp of a given concept is also an account of the nature of that concept itself. One respect in which that account may not be independently specifiable is that it may ineliminably use a concept, grasp of which, and so the nature of which, is being elucidated. This certainly prevents the account from being understood by one who does not possess the concept in question. But it does not prevent the account from being substantive, nontautologous, and individuating. It can be so, if in the account, the concept in question is not mentioned as such within the scope of the thinker's propositional attitudes (as opposed to being quantified over). If an account is not independently specifiable in that it violates this proviso, then there is indeed a circularity. But we have already seen in chapter 1 accounts of particular concepts that do not violate independent specifiability in this sense. In brief, we can distinguish an extreme demand for independent specifiability, which on my theory is in some cases not to be had, from this more moderate demand that the concept not be mentioned as such in the scope of the thinker's attitudes, a demand that can be met. The unmeetability of the extreme demand shows only that in some cases a complete account of a concept must use that concept. It does not show that complete accounts of a concept are impossible.[8]

2.4 Knowing-What-It-Is-For and the Explanations

I now turn to consider the notion of knowing-what-it-is-for and its role in the above explanations. I have leaned heavily on the notion in the Referential Explanation of the Generality Constraint. The notion has an intuitive appeal. It is highly intuitive that one cannot have any

propositional attitude of the sort in question in this chapter to the
content that p unless one knows what it is for it to be true that p. It
is equally intuitive that knowledge of what it is for it to be true that p
results from knowledge of what it is for things to be the semantic
values of its constituent concepts. But what is the status of the notion
of knowing-what-it-is-for, and how does it contribute to explanations?
My concern here is with grasp of conceptual content, and not immediately with the philosophy of language. But anyone interested in
applying these discussions to the philosophy of language will rapidly
see that what I have to say about grasp of concepts can be developed
equally for grasp of meaning.

Knowing-what-it-is-for seems to be distinct both from knowing that
and from knowing how. It is not reducible to knowing that, if my
account is correct, on pain of infinite regress. On my account, any
case of knowing that such and such rests upon several cases of knowing-what-it-is-for, namely, knowing what it is for things to be the values
of the various conceptual components of the content that such and
such. If these latter pieces of knowledge were in turn reducible to
knowledge that, we would be launched on an infinite regress.[9]

Nor is there any obvious reduction of knowing-what-it-is-for to
knowing how. I am trying to give a theory acceptable to a realist, so
knowing how to verify or how to falsify a thought are unavailable as
reductions to knowing how. It is true that some instances of knowing
how, for instance, knowing how to speak a particular language, suffice
for the possession of knowledge of what it is for things to be the
semantic values of the various concepts expressed in the language.
But it would be a nonsequitur to infer that knowing-what-it-is-for must
therefore be a form of knowing how. Many cases of knowing how
involve knowledge that: knowing how to prove Pythagoras' Theorem
would be an example. Knowing how to speak a language is plausibly
another. If it is, then by the regress argument, this route offers no
reduction either.

Is knowing what it is for something to be the semantic value of a
concept identifiable with knowing *when* to judge certain contents containing that concept? The problem with this is that a set of contents
does not in general determine whether it should be accepted in the
presence of given evidence. Two thinkers with the same conceptual
repertoire and in the same evidential position may differ in which

contents they are disposed to accept, because one is bolder, more imaginative, or more ingenious than the other. Can we then at least identify knowing-what-it-is-for with knowing what the constraints on the acceptance of contents are? If this means knowing *that* the constraints are such and such, it attributes unnecessary philosophical sophistication to the ordinary thinker. It is also vulnerable to the regress argument. The suggestion could be made more plausible by taking it to mean that there is some kind of knowledge of what the constraints are reflected in the thinker's willingness to make certain judgements for certain reasons. But in this sense, to say that someone knows what the constraints are on a given concept needs to be shown to be more than a stylistic variant on saying that he knows what it is for something to be its reference. Otherwise, it does not offer an illuminating reduction.

To say that someone possesses a particular concept is to make commitments about the kind of contents to which he is capable of having propositional attitudes. Propositional attitudes are at what Dennett (1978) distinguishes as the personal level, rather than his subpersonal level.[10] So if we accept the Identification of possessing a concept with knowing what it is for something to be its semantic value, knowing-what-it-is-for is at the personal level, not the subpersonal level. All the specific possession conditions I gave in chapter 1 were in fact at the personal level, and so are all those to follow in later chapters. Indeed, this must be so, because all possession conditions speak in one way or another of a speaker's reasons for forming beliefs (positive or negative). The statement that someone forms a belief for a particular reason is at the personal level, not the subpersonal.

The recombinability of constituents to form new contents is necessary for a type of content to be conceptual content, but it is not sufficient. Plausible computational theories of early visual processing make extensive attribution of contents, subpersonal contents, to states of the visual system that are produced prior to the production of visual experience. These contents are representational in that they have correctness conditions concerning things, properties, and magnitudes in the subject's environment. The components of these contents need not display full recombinability in respect of the range of states that the subject can instantiate. But even if it happened that there was such full recombinability for a particular subject, that would not suffice to make these contents into conceptual contents. (See also Davies 1989.) These contents would not be individuated by possession conditions formulated at the personal level. There would be no personal-level notion of knowing what it is for one of these contents to apply to something. Nor would there be any applicable notion of the person's reasons for being in the subpersonal states with these contents.

There are many skeptical positions that compete with the general position I have been taking in this chapter. Some such skeptical positions are defined by their claim that the notion of knowing-what-it-is-for is philosophically epiphenomenal. According to skeptical positions in this class, it is our practice to say that a thinker knows what it is for something to be the semantic value of a sense when we are prepared to attribute to him attitudes to contents containing that sense, and that is also the order of explanation, according to these skeptics. Talk of possession conditions or of knowing-what-it-is-for is, for them, nothing but redescription of certain facts about the legitimate attribution of propositional attitudes. Such redescriptions cannot be explanatory, they will insist, and certainly not causally explanatory.

I disagree. A thinker's meeting a possession condition for a particular concept can causally explain his judging a content containing the concept. This can be so even in circumstances that, as a matter of what is involved in possessing the concept, are sufficient for being prepared to judge the content. Take *red* again. A person can experience an object as having a particular shade clearly within the range of the spectrum covered by *red,* and he may also believe that he is not misperceiving in any way. This is not enough for him to be prepared to judge that the presented object is red, since these facts are jointly consistent with his not possessing the concept *red,* which picks out a particular, fuzzily bounded segment of the color spectrum. When a thinker is prepared to judge the object to be red, his possession of the concept *red* is an additional causal factor contributing to his readiness to do so.

Why should anyone deny this? One reason may be that, a priori, if a thinker has the concept *red,* enjoys an experience of an object as falling under a shade of red, does not discern any misperception, etc., he is prepared to judge that the perceptually presented object is red. This is not a good reason. Before it was known which chromosomal abnormality is responsible for Down's syndrome, we might refer to the abnormal property as "the D property." It would then have been a priori that if Down's syndrome is caused by a chromosomal abnormality, someone with Down's syndrome has chromosomes with the D property. It can hardly follow that having the D property does not cause Down's syndrome. No doubt it follows that there must be some other characterization possible of the D property. But there will also be other characterizations of a particular person's state of possessing a given concept: it is one of the aims of a subpersonal psychology to supply precisely this. (I discuss the relations between possession conditions and a subpersonal psychology further in chapter 7.)

A different reason that might be canvassed for saying that possession of a concept cannot be explanatory is an a priori conditional in the reverse direction. As the notions are used here, it is a priori that if someone can judge a content containing a given concept, then he possesses that concept. However, quite generally in the philosophy of mind and of language, there are capacities that can exist only if their existence has a causal explanation of a certain kind. Consider, for instance, the ability to hear the sentence "London is noisy" as meaning that London is noisy, that is, the ability to hear the occurrence of "London" as meaning London, and so forth. This ability can exist only if some states implicated in the perception of utterances contain the information that "London" means London, and so forth (Peacocke 1986a). These states causally help explain the person's hearing the utterance as meaning that London is noisy. But I doubt that we can conceive of precisely this capacity existing without its having an explanation of this sort.

There are further parallels between the explanation of someone's perception of an uttered sentence as having a certain meaning and the explanation of someone's ability to make judgements of given propositional contents. First, if someone no longer (subpersonally) possesses semantic information about the meaning of the word "London," then he no longer understands sentences containing it. Equally, if someone no longer knows what it is for something to be the semantic value of a given concept, then he loses the capacity to have propositional attitudes toward contents containing it. Second, both the subpersonally possessed semantic information and the knowledge of what it is for something to be the semantic value of a sense operate recursively. Third, both states help explain knowledge. Appropriate possession of the information that "London" means London results in perceptual knowledge that a certain utterance means that London is thus and so. A thinker's satisfaction of the possession condition for *red* is part of the explanation of his knowing that something is red when he experiences something as red and is, in suitable circumstances, taking his experience at face value. (I dip my toes into the ocean of issues surrounding the relations between possession conditions and epistemology in section 6.2.)

There are also two disanalogies, of course. The subpersonally possessed semantic information is information *that* such and such; I have been arguing that knowing-what-it-is-for cannot be knowledge of that kind. Second, I have claimed that knowing-what-it-is-for is at the personal level, not the subpersonal level.[11]

How can a skeptic who takes possession conditions to be epiphenomenal explain the truth of the Generality Constraint? The constraint cannot be explained as a trivial consequence of what is involved in a concept's having a certain significance range. If the object referred to by the singular mode of presentation *b* is in the significance range of the concept *F,* it does indeed seem to follow that the content *Fb* is intelligible, that it *could* be grasped by some thinker or other. Yet the consequent of the Generality Constraint speaks not of what could be grasped by some thinker or other but of what a thinker who satisfies the antecedent is actually in a position to know. It is hard to see how to derive that consequent without relying on the Identification.

Alternatively, the skeptic may say that conformity to the constraint is simply an additional requirement on the acceptability of a set of attitudes putatively attributed to a thinker by a radical-ascription procedure. If he says this, the skeptic need not reject the Identification, nor need he deny that we can write possession conditions for concepts of the sort I have been discussing. His view is just that they have no explanatory power. I close this chapter with a query for this kind of skeptic.

The query is whether we should try to explain any universal constraint on radical ascription in a way that relates it to what is fundamental to propositional-attitude psychology. Just saying that we attribute attitudes so as to make the constraint and other principles come out true leaves their status unexplained. The Referential Explanation, by contrast, grounds them in facts about making another thinker intelligible to us. A subject's thought and action has to be intelligible, given the way he represents the world to be, and representing the world to be a certain way involves knowledge of what it is for things to fall under the representing concepts. On the explanation I propose, systematicity is found wherever there is *Verstehen*.

2.5   Summary and a Further Application

In this chapter I have argued that the recombinability of concepts is inextricably tied to their referential properties. Such recombinability is not merely definitional, nor is it merely empirical. It is rather an inevitable concomitant of concepts' possessing semantic values that contribute to the determination of the truth value of thoughts containing them. In developing this position, I have made use of the notion of knowing what it is for something to be the semantic value of a concept and of knowing what it is for something to be the case. I have tried to elucidate that notion a little and to put it to some work. There remains much that is unclear about the notion. There also remains some promising, relatively undeveloped territory: the extension of the present approach to linguistic meaning and to the role of knowing-what-it-is-for in the elucidation of linguistic understanding. I hope that others too will explore this territory. With the results of such further exploration, we will be in a better to position to know whether the notion of knowing what it is for something to be the case can earn its keep.

3 Perceptual Concepts

A perceptual experience represents the world as being a certain way. What is the nature of the content it represents as holding? How is our mastery of observational concepts related to these perceptual contents? More generally, how are we to formulate possession conditions for observational concepts? These questions are of some intrinsic interest, but they are also crucial for a general theory of concepts.

Sometimes two sets of concepts stand in an asymmetrical relation of dependence. Possession of the concepts in one set presupposes, as a philosophical matter, possession of the concepts in a second set, while there is no converse presupposition of possession of concepts in the first set by possession of the concepts in the second set. Since our repertoire of primitive, unstructured concepts is finite, there will be at least one set of concepts that does not stand in the asymmetrical relation of dependence to any other set. It is very plausible that perceptual, relatively observational concepts are elements of one such set of concepts that does not depend asymmetrically on any others. A theory of concepts must explain the nature and the possibility of such conceptually basic sets.

In the course of addressing these issues, I will be identifying two kinds of representational content on which we can draw in giving accounts of concepts that have peculiarly close links with perception.

3.1 Scenarios Introduced

The representational content of experience is a many-splendored thing. This is true not only of the remarkable range of detail in the perceptual content but also of the range of different and philosophically interesting types of content that can be possessed by a particular experience. I begin with what is arguably the most fundamental type of representational content. The sense in which this type of content is arguably the most fundamental is that representational properties of all other sorts in various ways presuppose the existence of this first type of content.

I suggest that one basic form of representational content should be individuated by specifying which ways of filling out the space around the perceiver are consistent with the representational content's being correct. The idea is that the content involves a spatial *type,* the type being that under which fall precisely those ways of filling the space around the subject that are consistent with the correctness of the content. On this model, correctness of a content is then a matter of instantiation: the instantiation by the real world around the perceiver of the spatial type that gives the representational content in question.[1]

This intuitive formulation can be sharpened. There are two steps we have to take if we are to specify fully one of these spatial types. The first step is to fix an origin and axes. The origin and axes will not be a specific place and set of directions in the real world. This is precisely because we are here fixing a type that may potentially be instantiated at many different places in the real world. Nevertheless, it is important that the origin and axes be labeled by certain interrelated properties. It is this labeling by interrelated properties that helps to constrain what are instantiations of the spatial type we are determining. Thus, for instance, one kind of origin is given by the property of being the center of the chest of the human body, with the three axes given by the directions back/front, left/right, and up/down with respect to that center.

The use of a particular set of labeled axes in giving part of the content of an experience is not a purely notational or conventional matter. The appropriate set of labeled axes captures distinctions in the phenomenology of experience itself. Looking straight ahead at Buckingham Palace is one experience. It is another to look at the palace with one's face still toward it but with one's body turned toward a point on the right. In this second case the palace is experienced as being off to one side from the direction of straight ahead, even if the view remains exactly the same as in the first case.

To say that bodily parts are mentioned in the labeling of the axes is not to imply that the bodily parts are given to the subject in some visual or other sensory manner. It is not necessary, in experiencing something as standing in certain spatial relations to one's own body, to perceive one's own bodily parts. They may even by anaesthetized. The nature of the way in which bodily parts are given when they are appropriate labels for the axes is actually an issue of considerable interest. For present purposes, though, let me just note that in using this framework I am committed to the existence of some such way in which bodily parts are so given.

In giving the content of tactile experience, we would sometimes have to use as origin something labeled with the property of being the center of the palm of the human hand, with axes defined in relation to parts of the hand. Actually, in the specification of the representational content of some human experiences, one would need to consider several such systems of origins and axes, and to specify the spatial relations of these systems to one another. There are many other complexities too, but let me keep things simple at this stage.

Having fixed origin and axes, we need to take the second step in determining one of the spatial types, namely, that of specifying a way of filling out the space around the origin. Actually, in giving the content, we should strictly consider a set of such ways of filling out the space. By doing so, we can capture the degree of the experiencer's perceptual acuity. Greater acuity corresponds to restriction of the set of ways of filling out the space whose instantiation is consistent with the correctness of the representational content. I will understand this qualification as holding for the remainder of this chapter. In picking out one of these ways of filling out the space, we need to do at least the following. For each point (strictly, I should say point type), identified by its distance and direction from the origin, we need to specify whether there is a surface there and, if so, what texture, hue, saturation, and brightness it has at that point, together with its degree of solidity. The orientation of the surface must be included. So must much more in the visual case: the direction, intensity, and character of light sources; the rate of change of perceptible properties, including location; indeed, it should include second differentials with respect to time where these prove to be perceptible.

There is no requirement at this point that the conceptual apparatus used in specifying a way of filling out the space be an apparatus of concepts used by the perceiver himself. Any apparatus we want to use, however sophisticated, may be employed in fixing the spatial type, however primitive the conceptual resources of the perceiver with whom we are concerned. This applies both to the apparatus used in characterizing distances and directions, and to that employed in characterizing the surfaces, features, and the rest. I will return to the significance of this point later. The spatial type itself is not built up from concepts at all: it is well suited to be a constituent of a form of nonconceptual content.

I am now in a position to say, with slightly more precision, what one of the spatial types is. It is a way of locating surfaces, features, and the rest in relation to such a labeled origin and family of axes. I call such a spatial type a "scenario." Though I have been considering the content of visual experience for illustrative purposes, it should not be supposed in advance that the scenario contents of experiences in different modalities are totally disjoint. On the contrary, there are good reasons for saying that some overlap is possible. I will also return to this issue later.

With this apparatus, we can then say what is required for the correctness of a representational content of the sort with which I am concerned. Consider the volume of the real world around the perceiver at the time of the experience, with an origin and axes in the real world fixed in accordance with the labeling in the scenario. I call this a "scene." The content of the experience is correct if this scene falls under the way of locating surfaces and the rest that constitutes the scenario.

It is important to give for experiences a notion of their representational content that is evaluable as correct or incorrect outright, rather than merely as correct or incorrect relative to some assignment or other. The point parallels (and indeed is connected with) a familiar point in the philosophy of language. Consider a particular utterance of the indexical sentence "He is witty." A theory should provide a statement of the conditions under which this particular utterance is true outright, rather than merely the conditions under which it is true relative to any given assignment of objects to its indexical elements (Burge 1974). It is the content of the utterance assessable outright that concerns particular objects. Similarly, it is the content of a perceptual experience assessable outright that concerns particular places. For perceptual experience, I identify such an outright-assessable content with a *positioned scenario*. A positioned scenario consists of a scenario, together with (1) an assignment to the labeled axes and origins of the scenario of real directions and places in the world that fall under the labels, and (2) an assigned time. For a particular perceptual experience, the real directions and places assigned at (1) are given by the application of the labels to the subject who has the experience. If the origin is labeled as the center of gravity of the body, the real place assigned to it is the center of gravity of the perceiver's body, and so forth. (I oversimplify a little in aiming to capture the spirit of a position.) The time assigned at (2) is the time at which the perceptual experience occurs: perceptual experience has a present-tense content.[2] We can then say that the content given by the positioned scenario is correct if the scene at its assigned place falls under the scenario at the assigned time, when the scenario is positioned there in accordance with the assigned directions.

The requirement that any perceptual experience has a correctness condition imposes restrictions on what other forms of perceptual experience, besides those of human beings, are possible. Suppose it were said that there could exist a being whose perceptions have scenario-involving contents that have an origin but do not contain labeled axes. Now a correctness condition for a particular experience occurring at a given time is not fixed until its scenario is positioned in the real world. An origin alone does not suffice for this positioning: there will be many different ways of orienting it around the perceiver's location at the time of the experience. Until one of these orientations has been selected as being the appropriate one, no correctness condition has been determined. Even in the case of spherical organisms, existing in a fluid, whose perceptions are caused by the impact of light all over the surface of their bodies, the scenarios presented by such organisms' experiences must have axes labeled by parts of their bodies. (The parts mentioned in the labeling need not be limbs.) I will return to this labeling later.

I should also emphasize that the positioned scenario is literally meant to be the content itself. It is to be distinguished from any mental representation of the content. Subpersonal mental representations of several different sorts may equally have for their content the same particular component of a scenario. Possible mental representations with a given positioned-scenario content stand in a many-one relation to the content itself. For example, the orientation of a surface at a particular point may be given by specifying its slant and tilt, or equally by specifying components for its representation in gradient space (Marr 1982, 241–243). Mental representations that differ in the way such orientations are represented may nevertheless represent the same scenario as instantiated in their respective subjects' surroundings.

Since I have now touched on the issue of mental representation, it may be helpful for me to comment on the relation between the account being developed here and Marr's 2½-D sketch. There can be much in a positioned scenario that is not in the content of a 2½-D sketch. The 2½-D sketch has only retinocentric coordinates and does not include illumination conditions. My account, though, gives a natural framework in which to give the content of a 2½-D sketch if such mental representations exist.

Is my account committed at least to the existence of mental representations with roughly the properties of Marr's 2½-D sketches? In Marr's work, such representations are computed after the primal sketch and before any 3-D models are assigned to shapes in the environment. Is my philosophical treatment committed to the existence of such a temporally intermediate representation? It is not. What matters for the purposes to which this apparatus will be put is that there exist some mental representation at least part of whose content is given by the positioned scenario. It does not matter if the representation also has other, perhaps simultaneously computed, contents. It *will* matter that certain systematic connections hold between these scenario-involving contents and other contents that the representations may possess. I will be arguing that the identity of certain other contents depends upon the nature of their links with scenario-involving contents. But again, this does not require the existence of distinct mental representations with roughly the properties of Marr's 2½-D sketches.

A good theory must elucidate the appropriate correctness conditions for perceptual experiences if it is adequately to distinguish these experiences from states that do not represent the world as being a certain way to the subject. But the importance of elucidating representational content goes far beyond the need to draw that distinction in the right place. By perceiving the world, we frequently learn whether a judgement with a given conceptual content is true or not. This is possible only because a perceptual experience has a correctness condition whose holding may itself exclude, or require, the truth of a conceptual content.

Some conceptual contents are actually individuated in part by their relations to those perceptual experiences that give good reasons for judging those contents. I will give some detailed examples later. But in advance of the details, it should be clear that scenarios are a promising resource for anchoring notions of conceptual content in some level of nonconceptual content. For a scenario is a spatial type, and a positioned scenario is just a spatial type as tied down to a particular location, orientation, and time. A spatial type is quite different from a concept. The identity of a concept, as the term is used here, is answerable to Fregean considerations of cognitive significance. If the account in chapter 1 is right, a concept is also ultimately individuated by the condition required for a thinker to possess it. A spatial type is not. So a theory of nonconceptual content that employs the notion of a spatial type promises one way in which a hierarchy of families of concepts can be grounded in a noncircular way.

The notion of a positioned scenario I have been employing is one that can give the content of a fully perceptual experience and can equally give the content of a hallucinatory experience. But it is quite consistent with the apparatus I have introduced to hold that the fully perceptual case has a philosophical primacy and that nonperceptual cases have to be elucidated by the relations in which they stand to the fully perceptual case. Consider two different scenes the objects in each of which are distinct but that are perceived fully veridically and in the same way. We can regard a scenario as being the type that captures the similarity of two such different perceptual cases. It is then open to us to say that a hallucinatory experience represents the environment as being a scene of such a type, though there is no such scene there. In brief, the scenario account neither exacerbates nor by itself solves epistemological problems.[3]

3.2   Consequences and Comparisons of Scenarios

There are several desirable consequences of the thesis that the objective content of an experience is given in part by its positioned scenario. I note three of them.

First, writers on the objective content of experience have often remarked that an experience can have a finer-grained content than can be formulated by using concepts possessed by the experiencer. If you are looking at a range of mountains, it may be correct to say that you see some as rounded, some as jagged. But the content of your visual experience in respect of the shape of the mountains is far more specific than that description indicates. The description involving the concepts *round* and *jagged* would cover many different fine-grained contents that your experience could have, contents that are discriminably different from one another.

This fine-grained content is captured in the scenario. Only those ways of filling out the space around you that are consistent with the veridicality of your experience will be included in the scenario. The scenario will omit many ways that equally involve the appropriate mountains being rounded or jagged.

In describing the scenario, we do, of course, have to employ concepts. To fix on the scenario uniquely, we will have to use very fine-grained concepts too, to capture the fine-grained content. But it is crucial to observe that the fact that a concept is used in fixing the scenario does *not* entail that the concept itself is somehow a component of the representational content of the experience, nor that the concept must be possessed by the experiencer. The fine-grained concepts have done their work when they have fixed a unique spatial type. We should not confuse the scenario, the spatial type itself, with the infinitely various ways of picking it out. It is the type that is involved in the content of the experience, not descriptions of the type.

Correlatively, on this account we have to recognize the rather indirect way in which descriptions in ordinary language, which are always at least partially conceptualized, help to characterize the way in which someone is experiencing the world. The ordinary-language characterization of the scenario can be at most partial.

Second, in some of my own earlier writings (1986c, 1989c) I discussed the senses in which the type of content possessed by perceptual experience has an analogue character and is unit-free. Let me take its analogue character first. To say that the type of content in question has an analogue character is to make the following point. There are many dimensions—hue, shape, size, direction—such that any value on that dimension may enter the fine-grained content of an experience. In particular, an experience is not restricted in its range of possible contents to those points or ranges picked out by concepts—*red, square, straight ahead*—possessed by the perceiver. This fact is accommodated by attributing to the experience a scenario as part of its content. It is accommodated for characteristics of points in the environment because any values of a perceptible dimension may be mentioned in the ways of filling out the space around the perceiver that comprise the scenario. The restrictions on the environment determined by the veridicality of the experience need not be formulable using concepts possessed by the subject independently of the occurrence of the experience. With some important qualifications to be given below, nonpunctual properties, like shape, in the scenario will be determined by the assignments to points. Again, there will be no restrictions resulting from the thinker's repertoire of shape concepts on the shapes he may perceive things as having.

The unit-free nature of spatial perception is illustrated by the fact that when we see a table to have a certain width, we do not see it as having a certain width in inches, say, as opposed to centimetres. This is also explained by the distinction between the ways of characterizing a scenario and the scenario itself. Suppose we prescind here from qualifications about perceptual acuity. Then we can say that one and the same restriction on the distance between the sides of the table, one and the same restriction on the ways in which the space around the perceiver can be filled consistently with the experience being fully veridical, is given by doing either of these two things: saying that the sides are 39.4 inches apart, saying that they are 100 centimeters apart. The same point also holds for directions and the units in which they may be measured.

Third, the scenario account provides for the possibility of amodal contents of experience, in the sense that it allows for overlapping contents of experiences in different sense modalities. The restrictions on the environment required by the correctness of a visual experience may overlap with the restrictions required by the correctness of a tactile experience. This can be so if the positions of the origins and axes for the scenarios of each experience are fixed relative to each other by the subject's total conscious state. Both a visual experience and a tactile experience resulting from stretching out your arm at a certain angle may represent the existence of a surface in front of you at a certain distance. Because of this, if one takes one's experience at face value, the judgement "That surface is red and warm" does not rest on any identity belief, at any higher, concept-involving level, concerning the surface in question.[4] I will consider amodal conceptual contents further below.

There is a great deal more to be said on all aspects of this account. But even on this very primitive foundation, two considerations support the claim that an account mentioning scenarios cannot be dispensed with in favor of purely propositional accounts of the representational contents in question. By a "purely propositional account" I mean one that identifies the representational content with a set of propositions (whether built to Frege's, Russell's, or some other specification), where the constituents of these propositions do not involve scenarios directly or indirectly.

First, it is hard to see how a purely propositional account can be made plausible without being parasitic on something properly treated by the use of scenarios. Suppose you are in a field in the early autumn in England and see mist in a certain region. Can a theorist specify part of the representational content of your visual experience by means of the proposition that the region has the property of being misty? Consider in particular the Russellian proposition, which has the region itself as a constituent. This proposal seems inadequate for very familiar reasons. Suppose the region in question is to your north. Someone for whom the region is in a northeasterly direction may also see it to be misty, and the same Russellian proposition would be used by this theorist in specifying the content of his experience. But the region is clearly presented in perception in different ways to you and to the other person. Each of you sees it as being in a different direction relative to yourself, and your actions may differ as a result. Any description of the contents of your two experiences that omits this difference is incomplete. If we fill out the propositional theory to include "ways in which regions are perceived," the advocate of the scenario account will understandably say that these "ways" are a prime example of something only his account adequately explains.

To this the purely propositional theorist may reply that the relevant aspect of representational content should be formulated not just as "**R** is misty," where **R** is the region in question, but with a conjunction of Russellian propositions: "**R** is misty, and **R** is located in direction **D**." Here **D** is an egocentric direction.

The theorist of scenarios should say that this move is inadequate on either of the two ways of taking it. The two ways of taking it result from two different ways of construing "egocentric." Take first the construal on which seeing something to be in egocentric direction **D** involves merely seeing it as having a certain direction in relation to object **x**, where **x** is in fact the perceiver himself. This reading is too weak to capture what is wanted. This is because one can see something as having a particular direction in relation to an object **x** which is in fact oneself while not realizing that the object to which one sees it as bearing that relation is in fact oneself. Examples of persons seen in mirrors suffice to make the point.

This suggests that the propositional theorist needs rather the stronger construal. On the stronger construal, to see something as having an egocentric spatial property is to see it as standing in a certain relation to oneself, where this involves use of the first-person way of thinking in giving the content of the visual experience. But the second consideration I wish to develop is precisely that purely propositional accounts, unlike the theory of scenarios, make impossible an adequate account of the first-person way of thinking.

We have just seen that the pure propositionalist will have to mention the first-person way of thinking in giving the propositional contents of experience. For the pure propositionalist, propositional contents exhaust the nonconceptual representational content of experience. But this position is incompatible with the conjunction of two other principles that we have reason to accept.

One of these principles is what I call "Evans's Thesis."

Evans's Thesis   It is partially constitutive of a subject's employing the first-person way of thinking that he is prepared to make noninferential, suitable first-person spatial judgements on the basis of his perceptions when these are taken at face value. These will include "I am on a bridge" when he has an experience as of being on a bridge, "I am in front of a building," "There is a dog on my right," and so forth. (Evans 1982, chapters 6, 7)

The other principle is the Principle of Dependence of chapter 1. The Principle of Dependence states that there can be no more to a concept than is determined by a correct account of what it is to possess that concept. It was this which motivated the requirement that it should be possible to cast a good account of a concept in the $\mathscr{A}(C)$ form: concept F is that concept C to possess which a thinker must meet the condition $\mathscr{A}(C)$, where the concept F is not mentioned as such within the scope of psychological states ascribed to the thinker. The application of the principle of interest here is to first-person thought. If we accept Evans's Thesis, then the first-person way of thinking will be individuated in part by the rational sensitivity of present-tense spatial judgements containing it to the content of a thinker's perceptual experiences. But according to the propositionalist, these experiences themselves already have a first-person content not directly or indirectly explained in terms of scenarios. So the propositionalist will not have given an account of the first person that respects the Principle of Dependence. An account of mastery of a concept is still circular if it adverts, without further elaboration or explanation, to relations to perceptual states with a content requiring possession of the concept, the first-person concept, whose possession was to be elucidated.

This problem is not solved for the pure propositionalist merely by saying that he holds that neither experience nor thought is prior in the individuation of the first-person way of thinking (a "no-priority" view). As long as it is agreed that part of the account of mastery of the first-person concept involves a certain distinctive sensitivity of first-person spatial judgements to the deliverances of perceptual experience, there is an obligation to say what that sensitivity is without simply taking possession of the first-person concept for granted. If we accept the Principle of Dependence, an account of grasp of the first-person concept must distinguish it from all other concepts. Certainly the pure propositionalist does not have something individuating if he says that the first person (for a given subject) is that concept m such that his judgements about whether Fm display a certain sensitivity to experiences that represent Fm as being the case. This condition will be met by much else, including demonstrative ways of thinking of places in his immediate surroundings. A natural further condition is one that relates first-person, present-tense spatial judgements in a particular way to the scenario content of experience. But if this further condition is correct, the resulting treatment of the content of experience is not a purely propositional theory after all, for it employs scenario content.

The scenario account can respect the Principle of Dependence applied to the first person in the following way. The scenario account already says that a fundamental type of representational content is given by a scenario, a spatial type with a labeled origin and labeled axes. The rational sensitivity picked out in Evans's Thesis should be understood as a rational sensitivity of first-person, present-tense spatial judgements to the spatial relations that things are represented in the scenario of the experience as having *to the labeled central bodily origin and axes*. This avoids the circularity, and in an intuitive way.

Of course, I still owe a philosophical account of what it is for one scenario, with one set of labeled axes and origin rather than another, to be the content of an experience. But once we recognize the level of the scenario, there is nothing to make this problem insoluble.

Devotees of the theory of indexical thought will note that points exactly corresponding to those just made about first-person thought can be made about the indexical concept *here*. There would equally be a circularity in the philosophical account of mastery of *here* in its relation to perceptual experience if we were not able to make reference to the labeled origin in an experience's scenario.

It need not, of course, be any part of the scenario account to deny that the first person has to be mentioned in fully specifying the representational content of perceptual experience. It should insist on first-person contents, as it should equally insist on the partially conceptual character of the perceptual content when one sees something to be a dog or a tree. Again, the same applies to the conceptual constituent *here*. The issue is rather, in the case of the first person, whether or not the theorist can say more about the nature of first-person content, and similarly for these other conceptual constituents.

Despite the problems faced by the purely propositional approach, there is one range of phenomena for which the pure propositionalist may seem to have a superior treatment. These phenomena are experiences of "impossible" objects. The experience may be of an "impossible" depiction, or of an "impossible" three-dimensional object (Gregory 1970, 55). The problem such examples pose for my account results from the fact that there is no way of filling in the space around the perceiver in the region of the "impossible" object that is consistent with the correctness of the experience, for apparently the experience has an inconsistent content.

This problem is not satisfactorily resolved by leaving it unspecified, in such a case, what is in the region of the impossible object. That would not distinguish the experience of an "impossible" object from the quite different case of a subject who has a blind area, or scotoma, for that region. Nor would it be satisfactory to restrict the range of states said to have scenario content to those with a given locus of focal attention. It is true in some cases that the inconsistency of the properties of the "impossible" object can be established only with a shift of attention. But that does not hold for all examples, notably in cases in which the "impossible" object takes up a small region of the subject's visual field.

The experience of "impossible" objects should not be characterized at the level of scenario content at all. Though I have been arguing that scenario content cannot be replaced by pure propositional contents, propositional contents (even of a neo-Russellian kind) can still be important in characterizing further features of perceptual content once we have the level of scenario content in place. I will be arguing for just such a view in the next section. It will be a feature of this further level that it allows for an adequate account of experience of "impossible" objects.

3.3 A Further Level of Content and Its Applications

I have touched on one way in which scenarios can contribute to the individuation of a concept, the first-person concept. I turn now to discuss how some other conceptual contents are individuated in part by their relations to a level of nonconceptual representational content. I will be suggesting that we need to recognize a kind of nonconceptual representational content in addition to the positioned scenario.

How is mastery of such apparently partially perceptual-shape concepts as *square, cubic, diamond-shaped,* or *cylindrical* related to the nonconceptual content of experience? In the general framework developed in chapter 1, our task was to say how the various possession conditions for these concepts mention the nonconceptual contents of experiences. Take the concept *square* as the initial example for discussion. The concept intended is the relatively observational shape concept that can be possessed without the subject's awareness of any geometrical definition. It is also a concept that has inherently fuzzy boundaries.

We can enter the issues by considering a natural, simple suggestion about what is necessary for possession of the concept *square*. This simple suggestion is built up from the materials developed so far. Suppose that a thinker is taking his experiences at face value. Suppose too that in the positioned scenario of his experience, the area of space apparently occupied by a perceived object is square. Then, this simple account suggests, the thinker must find the present-tense demonstrative thought that the object is square to be primitively compelling.

 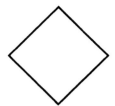

Figure 3.1

This simple account is not circular. It uses the concept *square* in fixing a certain sort of scenario; I emphasized earlier that this does not require the thinker to possess the concept *square*. This simple account can be written out in a way which makes it clearly capable of featuring as part of a longer story that, in the terminology of chapter 1, is cast in the canonical $\mathcal{A}(C)$ form. It proposes a noncircular description of a thinker's knowledge of what it is for something to be square. Indeed, it is plausible that any theory of possession of these relatively observational-shape concepts will have at some point to exploit this way of avoiding circularity.

The necessary condition proposed by the simple account is not, however, in fact necessary. That it is not necessary is already shown by Mach's (1914, 106) example of the square and the diamond (figure 3.1). A thinker, taking his experiences at face value and possessing the concept square, need not find it primitively compelling (without further reflection) that a floor tile in the diamond orientation is square. But it can still be that in the positioned scenario of his experience, the region of space apparently occupied by the floor tile is square, as indeed it will be if his experience is veridical.

The case illustrates one respect in which we need to qualify Evans's pioneering discussion of these issues. He wrote,

To have the visual experience of four points of light arranged in a square amounts to no more than being in a complex informational state that embodies information about the egocentric location of those lights. (1985b, 392)

Four points of light arranged in a regular diamond shape will produce an informational state that embodies information about the egocentric location of those lights. The informational state produced need not be an experience of them as arranged in a square.

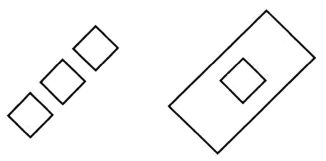

Figure 3.2
Figure 3.2 is reprinted from figure 14, parts (e) and (f), page 301, of Stephen Palmer's paper "The Psychology of Perceptual Organization: A Transformational Approach," in *Human and Machine Vision,* edited by J. Beck, B. Hope, and A. Rosenfeld (New York: Academic Press, 1983), with kind permission of the Academic Press and Stephen Palmer.

Mach's example does not show that scenarios are irrelevant to the difference between the concepts *square* and *regular diamond*. What it does show is that they cannot be used in so simple a fashion; they need to be supplemented with the use of further materials. I doubt that this can be done solely with the materials provided by scenario content. Certainly one should not impose the condition that mastery of the concept *square* is tied in some distinctive way to perception of squares in the orientation of the left-hand square in figure 3.1. It is possible to see a square at other orientations as a square. Indeed, as Stephen Palmer has emphasized (1983, 301), one can even naively see a square at a 45 degree angle as a square, rather than as a regular diamond, if the context is right (see figure 3.2).[5]

Intuitively, the difference between perceiving something as a square and perceiving it as a (regular) diamond is in part a difference in the way in which symmetries are perceived. When something is perceived as a diamond, the perceived symmetry is a symmetry about the bisectors of its angles. When something is perceived as a square, the perceived symmetry is a symmetry about the bisectors of its sides.[6] So intuitively, the simple account should be supplemented by requiring that, for the case it treats, the object apparently occupying the region in question be perceived as symmetrical about the bisectors of its sides. But does perceiving something as symmetrical require the perceiver to possess and make use of the concept *symmetrical*? If so, then what we will have done is simply to explain (this part of) mastery of the concept *square* in terms that require mastery of other concepts. We will not have anchored the difference between the concepts *square* and *diamond* at a level of nonconceptual content. If, on the other hand, there is a sense in which perceiving something as symmetrical does not require possession of the concept *symmetrical,* what is that sense? And how do we capture the nature of the additional content that distinguishes a case in which we not only have veridical perception of a symmetrical region but also have that symmetry perceived? I will sketch one way of answering these two questions.

I suggest that perceptual experience has a second layer of nonconceptual representational content. The contents at this second layer cannot be identified with positioned scenarios, but they are also distinct from conceptual contents. These additional contents I call *protopropositions*. These protopropositions are assessable as true or false. A protoproposition contains an individual or individuals, together with a property or relation. When a protoproposition is part of the representational content of an experience, the experience represents the property or relation in the protoproposition as holding of the individual or individuals it also contains. I write of proto*propositions* rather than protothoughts because protopropositions contain objects, properties, and relations, rather than concepts thereof. I write of *proto*propositions because in this account they are not determined as part of the content of an experience by being fixed by some conceptual content the experience possesses. The protopropositions that enter the representational content of ordinary human visual experience contain such properties and relations as SQUARE, CURVED, PARALLEL TO, EQUIDISTANT FROM, SAME SHAPE AS, and SYMMETRICAL ABOUT. (I use small capitals for a word to indicate that I am referring to the property or relation to which it refers, rather than to the concept it expresses.) These properties and relations can be represented as holding of places, lines, or regions in the positioned scenario, or of objects perceived as located in such places. There will, of course, be many equally acceptable set-theoretic ways of building up such propositions.[7]

Because protopropositions contain properties and relations, rather than concepts thereof, there is no immediate circularity in mentioning this level of representational content in individuating certain conceptual contents. As always, of course, we will want to have, one day, a substantive theory of what it is to be in perceptual states with proto-propositional contents.

Protopropositional content plays an important role in memory, recognition, and the subject's construction of a cognitive map of his world. When a subject perceives some of an object's properties and the relations of some of its parts, his memory of the object and for its perceptual type is greatly facilitated. When his experience has such protopropositional contents, the perceiver does not have to remember highly detailed scenario contents, with their specifications for each point. There is no need for so much detail if he can remember the salient properties and relations in which the object and its parts were perceived to stand. Protopropositional content is equally important to recognition. We may see an object and thereby acquire an ability to recognize it when we reencounter it. But the reencounter will frequently present the object from a different angle, a different distance, and the object's own orientation to its environment may vary too. If there were only a meagre protopropositional content in the original perception of the object, immensely complex operations on a highly detailed content would be necessary for perceptual recognition of the object. But with a detailed protopropositional content, the task is eased. That two lines are straight, that they form a right angle, that an object is symmetrical about one of its axes can enter the content of two experiences in which the same object is presented at very different angles and distances, or in a different orientation to its surroundings. A corresponding point applies to the construction of a cognitive map. The presence of protopropositional content reduces the demands on the thinker. As he moves, he can register that a certain line is straight and can enter this appropriately in his cognitive map after he has moved away, rather than having to transform one complex scenario content into a corresponding complex content for his map.[8]

Protopropositional content is not determined by positioned-scenario content. Two experiences can have the same positioned-scenario content but different protopropositional contents. Many familiar cases illustrate this. One illustration is given by the case in which one comes to see two shapes in the environment to be the same, one a tilted version of the other, say, even though the shape in question is quite unfamiliar. The experiences before and after seeing the identity of shape have the same representational content at the level of the positioned scenario. They differ in that the later experience has among its protopropositional contents that the two objects are of the same shape. An even more familiar case is given by certain differences in spatial grouping. When you see a two-dimensional array of elements as grouped in columns rather than rows, your experience has the protopropositional content that certain elements that are in fact vertically arranged are collinear. But there need not be any difference in the positioned-scenario content between the case in which the array is seen as grouped in columns and that in which it is seen as grouped in rows.[9]

The level of protopropositional content also makes possible a satisfactory description of the experience of "impossible" objects and figures, the topic that I left unfinished at the end of section 3.2. In the perception of an apparently impossible object, the protopropositional representational content of one's experience could include, for instance, that **x** is above **y**, that **y** is above **z**, and that **z** is above **x**. An experience can have such a set of inconsistent representational contents without any switches in attention or temporary indefiniteness. Similarly, a picture, perhaps one of Escher's drawings, may depict such a set of protopropositional contents as holding.

The reader will not be surprised to learn that it is in this level of protopropositional content that I propose to employ to avert the threatened failure to give an account of the difference between the concepts *square* and *diamond*. For something to be perceived as square, the symmetry about the bisectors of its sides must be perceived, and this is a restriction at the level of protopropositional content. When something is perceived as shaped like a regular diamond, the protopropositional content of the experience includes the proposition that the object is symmetrical about a line that bisects the object's corners. The difference between perceiving something as a square and perceiving it as a regular diamond is a difference between the protopropositional contents of the two perceptions.

Back in section 1.3, I identified a general connection between semantic value, possession conditions, and correctness. In chapter 5, I will be developing some closely related connections between possession conditions and rationality. It is worth noting how these links with correctness are present for this treatment of the observational concept *square,* and also worth noting some points about rationality involving this concept. I will later generalize these points in chapter 5. The nonconceptual protopropositional content of experiences of the kind mentioned in the possession condition for *square* will concern the straightness of certain lines, the symmetry of a figure about the bisectors of those lines, the identity of certain lengths, and the rightness of certain angles. Such experiences give a thinker who possesses the relatively observational concept *square* not merely reasons but good reasons for forming the belief that the demonstratively presented object is square. That they are good reasons is intimately related to the condition required for the belief "That's square" to be true. If the thinker's perceptual systems are functioning properly, so that the nonconceptual representational content of his experience is correct, then when such experiences occur, the object thought about will really be square. In this description of why the linkages are rational linkages, I make essential use of the fact that the nonconceptual content employed in the possession condition has a correctness condition that concerns the world. The account of the rationality of this particular linkage turns on the point that when the correctness condition of the relevant nonconceptual contents is fulfilled, the object will really be square. The correctness does not rest on any auxiliary or collateral empirical information about the property of being square.

This explanation of why the linkage is rational can proceed without appealing to the fact that the justifying experience mentioned in the possession condition represents the object as falling under the concept *square*. The experience will indeed also have a representational content involving that concept if the thinker possesses the observational concept *square*. The point is just that on this theory we do not need to appeal to that conceptual representational content in giving the possession condition for the concept *square,* nor in explaining the correctness and rationality of forming beliefs containing this concept in accordance with its possession condition. More generally, for a state canonically, i.e., at the level of the possession condition, to justify belief in a particular content containing a given concept, it is not required that the state have a representational content that contains that very concept. Acceptance of p and acceptance of q jointly and canonically justify acceptance of the conjunction p *and* q, but the concept of conjunction need not be present in either p or q.

It is high time to consider the objection that since what I have called protopropositional content is really a form of conceptual content, there is no need to postulate a level of nonconceptual protopropositional content. Consider the predicative component of the demonstrative content "That line is straight," judged on the basis of perception. Isn't what is judged here of the line the same as the way experience represents the line to be? So if the component of the content judged is conceptual, must not that of the perception be likewise? And cannot what I have called protopropositional contents be captured by such perceptually based demonstratives as "that shape," or even just "that property" (referring, say, to vertical symmetry)? And if the answers to these questions are affirmative, is not protopropositional content quite redundant?

There are three issues to be distinguished here, and I will address them separately:

1. Can the examples that I claim require the acknowledgment of protopropositional content be captured by nonindexical conceptual contents with such predicative components as the concepts *straight* or *symmetrical about*?

2. Can those examples be captured by indexical conceptual contents?

3. If the answer to either (1) or (2) is affirmative, is a level of non-conceptual protopropositional content redundant?

A negative answer to question (1) is supported by the existence of many examples in which a subject perceives a property or relation without conceptualizing it in any nonindexical fashion. If we take an observational concept we do in fact possess, then certainly we will have difficulty in successfully imagining an experience in which the observational property is perceived but not conceptualized as falling under that observational concept. This is not surprising. For those who possess an observational concept, it enters the representational content of their experiences and, derivatively, of their imaginings. But if we consider the question as applied to some third person, the possibility is unproblematic. We can ask someone who does not possess the concept of vertical symmetry to sort a set of inkblot shapes into those that look better to him than the others. Such a subject may separate out the vertically symmetrical ones on the basis of the way they look without any inference. He perceives the vertical symmetry without conceptualizing it as such. In my terminology, the property SYMMETRICAL features in the protopropositional content of this subject's experience.

The same point applies to auditory experience. There is a difference between hearing the interval formed by the notes middle C and the F♯ just above it as an augmented fourth and hearing it as a diminished fifth. I now follow DeBellis (forthcoming) in describing the difference between the two cases in terms of the relations in which the notes are perceived to stand. When the interval is perceived as an augmented fourth, the F♯ is perceived as the seventh of the scale with G as tonic, and the C as the fourth thereof. When the interval is perceived as a diminished fifth, the upper note is perceived as the fourth of the scale with D♭ as tonic, and the C as the seventh thereof. There is no question but that the interval can be perceived in either way by someone without even the most rudimentary, personal-level knowledge of the classifications of music theory, that is, by someone without the apparatus for conceptualizing in any nonindexical fashion the relations he perceives.

A third case is supplied by the perception of language. Consider the two most salient ways of perceiving an utterance of the familiar sentence "Visiting royalty can be boring." It seems correct to me to say of an English hearer of an utterance of this sentence that he hears it under one rather than another of its structural descriptions. What this involves in one of the two cases is the hearer perceiving it as, roughly, the royalty of which boringness is being predicated, rather than that of a certain kind of visit. When heard this way, the components of the uttered sentence are heard as standing in certain relations to one another. But I doubt that the ordinary speaker-hearer has to have, at the personal level, the apparatus for conceptualizing these relations in syntacticosemantic terms. I doubt that the ordinary speaker-hearer has to be capable of any thoughts about these syntacticosemantic relations. The ordinary speaker-hearer either hears the utterance as meaning that it can be boring to visit royalty, or he hears the utterance as meaning that when royalty visit, they can be boring. It is not that talk of one structural description's being perceived rather than another is merely projected backward from the sentence's being heard as having one complete meaning rather than another. Take someone who

understands much of English, including the "-ing" suffix applied to
verbs, but who does not understand the verb "to bore" as intended in
the example. This person can still hear the sentence under one rather
than another of its structural descriptions. The plausible hypothesis,
it seems to me, is that far from perception of structural descriptions
being projected backward from perceived meaning, it is rather that
perception of the sentence as structured one way rather than another,
or what underlies such perception, positively contributes to the hearer's perception of the sentence as having one meaning rather than
another. As in the musical and the spatial cases, the syntacticosemantic relations are perceived but not conceptualized in any nonindexical
way.

I now turn to question (2). The prospects of capturing the contents
I have called "protopropositional" by means of demonstrative conceptual contents are much more promising. The case for employing demonstrative concepts in predicative, as well as singular, position has
been made and developed by McDowell (forthcoming) and Sedivy
(1991). On this approach, even the musical example would be captured
by a conceptual representational content of the form "*Those* notes are
thus," or even just "*that* is *thus*." These demonstratives, like other
perceptual demonstratives, express concepts made available to the
thinker by his perceptual state. Such demonstratives may pick out a
shape property, a shade, or musical relation without the subject possessing a nonindexical way of thinking of the property or relation.

There surely are such fine-grained perceptual demonstratives. A
treatment of them has to avoid a well-known, and far from fully solved,
problem that afflicts this territory. It is pretheoretically tempting to
suppose that a perceptual demonstrative "that shade" refers to a shade
sliced at a fineness of grain that ensures the following: perceived
shades **s** and **s**' are identical if and only if **s** is not discriminably
different from **s**'. The nontransitivity of nondiscriminable difference
("matching") entails that there is no way of dividing the spectrum into
shades that meets that condition. Take an example in which, in respect
of color, **x** matches **y**, **y** matches **z**, but **x** does not match **z**. To conform
to the above principle about shades, the shade of **y** would have to be
identical with shades that are distinct from one another.

This problem, though, need not prevent us from capturing the relevant contents with perceptual-demonstrative concepts. One way to

preserve coherence is to use Hartry Field's (1974) notion of partial denotation. A content containing a perceptual-demonstrative reference to a shade can be treated as true outright if it is true under all acceptable assignments of a referent to the demonstrative of a maximally finely discriminated shade. Acceptable assignments are those that assign a finely discriminated shade not discriminably different from that of the perceived object in question. Maximally finely discriminated shades can be taken here as having the very strict identity conditions that Goodman (1977) gives for qualia in *The Structure of Appearance*. (In emphasizing the possibility of this treatment of demonstratives for perceptible properties, I dissent from one of the arguments in Cussins's important 1990 paper, pages 406–407.)

There is, then, a plausible case to be made for a positive answer to question (2). Whether this plausible case is correct would require further discussion. My present reason for interest in the issue is its connection with the issue raised in question (3). Does a positive answer to (2) entail that it is unnecessary to postulate a level of nonconceptual protopropositional content? I claim that it would be a nonsequitur to move from the premise that there cannot be two experiences differing in representational content but not differing in their conceptual representational content to the conclusion that nonconceptual representational content is redundant. Even if the premiss is true, the conclusion could still be false if nonconceptual representational content is needed in the philosophical explanation of the perceptual-demonstrative concepts used in arguing for the premiss. This, I claim, is the actual state of affairs.

I have already emphasized that one and the same shape can be perceived in two different ways. Perceiving a shape as a rotated square and perceiving it as an upright regular diamond is such a case. The different perceptual demonstratives of the form "that shape" associated with each of these two cases will be different concepts that pick out the same shape. But what is it for one of these demonstrative concepts rather than the other to enter the content of a subject's perceptual experience? It seems to me that this has to be elucidated in terms of nonconceptual protopropositional content. I have already noted the different properties and relations that are perceived when the shape is perceived as a square rather than a diamond. It is these differences that we have to draw upon in saying what it is for one demonstrative concept rather than another to enter the representational content of a subject's experience. Equally, it is these differences that would also constitute the difference between the two possession conditions for these two demonstrative concepts. Perhaps an objector would reply that these differences too are really conceptual. He might say that the basis of the difference between perceiving something as a square and perceiving it as a diamond is to be explained in terms of conceptual demonstrative representational content. But even when the property of being symmetrical about the bisectors of its angles is conceptualized in demonstrative rather than nondemonstrative terms, it is not plausible that such a concept has to enter the representational content of the experience of anyone who sees something as a regular diamond. It can take reflection to see that the diamond has that property even when it is demonstratively conceptualized, but the diamond is seen as a diamond before any such reflection takes place. In any case, this objector's response only postpones the question. The issue of the possession conditions for these additional demonstratives has also to be addressed.

The remaining objection from this cluster was that the same content *straight* enters both the representational content of certain experiences and the judgement "That's straight" based on those experiences. There is indeed a conceptual component of the judgement intimately related to experiences with protopropositional contents that certain perceived things are straight. But this conceptual content is individuated in part by certain of its relations to those protopropositional contents. In an earlier section I discussed the way in which the individuation of the first-person (type of) concept has to mention the origin of the scenario presented in perceptual experience. I emphasized that it was no part of that account that experiences do not have the content of a first-person conceptual representation. They do; it is just that the content cannot be used without circularity in the individuation of the first-person concept. Similarly, it is not part of the present position that perceptual experiences do not have conceptual contents involving the concept *straight*. They do in general have such conceptual content. What matters to my position is that if we are to have a noncircular and individuating account of mastery of the perceptual concept *straight,* that mastery must be related to some feature of experience that does not have to be explained in terms that presuppose possession of the concept. We cannot supply this by relating the mastery to experiences whose positioned scenarios require for their correctness that a certain line be straight, for that can be so without the straightness being perceived. Having the property STRAIGHT in the protopropositional content respects that point, without threatening a circular account of mastery.[10] These points, made just for properties and certain concepts of them, also have structural analogues for perceptual-demonstrative modes of presentation of individual objects.[11]

A congenitally blind man can possess the perceptual concept *square* and apply it on the basis of his tactile experience of the world. There is a good case to be made that *square* and other perceptual shape concepts are not modality-specific, are amodal, as I will say. There is a natural criterion for the amodality of a concept within the framework of possession conditions. A concept is *amodal* if there is no particular sense modality such that the possession condition of the concept mentions the thinker's sensitivity of beliefs containing the concept to experiences in that particular modality. This criterion treats amodality as a property of the concept itself, as opposed to a property dependent upon one among other means of grasping it. By this criterion, the modified simple account of the concept *square* can itself be a fragment of a possession condition for an amodal shape concept. Suppose that a possession condition for a concept mentions a sensitivity of certain beliefs whose contents contain it to states with scenario-involving contents, protopropositional contents, or to anything else that can equally be present in more than one sense modality. Suppose too that it does not mention anything else that requires experiences in a particular modality. When these suppositions hold, the concept is amodal. Despite the departure already made from it, this is very much in the spirit of Evans's idea. On my account, there remains a "single conceptual capacity," which is exercised in response to both visual experience and tactile experience when, in response to experiences of each kind, a thinker judges something to be square (Evans 1985b, 374).

On the present criterion for the amodality of a concept, it is a nonsequitur to deny the amodality of a particular concept *F* solely on the ground that some particular subject can experience things as *F* in one modality but not in another. For it may be that experiences in one modality have protopropositional contents lacking in that particular subject's experiences in the other modality. So, for example, symmetry and parallelism are not made salient in the protopropositional content of our tactile experience in nearly so wide a range of cases as they are in visual experience. Since this is so, some shape concepts may be applied on the basis of visual experience of an object, while they are not immediately applied when the object is touched. It does not follow that the concepts are modality-specific in the way in which the concept *red* is. Rather, we may be able to explain the difference by citing the different properties entering the protopropositional contents of visual and tactile experiences.

The remarks of this section cannot purport to give a full possession condition for the concept *square*. A full possession condition must elucidate a thinker's ability to judge that an unperceived thing is square. Many intriguing issues arise in the attempt to elucidate that ability. One of them is the nature of a thinker's understanding that imperceptibly small things can be square and that objects too large to perceive can also be square. Another such issue is the relation of this understanding to the ability to judge, of an unperceived but perceivable thing, that it is square. Pursuing these issues here would take us too far from my agenda. It is worth noting, though, that the partial possession condition developed so far has a bearing on these issues. Consider, for instance, a thinker's ability to judge, of some unperceived but perceptible thing, that it is square. A theorist might try to explain this as follows. Just as the nonconceptual content of perception is given by a spatial type, so the nonconceptual content of a cognitive map is given by a way of assigning objects, properties, relations, and so forth in the space in which the subject is embedded. So far this is tempting and plausible. But suppose that the theorist goes on to say that to judge an object at a specified, unperceived location to be square is simply for the thinker's map to have, as part of its correctness condition, that the object at that location has the property of being square. If a map is a way of assigning objects, properties, and relations in the appropriate space and the property (as opposed to the concept) of being square is the same as that of being shaped like a regular diamond, then a map that represents the object at a given location as square is equally a map that represents that object as shaped like a regular diamond. Yet judging that the object there is square is different from judging it to be diamond-shaped. The distinctions between perceptual contents infuse our thought about the nonperceptual cases too.

As I have implied at several points, my treatment of perceptual-shape concepts is consistent with acknowledging that experiences have conceptual content. In Evans's work (1982), experiences are conceived of as not having a conceptual content at all (see also McGinn 1989, 62). This part of Evans's conception is not obviously obligatory. There is no good reason for denying the overwhelmingly plausible view that we see things as trees or hear a sound as that of a car approaching. However, accepting the overwhelmingly plausible view does not immediately give us a new resource to use in building possession conditions for perceptual shape concepts. If we try to make the possession condition for the perceptual concept *square* a matter of sensitivity to experiences with a content containing the concept *square,* we will be open to the charge of circularity. This circularity is parallel to that suffered by the propositional theorist, noted earlier, who tries to make possession of the first-person concept a matter of the sensitivity of thoughts containing it to features of experiences that already have first-person contents. Like that theorist, we would be attempting to individuate a concept by reference to something that already takes for granted the thinker's possession of the concept in question, namely, the capacity to have experiences whose contents contain the concept in question. The circularity is no less present when the mental state whose content contains the concept is perceptual experience than when it is judgement or belief. (This problem was noted, but far from satisfactorily resolved, in Peacocke 1983.)

It may be tempting to conclude from these points that a possession condition that genuinely instantiates the $\mathcal{A}(C)$ form simply cannot mention the conceptual representational content of experience (although, of course, someone who defends the form may still agree that experiences do have a conceptual representational content). This, though, would be a hasty conclusion. It is indeed true that the sketch I have offered of some parts of possession conditions for perceptual concepts have not themselves mentioned the conceptual representational content of experience. That is one way of developing an account in accordance with the $\mathcal{A}(C)$ form, but it is not the only way. Other ways are highly worthy of investigation. Other ways of instantiating the $\mathcal{A}(C)$ form are possible precisely because we can make the same move for the conceptual content of experience that I earlier made for the conceptual content of belief and judgement. We may individuate a perceptual concept C in part by a statement of this form: it is that concept C to possess which a thinker must be willing to judge that certain things are C in such and such circumstances in which he perceptually experiences them as falling under C, etc. That last occurrence of the variable C is crucial in avoiding circularity. For any such account to be genuinely individuating, it must contain additional material giving further conditions on the experience representing something as falling under the concept C. No doubt there will need to be reference to nonconceptual representational content and a great deal more at this point. Indeed, the sketches of parts of possession conditions for *square* and *shaped like a regular diamond* could be recast in this form.

The possibility of developing the account of the $\mathcal{A}(C)$ form in this way is philosophically important. It means that endorsing the constraints that lead to a commitment to the $\mathcal{A}(C)$ form is in no way incompatible with insisting, for perceptual concepts, on the constitutive nature of the relation between experiencing something as falling under the concept and judging that something falls under it. If one thought that the only way such constitutive relations could be acknowledged is to use the very concept within the scope of a thinker's mental state in a specification of mastery of the concept, then the $\mathcal{A}(C)$ form would be highly questionable. But it is not the only way, and the requirements of the $\mathcal{A}(C)$ form can still be met. That is just as well too, for the arguments in favor of the $\mathcal{A}(C)$ form remain in place.

To conclude this section, I note that while the direction of constitutive explanation has so far been running from experience to concept possession, it is essential also to allow that some causal explanations are in the opposite direction. Once a thinker has acquired a perceptually individuated concept, his possession of that concept can causally influence what contents his experiences possess. If this were not so, we would be unable to account for differences which manifestly exist. One such difference, for example, is that between the experience of a perceiver completely unfamiliar with Cyrillic script seeing a sentence in that script and the experience of one who understands a language written in that script. These two perceivers see the same shapes at the same positions. The positioned scenarios and the protopropositional contents of their respective experiences can be identical. The experiences differ in that the second perceiver recognizes the symbols as of particular orthographic kinds, and sequences of the symbols as of particular semantic kinds. The questions of the nature of this difference and, more generally, of what constitutionally makes an experience have a conceptual content remain as urgent and open as ever.

3.4 Spatial Reasoning and Action

Is nonconceptual representational content autonomous? Is there, or could there be, a creature in states with nonconceptual representational contents, even though the creature does not possess any concepts? Some passages in Evans suggest that he was tempted by such a claim of autonomy for his nonconceptual contents (1982, 124, 158).[12] But such a thesis of autonomy is not obligatory.

Even for the most primitive level of scenario content, there are strong arguments against such autonomy. Scenario content is spatial representational content. Specifically, spatial content involves more than just a sensitivity to higher-order properties of stimulation patterns. I doubt that we could ever justify attributing genuinely spatial content to an organism's states of a kind going beyond such sensitivity unless the subject were on occasion to employ states with these contents in identifying places over time. Such an identification might on occasion consist in identifying one's current location with one previously encountered. The possibility of such identification is also involved in the subject's appreciating that the scene currently presented in his perception is something to which his own spatial relations can vary over time.

Identification of places over time requires that states with scenario content contribute to the construction of a cognitive map of the world around the subject. It is also highly questionable whether we can make sense of the subject's engaging in such construction unless he employs at least a rudimentary form of first-person thought, that is, unless he possesses at least some primitive form of the first-person concept. If this is correct, scenario content is not autonomous. On the approach I am advocating, then, nonconceptual content is not a level whose nature is completely explicable without reference to conceptual content. It is rather a type of content that, though nonconceptual, cannot be explained except in part by reference to its relations to certain primitive conceptual contents. At the most basic level, conceptual and nonconceptual content must be elucidated simultaneously. The most basic elements of the scheme themselves form a local holism.

To identify places over time requires the subject to be able to integrate the representational contents of his successive perceptions into an integrated representation of the world around him, both near and far, past and present. I label this the ability to engage in spatial reasoning. Some parts of spatial reasoning may be conceptual. Some parts, though not conceptual, will still be propositional. (I earlier emphasized the role of protopropositional contents in building a cognitive map of the environment). But where spatial reasoning involves only scenario content, the reasoning will be neither conceptual nor propositional.

Spatial reasoning involves the subject's building up a consistent representation of the world around him and of his location in it. It is worth remarking on what "consistent" means here, since scenario content is neither conceptual nor propositional. One of the distinctive relations to which spatial reasoning is answerable is the following notion of consistency: that of the positioned scenario of a given perceptual experience being consistent with a given cognitive map. What this consistency means is that there are ways of filling out the mapped space around the subject that both conform to the way of locating features in it required by the cognitive map and are sufficient for the correctness of the positioned scenario.

Whenever we claim that a certain role in reasoning is essential to a particular kind of content, we incur an obligation. The obligation is to elucidate the relation between that role in reasoning and the correctness (truth) conditions of such contents. This is a natural generalization of the previously discussed obligation to provide, in the conceptual case, a determination theory (section 1.3). Ideally, I would like to have a theory of how a role in spatial reasoning determines the correctness of assigning one positioned scenario content rather than another to an experience. The task of providing this theory is one of the many that lie in intriguing regions visible from the main route of this chapter. The task is not, of course, precisely analogous in detail to that which arises for conceptual contents. For in those cases the concepts are individuated by their possession conditions, whereas, I have been emphasizing, a scenario (a spatial type) is not so individuated. Nonetheless, the obligation to say what it is for one spatial type rather than another to be involved in the content of an experience still exists and must be met in part by its detailed role in spatial reasoning.

Genuine spatial reasoning must be capable of explaining the spatial properties of a thinker's actions. The spatial property may just be the minimal property of being carried out at a particular location. The fact that such properties are included in the explained spatial properties leaves room for the possibility of a minimal case, alluded to earlier. This is the case of a being that is not capable of initiating changes in its own configuration or location but whose nonspatial actions (such as changes of color or of the acidity of its surfaces) are controlled by its representation of the locations of itself and other things in its cognitive map. Human beings are, though, obviously capable of controlling a much wider range of spatial properties of their actions, and in the remainder of this section I will consider the role of scenario content in this control. This further role cannot be taken as unconditionally constitutive of having experiences with scenario content, since the minimal case is possible. But the further role is crucial to the content-involving explanation of human action.

To characterize the further role, we must first remind ourselves of the distinctive kind of knowledge that a subject has about the position of his limbs and the configuration of his body. As Wittgenstein (1980, 770–772, 798) and Anscombe (1981) emphasized long ago, this knowledge is not inferred from, or even caused by, sensations. You can know the position of your own arm even when it is anaesthetized and even when you are not seeing it or feeling it with another limb. What is important for us is that in the content of this distinctive kind of knowledge, the location of a limb is given egocentrically, in relation to the subject's body. It is given in the same kind of way in which a location is given in the positioned scenario of an experience: the scenario is labeled with bodily axes.[13]

In characterizing the distinctive type of knowledge in this way, I differ in some respects from Brian O'Shaughnessy's penetrating treatment (1980, "The Subintentional Act"). O'Shaughnessy's insight is that knowledge of the position of our "bodily extremities" is "non-conceptual" and "non-propositional" (p. 64). But he also says that this knowledge is "entirely practical" and that its content "is exhaustively manifest in a set of physical acts" (p. 64). It is certainly not true that a person's knowledge of the position of his limbs and body at a given time is exhaustively manifest in actions he actually performs. Much of this knowledge possessed at a given time is not put to use in action at all. Perhaps O'Shaughnessy would rather say that the distinctive knowledge consists in certain dispositions to act. There is something right about mentioning dispositions to act, and I will return to them soon. But we will not get a proper understanding of the knowledge in question until we acknowledge its content. For it seems clear that the content of the distinctive knowledge has correctness conditions, which may or may not obtain. As a result of drugs or neural damage, a subject's belief about the location of his hand may be false. We cannot accommodate this just by saying that a false belief is one that, when manifested in action, does not lead to success. A distinction between the success and failure of an action depends upon a notion of the content of its generating intentional or subintentional state, a content whose correctness condition may obtain (success) or not (failure). And the content of these (sub)intentional states is of the same kind as the content of one's knowledge when one knows that one of these states has succeeded.[14]

It is not surprising, given his views, that O'Shaughnessy says there is a structural parallel between subintentional states and sensations. On my account, the content of the subintentional state has a correctness condition on the external, objective world. The sensation does not (or at least does not have a correctness condition of that kind). So there is no structural parallel of that sort on my position. Absence of conceptual content does not mean absence of all genuine content.

Now let us return to the further role of scenario content in human action. In supplying a subject with information about the location of things relative to bodily axes, perception supplies that nonconceptual information in a form immediately usable if the subject wants to move his body or some limb toward, from, or in some other spatial relation to what he perceives. Bodily based, scenario-involving contents are involved in three kinds of states: in perception, in our distinctive knowledge of bodily position, and in our immediate (sub)intentional tryings. It is this threefold presence that makes the information in perception immediately usable in performing actions. When a propositional attitude has a conceptual constituent individuated in part by scenario content, it can play an intermediary role between perception and action.

This intermediary role, made possible by scenario contents with labeled (bodily) axes, explains more fully a connection I mentioned in earlier work (1986c, 1989c) between the nonconceptual contents of perception and bodily action. A normal individual, asked to direct the beam of a spotlight in a forest onto a tree 47 degrees to the right of straight ahead, will not know, in the sense relevant to action, where to point the beam. The normal individual does not know which perceptually individuated direction is 47 degrees to the right of straight ahead. He will, though, have no difficulty if the tree in question is marked so that he can see in which precise direction it lies.

It is helpful here to consider an explicit statement of the subject's practical reasoning in this second case, in which the normal individual has no difficulty in carrying out the task. He forms an intention with content (1).

(1)   I will move my arm in the direction of that tree.

He also knows from his perceptual experience that (2).

(2)   That tree is in direction **d** (identified egocentrically from scenario content).

So he forms the intention with content (3).

(3)   I will move my arm in direction **d**.

He can then carry out this intention without further practical reasoning. This description makes it clear that the connections between perception and action rest on two links. The first is the link between the perceptual demonstrative "that tree" and the availability of perceptually based knowledge of (2), which contains that demonstrative way of thinking. The second is the link between the egocentric mode of identification of directions and the subject's "basic" actions. If either of these links does not hold for some other mode of presentation in place of "that tree," such connections between perception and action will not hold, *ceteris paribus*.

Actually, even if both these links hold, this is not strictly sufficient for the link between perception and action to hold, because of the phenomenon known as "optic ataxia." A subject with optic ataxia cannot reach accurately for visually presented objects, nor can he orient his hand correctly to fit into a slot he sees. We should not conclude from such cases that the representations that control bodily movements do not involve scenario content. A better hypothesis is that the representations that control the limbs do use scenario content, but that in the cases of optic ataxia the contents of visual experience are *inaccessible* to the motor-control systems. That is, we have two different representations, not two different kinds of content (which would need some kind of "translation" procedure). This is a better hypothesis because subjects with optic ataxia display a "well coordinated, rapid and accurate pattern of movements directed at the body."[15]

There are also unusual cases in which two or more systems of labeled axes are properly used in giving the positioned-scenario content of a single experience, but in which the spatial relation between those two systems is not specified in the content of that experience. There are, for instance, certain positions in which, when lying on your back, you can twist your arms up behind your head. A piece of furniture touched with a hand of the twisted arm may be experienced as standing in certain spatial relations to one's hand, fingers, and wrist, but not as standing in any particular relation to the rest of one's body. In such a case of fragmentation, there is also fragmentation of the person's systems of knowledge, which help to explain bodily actions. The subject will know what to do to move his fingers away from the touched furniture but, without further reasoning, not how to move them closer to his torso.

Of the many substantive questions that arise in this area, one that seems somewhat more tractable than the rest is this: what gives a subintentional state or trying one nonconceptual content rather than another? One subpart of this question concerns the labeling of axes in a scenario. I need to say something illuminating about this labeling that does not take for granted a partially scenariolike, nonconceptual content that already has labeled axes.

I should emphasize that the problem here does not concern merely notational variants of particular axes and coordinate systems. One notational variant of the basic human axes would rotate them by 45 degrees and adjust coordinates in specifying a scenario in a compensating fashion. That this is a purely insubstantial, notational matter should be especially clear in the case of scenario content, for it is clear here that the variation is solely in the chosen means of specifying one and the same spatial type. The important question is rather this: why are axes labeled in *some* way involving particular bodily parts and limbs appropriate in giving the spatial type, which is in turn used in giving the content of a trying and of other subintentional states? The point could be encapsulated by saying that the question is about frames of reference for spatial types, rather than about coordinate systems.

Here is one possible answer. Let me say that two instructions ("tryings") of a given subject are of the same type if they differ only in the reference of their "now" component. So, trying to move one's left hand to a particular position in front of oneself at 9 A.M. and trying to do so at 10 A.M. are instructions of the same type. Now take a given type of instruction with a nonconceptual, partially scenariolike content. I suggest that the frame of reference to be used in labeling the axes of its scenario is that frame with respect to which instructions of the given type always have the *same* effect in all normal spatiotemporal contexts when characterized in relation to that frame (and when the efferent nervous system is functioning properly). When an instruction is an instruction to move one's hand so that it has a certain relation to one's body, it will have the same effect, described in relation to a bodily frame of reference, whether the thinker is in London or in Edinburgh. It will not have the same effect if the bizarre choice were made of a frame of reference involving longitude and latitude. It will not always have the same effect (when the thinker is functioning properly) in any other frame of reference defined by objects with respect to which the subject can move. Nor will descriptions of the effect in terms of muscle changes be the same in all spatiotemporal contexts. For the changes will depend on the starting point of the hand. This criterion can be called the *constancy* criterion for fixing the frame of reference, and thus the labeling, of any axes used in individuating the scenarios for a given subject's subintentional states. The constancy criterion is a small first step toward the formulation of a substantive theory of the nonconceptual content of subintentional states.

3.5 Summary and Open Questions

I have been arguing that we should recognize scenario and protopropositional contents as forms of nonconceptual representational contents. These nonconceptual contents must be mentioned in the possession conditions for perceptual and demonstrative concepts. A proper appreciation of their role allows us to explain the possibility of noncircular possession conditions for these very basic concepts and to given an account of the relations between perception, action, and a subject's representation of his environment.

At several points I have indicated philosophical issues arising out of the approach of this chaper. Before closing, I wish to mention very briefly some of the links between, and open questions about, the types of nonconceptual representational content I have been discussing and issues in the cognitive sciences.

Suppose, with Roger Shepard (1981), that we regard the task of the mechanisms of visual perception as that of computing an inverse of the projective mapping from the environment to the retinal image. From this lofty perspective we would certainly expect representations with positioned-scenario and protopropositional contents to be computed along the way, for it is the real scene, in my sense, that produces the retinal image. In a content-involving psychology, we would expect the early stages of vision to compute and combine various partial specifications of the scene around the perceiver. The several feature maps and the integration thereof, studied by Anne Treisman and her colleagues (Treisman and Gelade 1980, Treisman and Schmidt 1982) are just such partial specifications. They also begin to suggest mechanisms by which protopropositional content is made explicit in mental representations. If we want the explanatory power that only a content-involving description of a computation can supply, we should use positioned scenarios and protopropositions in describing the mechanisms outlined in that research.

If the claims in this chapter are correct, then an important item on an interdisciplinary agenda should be the construction of a theory of the ways in which the various types of representational content proposed here are mentally represented. We should certainly want to know the relation between these types of content and the theory that mental images are interpreted, symbol-filled arrays (Tye 1991, 90–102).

It is also important to understand the possibilities for the realization of states with scenario content in connectionist systems. We need to consider the following proposal. We might partition the three-dimensional space around the subject into suitably small cells. Each cell could be represented by a "binding" unit, which is connected to three other elements. These three other elements each represent the values of the cell on the labeled axes of the scenario. The binding unit can then have connections to other assemblies for the features represented as instantiated at that cell. And so forth. Do problems about binding make this too costly and implausible? A third, closely related area in which interdisciplinary questions arise is that of the mental models discussed in philosophical terms by Colin McGinn (1989).[16] Are mental models peculiarly appropriate representations for nonpropositional contents? With prospects of further understanding of mental representation and potentially of content itself emerging from work on such an interdisciplinary agenda, the ending of this chapter must be open-ended.[17]

4 The Metaphysics of Concepts

4.1 The Problem

Concepts are abstract objects. The paradigmatic general form of an individuating condition for a concept, the $\mathcal{A}(C)$ form of chapter 1, is that concept F is the unique concept C to possess which a thinker has to meet the condition $\mathcal{A}(C)$. Any true instance of this form quantifies over concepts and is committed to their existence. At the end of section 2.1, I noted that this commitment cannot be avoided by reading this quantification as substitutional. To do so would undermine the point of the $\mathcal{A}(C)$ form. Further, I have made characteristic neo-Fregean claims that strongly appear to require a domain of concepts as entities, such as the claim that concepts can be combined into complex, structured contents. I have conceived concepts as not having any spatiotemporal locations. By themselves, that is, apart from any mental states, they do not participate in causal interactions. Thus the question of the nature of the ontology of concepts is pressing for the approach I am developing in this book. In this chapter I will address the question of how it is possible for mention of concepts, those abstract objects, to play a significant part in the description of the empirical mental states of thinkers.

This question is in a broad sense metaphysical rather than epistemological. Like other abstract objects, concepts do raise epistemological problems aplenty. I believe that a correct answer to the metaphysical question can considerably alleviate the epistemological problems. In any case, my primary concern here is with the metaphysical issue. Even among those who most enthusiastically embrace a domain of abstract objects as the contents of propositional attitudes, the answer to the metaphysical question is almost always left in the shadows of obscurity. Frege himself wrote, "[The grasping of a thought] cannot be completely understood from a purely psychological standpoint. For in grasping [the thought] something comes into view whose nature is no longer mental in the proper sense, namely the thought; and this process is perhaps the most mysterious of all" (1979, 145).

I will here be treating the metaphysical issue as a special case of the general problem of how reference to abstract objects functions in the description of the empirical world. When we take this approach, it is convenient to isolate what we can call the *pure theory* of concepts.

Strictly, we should fix on a given collection of concepts and specify the pure theory of that collection of concepts, since concepts form an indefinitely extensible totality. The appropriate theory for some given collection of concepts is pure in two respects. It does not attribute any particular concepts or attitudes involving them to any particular thinker. It is also pure in that it has a relatively a priori status.

The pure theory consists first of a statement of a possession condition for each concept in the set of concepts in question. As always, a possession condition for a single concept has to instantiate the form "Concept F is the concept C to possess which a thinker must meet the condition $\mathcal{A}(C)$," or the corresponding form appropriate when there is a local holism that requires several concepts be treated simultaneously. Instances of either form quantify over the concepts they purport to individuate. A possession condition will also be ontologically committed to any other concepts it claims that a thinker must have to possess the concept it individuates. Second, the pure theory of concepts must classify its domain of concepts into categories of singular concepts, first-level predicative concepts, second-level predicative concepts, and so forth. For categories other than the singular, the degree must also be indicated. If the concepts in the set treated include variable-binding operators, there must also be some apparatus to handle the concept-theoretic analogue of an operator's binding one particular place in an open sentence. Third, the pure theory will contain principles to the effect that concepts of suitable categories can be combined to form complete thoughts, over which the pure theory also quantifies. So the pure theory will entail, for instance, that if a and b are singular concepts and R is a binary first-level concept, then there exists a thought that consists of the binary concept R in predicational combination with a and b, taken in that order.

In addition to these three kinds of principles within the pure theory itself, there are general constraints upon acceptable pure theories. The requirement that a possession condition, possibly together with the world, fix a semantic value for the concept it treats is one such general constraint. This is the requirement that I earlier formulated by saying that there must exist a determination theory for any given possession condition. Another requirement on acceptable pure theories can be summarized by saying that the possession conditions put forward by the theory must be collectively *grounded*. A theory is unacceptable if it advances a possession condition for a concept F that presupposes that the thinker already has the concept G, and then goes on to suggest a possession condition for the concept G that presupposes that the thinker already has the concept F. Similarly, there should not be finite circles of a similar kind.

4.2 A Ready-Made Solution?

Of a pure theory of concepts that meets these constraints, I can now raise the question, How can the abstract objects it postulates be of use in describing the empirical mental states of thinkers? There is one general position on certain kinds of abstract objects that may seem tailor-made to answer this question. This is a position that emerges from certain passages in Frege 1953 (sections 64–66) and Dummett 1956, but has been developed in most detail by Crispin Wright (1983, 1988). Take the following famous biconditionals:

The direction of line **j** = the direction of line **k**
  iff **j** is parallel to **k**.

The number of Fs = the number of Gs
  iff there is a one-one mapping from the Fs to the Gs.

On the view in question, these biconditionals show the ontologies of directions and numbers to be legitimate and relatively unproblematic. The biconditionals are regarded as disclosing ontological commitments already present in the statements on their right-hand sides. These right-hand sides make no reference to the abstract objects in question. So on this view, the statements on the left-hand sides can be no more problematic metaphysically or epistemologically than their right-hand-side equivalents.

Can this platonism without tears be applied to the statements of the pure theory of concepts, and so answer our question? The first step would be to find some suitable biconditionals. To be suitable, a biconditional must meet two conditions. First, if the Wright paradigm is to apply, the right-hand side of the biconditional must not make reference to concepts. Second, if the biconditional is to serve my purposes, it must supply an account of the application of the apparatus of concepts and thoughts. Since concepts can be senses of expressions, we might try this:

The concept expressed by **A** = the concept expressed by **B** iff necessarily, any thinker who understands **A** and understands **B** judges that **S(A)** iff he judges that **S(B)**, for any suitable linguistic context **S( )**.

I doubt, though, that instances of this biconditional meet the first of the two required conditions. If understanding an expression is knowing which concept it expresses, then the right-hand side cannot be elucidated without making reference to concepts. This contrasts with the right-hand sides of the biconditionals about directions and numbers. This biconditional about concepts is also not going to capture those concepts that are not, and perhaps in some cases cannot be, fully expressed in the thinker's language, such as perceptual-demonstrative singular concepts and memory demonstratives.[1]

Does the biconditional at least deliver an account of the application of the apparatus of concepts and thoughts? Perhaps there is reason for taking as a starting point something that mentions expressions if one holds that language is in some way fundamental to the individuation of conceptual contents. But whether it is or not, the biconditional does not tell us how to apply the pure theory of concepts. It does not give an account of the application of concepts in the description of thinkers' mental states, for the identity on the left-hand side of the biconditional does not involve propositional attitudes at all. This is another point of contrast with the biconditional about natural numbers, because in that case the notion "the number of Fs," which features on the left-hand side, *is* the fundamental notion used in applying the natural numbers to the empirical world.

A theorist might attempt to meet these points within a Wright-like framework by proposing a biconditional of the following form:

The content of mental state **M** = the content of mental state **M'** iff ____ **M** ____ **M'** ____.

For the proposal to meet my two requirements, the mental states here must be taken as actual empirical states of particular thinkers. If the range of the variables "**M**" and "**M'**" were taken to be all possible mental states, the proposal would be vulnerable to the charge that this range depends upon the ontology of concepts and thoughts. The argument would be that the range of possible mental states is dependent upon what concepts and thoughts are available to be the contents of those states. But if the variables "**M**" and "**M'**" are for this reason taken to range only over actual states of thinkers, we can know in advance that any proposal of this form is too weak, however the blanks are filled in. In general, a pure theory of concepts acknowledges the existence of infinitely many complete propositional thoughts. There will be many that are not the content of any actual thinker's thoughts.[2]

These points suggest that we will have to give an adequate vindication of the pure theory of concepts by a rather different account of abstract objects. There is independent evidence that some other account must exist. For there are relatively uncontentious kinds of abstract objects for which the Wright-like account is not available. Consider the humble case of the pure theory of expression types. Let "**x**" and "**y**" range over expression tokens. Then the natural starting-point for a Wright-like account is the following true biconditional:

The type of **x** = the type of **y** iff **x** is equiform with **y**.

If we take the terms on the left-hand side as referential, this biconditional will certainly ensure that every token has a type (since every token is equiform with itself). But the pure theory of expression types has as a theorem that for any two expression types **S** and **T**, there is a third type **U** that consists of the concatenation of **S** and **T** (taken in a given order). There can be tokens of **S** and tokens of **T** without there being any tokens of **U**. This point remains correct even on the most generous standards of what a token is. It is correct even if tokens are merely the appropriately shaped regions of space, since the universe may be finite. (Mere possibility is enough: the pure theory of expression types is not meant to be contingent!) So the existence of the type **U** is not guaranteed by the above biconditional about the types of tokens together with a Wright-like attitude to the biconditional. This is an analogue for expression types of the problem that arises in the theory of concepts for a Wright-like attitude to any biconditional of the form "The content of mental state **M** = the content of mental state **M'** iff. . . ."

This suggests a classification of the kinds of domains of abstract objects for which the Wright-like position is available. Domains of abstract objects are characteristically closed under some operation distinctive of that domain. The domain of expression types is closed under concatenation, that of the natural numbers is closed under the successor function, and so forth. Take a given domain, and suppose that we have selected a fundamental biconditional for the domain, one that stands to it as the famous biconditionals about directions and numbers stand to their respective domains. We can suppose the biconditional has the following form:

The ϕ of **X** = the ϕ of **Y** iff **R(X, Y)**.

Here the range of ϕ is the domain of abstract objects in question and "**X**" and "**Y**" take as values something outside that domain. The Wright-like attitude is available if every abstract object in the given domain is the ϕ of some **X** outside the domain. When that condition is met, the biconditional guarantees the existence of the objects required by closure under the distinctive operation. It is well known that a natural inductive generalization of this condition is met by the natural numbers. The existence of the number 0 follows from the biconditional for nonnegative integers (since we can take any contradictory concept for '*F*'). For any number **n**, there will also be some concept with **n** instances, since the concept *predecessor of n* is just such a concept. A natural generalization of the condition for the availability of the Wright-like approach is also arguably met by predicative sets. But the condition is not met by all domains of abstract objects, the domain of expression types being perhaps the simplest for which it fails. While numbers can themselves be counted and sets can be members of sets, acknowledging the existence of expression types does not widen the class of acknowledged expression tokens.

If there were something obscure or questionable about expression types, this would be an appropriate point at which to address the question of whether perhaps the availability of the Wright-like attitude is a necessary condition of the legitimacy of an alleged domain of abstract objects. But it seems very implausible to hold that the pure theory of expression types suffers from such obscurity. On the contrary, one of the main reasons that it does not is that we have a very

clear notion of how the world would have to be for an actually uninstantiated expression type to be instantiated. The case suggests that
there must be some other way of showing a domain of abstract objects
to be legitimate when the Wright-like stance is unavailable. I will be
exploring such a possibility for the domain of concepts.

4.3 A Proposal

I want to consider a different parallel between concepts and numbers.
We can compare the following two sentences:

(1)   The number of the planets is nine.

(2)   John believes that Lincoln Plaza is square.

We have the familiar fact that sentence (1) about the number of the
planets is logically equivalent to the conjunction of the two sentences
(3) and (4) below:

(3) $\exists x_1 \ldots \exists x_9[x_1$ is a planet & $\ldots$ & x_9 is a planet
      & $0 < i < 10\ (x_i \neq x_j)$
      & $\forall y(y$ is a planet $\rightarrow y = x_1 \vee \ldots \vee y = x_9)]$

I abbreviate (3) as "_____ planet _____ ," and I use this abbreviation in
writing (4):

(4)   Nine is the unique number n such that necessarily, for every
      property P, there are n things that are P iff _____ P _____.

We can imagine someone asking the following metaphysical question
about numbers: how is it possible for us to mention numbers, those
abstract objects, in describing the empirical world? For the restricted
case of natural numbers and sentences like (1), the logical equivalence
of (1) to the conjunction of (3) and (4) supplies a satisfying answer to
that question. In effect, the content of the statement about the number
of the planets is split up into an entirely empirical component (3),
which does not mention numbers at all, and a theoretical component
(4), which is part of a pure, relatively a priori theory of the natural
numbers. The pure theory specifies, in sentences such as (4), the
conditions under which the numbers can be applied. The fulfillment

of the application condition so specified is an empirical matter, and it does not need to mention numbers.[3] In a statement like (1), reference to a number serves as a means of encoding a condition on the property of being a planet, a condition that can be formulated without any reference to numbers.

The proposal I want to explore is that something structurally similar holds for thoughts. According to this proposal, there is some relational property **R** with two characteristics. First, the relational property **R** can be specified by mentioning no relations to concepts or thoughts but only relations to other empirical things and states. Second, "John believes that Lincoln Plaza is square" is equivalent to the conjunction of (5) and (6):

(5)   John is in some state **S** that has the relational property **R**.

(6)   The content that Lincoln Plaza is square is the unique content p such that necessarily for any state **S**, **S** is a belief that p iff **S** has the relational property **R**.

In fact, since contents are built up from concepts and are not neo-Russellian propositions, I should not speak of *the* content that Lincoln Plaza is square. Let us take it for the moment that we have fixed on one particular mode of presentation of that plaza and on one particular mode of presentation of the property of being square. The proposal, then, is that (2), so understood, stands to the conjunction of (5) and (6) as (1) stands to the conjunction of (3) and (4). Reference to a content in describing a mental state serves as a means of encoding a condition on that mental state, a condition that can be formulated without making reference to contents. Under the proposal I am developing, concepts in turn pull their weight in the description of the empirical world by making a systematic contribution to the condition a mental state must satisfy if it is to be a state with a given complete propositional content.

The crucial task facing this proposal is, of course, that of saying how the relevant relational property **R** of a state is fixed from a given content.[4] This is a completely general question, and it requires a completely general answer, one that can be applied to any propositional content whatsoever. It is not enough to have plausible specifications of the relevant relations for certain particular contents. We must be given a rule for going on to new cases. Also, the rule must draw only upon those components of a theory of concepts that are present for any belief content whatsoever.

I suggest that the relations required of a state if it is to be a belief with a given content are fixed by the possession conditions of the constituent concepts of the content. My task is to say how they are so fixed. A possession condition for a particular concept specifies a role that individuates that concept. The possession condition will mention the role of the concept in certain transitions that the thinker is willing to make. These will be transitions that involve complete propositional thoughts involving the concept. In some cases they are inferential transitions; in others they are transitions from initial states involving perceptual experience. Normally, a possession condition has several clauses, each treating of a different kind of case. The division into the various cases it treats may be given by a classification of certain sorts of inference, as in a plausible treatment of the logical constants. For instance, a possession condition for the concept of conjunction will have three clauses requiring some designated kind of acceptance of instances of the two elimination rules and one introduction rule for conjunction. The division into several clauses may also be given by a classification of the thinker's circumstances vis-à-vis some designated kind of thought involving the given concept. So, for relatively observational concepts, it is plausible that the possession condition should have one clause relating to certain conditions in which the concept is perceptibly instantiated by the object thought about and a second clause relating to circumstances in which it is not. Quite generally, each clause in the possession condition for a concept that occurs in a given complete propositional content makes a distinctive contribution to the requirements for a belief to have that propositional content. The totality of requirements derived by considering the contribution of each clause of a possession condition of each concept that occurs in the content fixes the relational property required for a belief to have that content.

The contribution to such requirements made by the clauses of the possession condition for a logical constant are relatively straightforward. In the simplest case of conjunction, a state is a belief with a content of the form *p and q* only if the thinker is willing to move into that state from the two beliefs that p and that q and is willing to form each of those beliefs when in that state. But the contribution to the totality of requirements made by concepts in predicational combination is more complex, and it needs more discussion.

I can illustrate the nature of the contributions by working it out for a particular belief, the belief that Lincoln Plaza is square. We need possession conditions for the concepts comprising this content. Let me assume that we are concerned with a recognitionally based, singular way of thinking of Lincoln Plaza and with a relatively observational (and so fuzzy) shape concept *square*. Getting the possession conditions for these particular concepts exactly right is not crucial for present purposes, since what most concerns us is the route from possession conditions to relational properties of belief states. We can work with the following formulations.

Possession Condition for the Concept *Square*   For a thinker to possess the concept *square* (C)

(S1)   he must be willing to believe the thought Cm_1 where m_1 is a perceptual demonstrative, when he is taking his experience at face value, the object of the demonstrative m_1 is presented in an apparently square region of his environment, and he experiences that region as having equal sides and as symmetrical about the bisectors of its sides (I summarize this by saying that "the object has appearance Σ"), and

(S2)   for an object thought about under some other mode of presentation m_2, he must be willing to accept the content Cm_2 when and only when he accepts that the object presented by m_2 has the same shape as perceptual experiences of the kind in (S1) represent objects as having.

Each of these clauses needs some comment. The possession condition is relying on a notion of the nonconceptual representational content of an experience, as clause (S2) makes clear. The use of the phrase "apparently square" in clause (S1) does not presuppose that the perceiver possesses the concept *square*. Rather, it alludes to the point that in the circumstances covered by the first clause, the spatial type that the experience represents as instantiated around the perceiver is one in which the perceptually presented object occupies a square region. "Square" is here used in specifying a spatial type, a scenario of chapter 3. This clause of the possession condition can draw on the materials developed in that chapter. It must also include the requirements on protopropositional content discussed in section 3.3 of that chapter.

Clause (S2) must be understood to cover not only the case in which the singular mode of presentation m is not a perceptual demonstrative but also that in which, although m is a perceptual demonstrative, the thinker does not meet the other conditions in (S1) for one reason or another. Clause (S2) is also not meant to require that anyone who possesses the concept *square* also has the concepts of perception and representation. Rather, it alludes to the role that the concept *square* has in spatial reasoning and thought. We can perceive and reason to the conclusion that an object is the same shape as one (or several) we have experienced in the past. This ability, which seems to me to merit much more philosophical attention than it has received hitherto, is essential to possession of the relatively observational concept *square* in question. So much for a possession condition for *square*.

Next we need a possession condition for the recognitionally based way of thinking of Lincoln Plaza. For each recognitional way of thinking that a subject employs, there seems to be a *presupposed range* of objects within which it attempts to secure a reference. You may think of a friend you can recognize as having a certain appearance, but this does not commit you to thinking that the appearance is unique in the human race. You may be able to recognize your local bank, and you may use in your thought a recognitionally based way of thinking about it. If a film director builds a replica of the bank on a film set in Los Angeles, you are not committed to thinking that the replica *is* your local bank. The presupposed range within which an object must lie to be the referent of a recognitionally based way of thinking of an object heavily depends on context. You do not acquire a recognitional way of thinking just by looking at one egg among thousands in a supermarket. But you may recognize one egg out of the two in your lunch pack as the one you purchased at a particular place. In outline, when all is working properly, the object that is the referent of your recognitional way of thinking and its causal source is the unique object in the presupposed range that has a certain appearance. At any rate, let us rest content with this for present purposes. There is an excellent discussion of further complexities in Evans 1982, chapter 8.

With these points in mind, we can now make an attempt at formulating a possession condition for the recognitionally-based way of thinking of Lincoln Plaza, *Lincoln Plaza*. I suggest this:

Possession Condition for the Concept *Lincoln Plaza* *Lincoln Plaza* is that mode of presentation m of an object x such that for a thinker to possess m is for there to be a certain appearance Δ of x, which the thinker has perceived x as having, and such that the thinker's ability to employ m stems from that perceptual encounter; and for there to be a certain range of objects such that

(L1)   the thinker is willing to judge of an object perceptually presented under c that $c = m$ when he is taking his experience at face value, perceives the object as having appearance Δ, and is taking it for granted that the object is in the presupposed range, and

(L2)   for an object thought about under some other mode of presentation k, if the thinker accepts that the object is in the presupposed range, then he is willing to accept that $k = m$ when and only when he accepts that the object is as appearance Δ represents the object as being.[5]

We now have before us at least first approximations to possession conditions for the singular recognitional concept *Lincoln Plaza* and the predicative, relatively observational concept *square*. My task is now to trace out the consequences of the combined requirements of the possession conditions for *square* and *Lincoln Plaza* to formulate a statement of what is required if a belief is to have the relevant content that Lincoln Plaza is square. To trace out these consequences, we have to consider four combinatorial possibilities: (L1) with (S1), (L1) with (S2), (L2) with (S1), and (L2) with (S2). To each of these combinations there corresponds a requirement for a state **S** to be the relevant belief that Lincoln Plaza is square. In accordance with the batch of antecedents at the start of the possession condition for the singular concept *Lincoln Plaza*, let us suppose that there is a certain appearance Δ of Lincoln Plaza, which the thinker has perceived it as having, and such that the thinker's ability to employ *Lincoln Plaza* stems from that perceptual encounter. Let us also suppose that there is a certain presupposed range of objects associated with this singular mode of presentation. Then, in the case of (L1) with (S1), we have the requirement that the thinker be willing in these circumstances to be in state **S** when he is taking his experience at face value, experiences some object as having both appearance Σ and appearance Δ, and takes it for granted that the object is in the presupposed range. In the case of (L1) with (S2), we have the requirement that when the thinker takes his experience at face value, experiences something with appearance Δ, and takes it to be in the presupposed range, he is willing to go into state **S** iff he accepts that the presented object has the same shape as appearance Δ represents objects as having. The other two cases can be treated analogously. Martin Davies suggested to me that I call the operation in which I have just engaged *multiplying out* the clauses of the two possession conditions, and I will henceforth adopt this apposite label. By multiplying out the clauses of the two possession conditions, we obtain four requirements for state **S** to be a belief that Lincoln Plaza is square. On this general approach, I suggest, these requirements are jointly sufficient in the sense that if **S** is a belief state, fulfillment of these four requirements is sufficient for it to be the relevant belief that Lincoln Plaza is square.

A belief that Lincoln Plaza is square can be reached by indefinitely many transitions other than those mentioned here, and its content can also be rejected by indefinitely many other transitions. Anything from map reading through testimony up to the theoretical interpretation of satellite photographs may be involved. What the requirements here aim to do is to state the (often counterfactual) relations in which a belief state must stand if it is to be the relevant belief that Lincoln Plaza is square. Two belief states that both meet these requirements may differ radically in their other actual and counterfactual relations. I am in effect using a notion of a canonical conceptual role for a belief with a given propositional content. That role is fixed by the canonical roles, the possession conditions, of the conceptual constituents of the complete propositional content. My approach is, then, a kind of conceptual-role semantics, under which attribution of states with conceptual content allows us to classify together two individuals with very different beliefs and overall psychological economies.[6] This approach allows us to do this in virtue of the properties of the two individuals' mental states at the level of broadly Fregean *Sinn,* and not merely at the level of reference.[7]

The possession conditions for a given concept may take for granted that the thinker already possesses certain other concepts. In such cases the requirements for a belief state to have a particular content containing the given concept will themselves presuppose that the thinker has various other concepts. This is particularly clear when the requirements are traced out for logical concepts, whose possession conditions mention inference patterns. Here the relevant requirements for a belief containing a logical constant will concern the thinker's rejection or acceptance in specified circumstances of the contents on which the constant operates. The general point will also hold for some concepts that are not themselves operators on other contents. The possession conditions just sketched for a capacity to recognize Lincoln Plaza and for the concept *square* themselves presuppose the thinker's grasp of identity, and they also quantify over other concepts. So the conditions for a belief to have a given content will often have to be elucidated further. The further elucidation will result from tracing out the consequences of the possession conditions of conceptual contents that have been taken for granted, and these in turn may need further elucidation. Similarly, there will have to be a more complex elucidation when there is existential commitment in a possession condition to a thinker's having some other concepts meeting certain conditions. When this process of elucidation can be carried no further, we will have a statement of what it is for a belief state to have a certain conceptual content that does not take for granted the thinker's possession of any conceptual contents.[8] This process will terminate if the further elucidation always involves the thinker's possession of families of concepts earlier in the partial ordering fixed by the relation mentioned in chapter 1: set **K** of concepts is earlier than set **K'** just in case possession of **K'** presupposes possession of **K** and possession of **K** does not presuppose possession of **K'**.[9]

It may seem strange to try to give the requirements for a belief to have a given content solely by considering the conceptual components of that content. Can the level of reference really be irrelevant to the formulation of these requirements? It is indeed not irrelevant, nor is it treated as irrelevant by the account outlined. In some cases a mode of presentation will refer to an object, and the possession condition for that mode of presentation will advert to the relations in which the thinker stands to that referent. Such was the case for the recognitional mode of presentation of Lincoln Plaza. It will also be the case for perceptual-demonstrative modes of presentation when they refer to an object if an account of their possession adverts to the thinker's use of perceptual information about the referent. In all such cases, the requirements in the possession condition that relate the thinker to the referent will be taken up in this account and incorporated into requirements for a belief to have a content containing such a mode of presentation. In the terminology of conceptual-role semantics, my approach falls into the category of *wide* canonical conceptual-role semantics.

I have been cautiously saying that the requirements obtained by multiplying out the clauses of the possession conditions give us sufficient conditions for a belief state to have a given content. I have held back from saying that the combined requirements are sufficient for a state to be a belief with that content. Intuitions differ on this matter of sufficiency, but I think that the proposal I have been developing can be accommodated by each of the main parties that differ over sufficiency. If the combined requirements are sufficient, the account can stand without supplementation. If the combined requirements are not sufficient, that is likely because those requirements do not guarantee that the beliefs in interaction with desires produce intentions and action, an interaction characteristic of belief. According to likely proponents of this view, there could be a system of states that shadow the real beliefs but do not produce intentions and action. The states in that system would not be beliefs, they say, even if they met the requirements derived in the above way from possession conditions. At this point we should remember my aim of explaining (2) as equivalent to the conjunction of (5) with (6). If, to fulfill this aim, we are to use the relational property of states derived by combining the requirements of several possession conditions, we must have genuinely sufficient conditions for a state to be a belief with a given content, and not merely conditions that are sufficient within the class of beliefs.

In this project it would be inept simply to add into the relational property, besides those requirements on a state derived from the possession conditions, the additional demand that the state be a belief. For a state to be a belief is for there to be some content p such that

the state is a belief that p. Adding this demand without further elucidating it would simply be trading an existential quantifier over some
of the entities in the domain of the pure theory of concepts for specific
commitments to such entities found in the original sentence (2). So
the maneuver prevents the approach from answering the original metaphysical question.

A more promising reaction is to explicitly write into the relational
property required for a state to be a belief with a given content the
requirement that there be desirelike states with which it is capable of
interacting to produce intentions and actions. I can give at least a
programmatic indication of how this might run. So far I have sketched
an outline, using the apparatus of possession conditions, of what it is
for a state to be a *putative belief* that p. So what I have to indicate is
what distinguishes those putative beliefs that really are beliefs from
those that are not. One way to do so is to carry out the following two
tasks. The first task is to explain how desires have their contents
partly in virtue of their relations to putative beliefs with given contents.
This would involve such principles as that a desire that p no longer
produces intentions when the subject comes to have a putative belief
that p. The second task is to explain how putative beliefs are genuine
beliefs when there are desires with which they interact in the ways
characteristic of propositional-attitude psychology. In this way the
approach could be squared with the views of those who hold that the
combined requirements are not sufficient for a state to be a belief with
a given content.

The approach I am suggesting depends, then, on further work on
several matters that are far from fully understood at present. First,
the tasks just mentioned concerning putative belief and desire need to
be carried out. Second, if the treatment in (5) and (6) is to be extended
to other propositional attitudes, as it must if it is to be general, then
belief must somehow be taken as primary and other attitudes explained
as inheriting their contents from their relations to beliefs (or putative
beliefs). Third, the account rests on the notion of the nonconceptual
representational content of experience, a notion elaborated in chapter 3
but still certainly in need of much philosophical explanation.

Nonetheless, it does seem to me that if these three matters are
adequately resolved, then the technique of deriving requirements on
belief states from the combined requirements of the possession con-

ditions of constituent concepts and then using the resulting relational property in the treatment in (5) and (6) does give an answer to the initial metaphysical question. The treatment shows how the pure theory of concepts can be applied to the empirical states of thinkers. It promises to make unproblematic what Frege said is perhaps the most mysterious of all.

4.4   Aspects and Consequences of the Proposal

I now turn to consider various aspects of the above proposal and its bearing on other issues about conceptual content.

First, the above account can be seen as outlining the contribution of predicational combination to the empirical application of the apparatus of concepts. The model on which (2) is equivalent to the conjunction of (5) and (6) gives, in the first instance, an account of the empirical application of complete thoughts rather than concepts. Concepts in turn can be used in classifying the empirical mental states of thinkers because of the systematic contribution made by their possession conditions to the classification of empirical mental states by attitudes to complete thoughts.

To appreciate why there is a task that had to be accomplished, it is interesting to compare the pure theory of concepts with other pure theories of abstract objects. In the case of the pure theory of expression types, linking the concatenation operation on expression types with empirical application is trivial: an instance of the expression type **A^B** is any token that consists of an instance of **A** followed by an instance of **B**. Nothing analogous holds in the pure theory of concepts. In the sense in which concepts have instances, the way in which a predicational combination of two concepts is applied in classifying mental states is *not* given by some operation on the objects to which those concepts apply! The ontology of concepts pulls its weight in the description of the empirical world only via its role in fixing the application conditions for complex thoughts to be used in the classification of mental states.

There is another kind of difference from the pure theory of natural numbers. The operations recognized in the pure theory of natural numbers, such as successor and addition, do not take one outside the domain of natural numbers. So, given a general account of the application of natural numbers, by reference (say) to their role in the numerical quantifiers, the significance of operations on the natural numbers, for applications, is thereby determined. For example, given the standard recursion equations for addition and the appropriate generalization of (4) to all natural numbers, it is determined what number-free condition is logically equivalent to "There are $(n + m)$ Fs." A similar situation is not present in the pure theory of concepts, because, given an initial subdomain of unstructured concepts, the operation of predicational combination has a range, the complete thoughts, that is outside that initial subdomain of concepts. I emphasized, though, that the possession conditions for concepts themselves do specify roles in complete thoughts. It is for this reason that a statement of the contribution to application of predicational combination does not need to draw on resources outside the pure theory of concepts.

Second, the above account of the application of the pure theory of concepts provides additional underwriting for the condition of adequacy on the possession conditions offered by the pure theory that they be collectively grounded (see section 4.1). The requirement of groundedness is naturally and intuitively motivated by the idea that a set of putative possession conditions that violates it is offering a circular account of some of the concepts it treats. For at least some of the concepts it mentions, no account of their possession will have been given that does not at some point take for granted the thinker's possession of those concepts. But a circularity would also block any account of application on the above lines for an allegedly ungrounded set of possession conditions. A circularity would have the consequence that it is not possible to state the relations in which a state must stand to be a belief involving one of the concepts in question without at some point mentioning that concept (as that concept) within the scope of the thinker's propositional attitudes. We would have no condition analogous to (6), and we would not have returned an adequate answer to the metaphysical question.

Third, the approach to applications I have been developing is equally consistent with two different attitudes to the states in the range of the variable "S" in (5):

John is in some state S that has the relational property R.

The *bold* view is that the range of the variable "**S**" here can be taken as subpersonally characterized states whose individuation does not presuppose conceptual content at all. Anyone is committed to the bold view who believes an identity theory of mental states on which each particular mental state of an individual at a given time is identical with some nonmentally individuated states. So is anyone who holds that each such mental state is realized or constituted by some nonmentally individuated state. It is clearly a central question in the philosophy of mind whether the bold view can be sustained. Part of the discussion in chapter 7 below will return us to this issue. If the bold view can be sustained, and on relatively a priori grounds, then the parallel is exact between this approach and the case of application of natural numbers.

By contrast, it might be held that there is no way of saying what the states that lie in the range of the variable "**S**" in (5) are without using the notion of conceptual content. We can call this the *unassuming* view. One who holds the unassuming view will think that no relation—be it one of identity, realization, constitution, or anything else—can relate propositional attitudes and nonmentally individuated states in the way required for (2) to be equivalent to the conjunction of (5) and (6), where "**S**" ranges over nonmentally individuated states.

The unassuming view does not make pointless the approach of this chapter to the empirical application of the pure theory of concepts. For, first, we can take (5) as using a general, open-ended notion of a state, and (5) is also fully elaborated so that its relational property **R** makes no reference to concepts or thoughts. It would then follow that a suitable instance of (5), in giving the empirical contribution of (2), can be understood by someone who has no grasp of the pure theory of concepts. Second, the holder of the unassuming view can still acknowledge that to be a belief with a certain content, a state has to stand in such and such relations to other states, events, and objects in the empirical world. The metaphysical question would still have received an answer. On the unassuming view, there would not, though, be an exact parallel with the treatment that involves seeing numerical examples such as (1) as equivalent to the conjunction of (3) and (4). Formula (3), when fully written out in first-order logic with identity, involves no reference to numbers at all.

Fourth, several writers, including Paul Churchland (1979) and Hartry Field (1981, postscript) have compared the use of propositions in characterizing mental states with the use of numbers in the characterization of physical and other magnitudes in the empirical sciences.[10] This comparison stands up well if the present account of application is roughly correct. In accordance with standard treatments in the theory of measurement, assigning a number to a physical magnitude possessed by an object can be seen as a means of characterizing certain physical relations in which that object stands. The underlying physical relations do not involve the ontology of numbers. Similarly, assigning conceptual contents to a mental state is a means of characterizing a system of relations in which that state stands, a system of relations that can be characterized without referring to the ontology of concepts and thoughts. If the bold view is correct, the state that stands in these relations can also be so characterized.

Fifth, it is a major issue in the theory of content whether the nature of concepts and contents built up from them can be elucidated without reference to language, the position of the theorist of thought, or whether any adequate elucidation must mention language. I have placed any full discussion of this large issue outside the scope of this work. But I can note briefly that this treatment of the ontology of concepts is germane to one part of that large issue. This treatment can assist the theorist of thought in meeting the objection that the structure of thoughts is but a reflection of the semantic structure of sentences. On my account, to say that a thought has a particular concept at a particular place in its treelike structure is to say that the possession condition for that concept makes a certain contribution to the complex relational property that a belief must possess if it is to have that thought as its content. More generally, facts about the structure of a thought and its constituents are explained in terms of characteristics of the relations required of a belief if it is to have that thought as its content. This gives an explanation of what it is for a thought to have a certain structure and constituents that does not immediately appeal to the notion of a sentence and its constituents.

It would be quite wrong, of course, to claim that the treatment of ontology that I have been offering is any kind of conclusive argument in favor of the thought theorist. There is much still in dispute between the theorist of thought and his opponent, some of it concerning notions I have taken for granted here. In dispute are the nature of belief states, their required connections with the possibility of expression, and much else. Yet this treatment of ontology does support the conditional that if the thought theorist can overcome these other challenges, the sentencelike structure of thoughts will not provide an insuperable obstacle for him.

It remains a question why both thoughts and sentences have the kind of structure they do. It seems to me that the answer to this question should advert not to the level of concepts but to the level of reference and semantic value. The elucidation of the correctness conditions of thoughts and sentences involves at the fundamental level the notion of an atomic predication, whose correctness in turn involves an object or objects having a monadic or relational property. The possibility of other constituents of thoughts and sentences rests ultimately on the existence of this fundamental level of atomic predications (a *Tractatus*-like remark). Once this is acknowledged, it seems to me that we have all we need to explain the common structure that both thoughts and sentences share. It is the kind of structure one would expect when both these conditions are met: the correctness of the whole and of any suitable complex constituent is a systematic function of the semantic values of its immediate constituents, and at the basic level we have predicational combination. This is sufficient to explain the characteristic treelike structure of thoughts and sentences.

4.5 Ontology and Legitimation by Application

The above treatment of concepts is a special case of a general strategy. The general strategy is that of legitimizing discourse apparently about a domain of abstract objects by giving an account of their empirical application. I use the cagey word "legitimize" to take account of the point that such legitimation could be acknowledged by someone who thinks that the alleged domain of abstract objects should be given an instrumentalist or what Hartry Field calls a "fictionalist" treatment.[11] I will return very briefly to the whole issue of fictionalism in a few paragraphs. Before then, let us consider what legitimation by application involves.

It involves, first, specifying a kind of statement in which the putative abstract objects are applied to the empirical world, either to its objects or to properties of its objects. Such types of statement will include "The number of Fs = **n**," "Expression token **t** is of type **A**," and, if the above arguments are correct, "**x** believes that p." Instances of these various kinds I call "application statements." Second, legitimation by application involves specifying, for each application statement, something equivalent that can be understood even by someone who does not possess the concepts of the appropriate pure theory of abstract objects. This too is a cautious formulation, designed to include the case of the "unassuming" view mentioned in the last section. (That the equivalents can be *understood* without possessing concepts of the appropriate theory of abstract objects does not imply that the equivalents can be *true* without such abstract objects existing.) It is a sufficient condition for the legitimacy of some proposed ontology of abstract objects that each of its objects meet one or the other of the following two conditions. (1) It can be associated with an application statement and an equivalent of the kind just mentioned. (2) It is associated in the theory with something that makes an essential contribution to fixing equivalents for objects that meet condition 1. I have been arguing that complete thoughts meet condition 1 and that concepts, as associated with possession conditions, meet condition 2.

Specifying equivalents of the application statements seems always to involve finding a certain property. The property, which may be a higher-level property, is selected for the abstract object so that the equivalent of the application statement says that the empirical entity in question has the selected property. It is because of its clear conformity to this model that the ontology of expression types is so unproblematic, despite its nonconformity to Wright's paradigm. We know exactly what shape property a token has to have to instantiate an actually uninstantiated type. It is, of course, an important question whether all abstract objects we seem to speak about can enjoy legitimation by application. For the real numbers and the higher reaches of set theory, it is a complex and fascinating issue. It is also one that we can bracket here. We can bracket it because what matters for present purposes is that the existence of a legitimation by application seems to be a sufficient condition for the intelligibility of discourse apparently about a domain of abstract objects. The model can be applied to the case of concepts whether or not legitimation by application is also a necessary condition of intelligibility.

On this view, concepts are legitimate in their own right, at least to the extent that natural numbers, predicative sets, and expression types are. This view contrasts with a position developed by Stephen Schiffer, who complains that modes of presentation, concepts here, do not meet a required "Intrinsic-Description Constraint." He writes,

> The Intrinsic-Description Constraint holds that if a thing [is a mode of presentation] then it must be intrinsically identifiable in a way that doesn't describe it as a mode of presentation or as a possible mode of presentation. In other words, it must be possible to answer the question "What is the mode of presentation of so and so?" in terms of an intrinsic characterization of the mode of presentation whose meaning implies nothing about the thing it applies to being a mode of presentation. If a thing is a mode of presentation, then it must be intrinsically identifiable as some other kind of thing. (1990, 253)

In my judgement, the intrinsic-description constraint is quite generally false of abstract objects, and its falsity for concepts or modes of presentation is a special case of this general falsity. Suppose we put forward the view that the number 3 is individuated by stating the following:

Three is the unique number **n** such that necessarily for any property **P** there are **n** things that are **P** iff there exist distinct objects **x**, **y**, and **z** that are **P** and anything that is **P** is identical with one of **x**, **y**, and **z**.

We can then imagine someone motivated by Schiffer's intrinsic-description constraint saying, "You have stated that the number 3 plays a certain role in numbering things with a given property, but what is it *intrinsically* apart from this role? Can you identify the number 3 for me as a thing of some other kind in a way that does not imply that it numbers things of a given kind?" It seems to me that this is not a good question, and that it is a mistake to look for some other identification of the number 3. Nothing more than the displayed identification is necessary, and nothing very different from it is possible. (We can individuate 3 as the successor of 2, but then for 2 or for one of its predecessors we have eventually to individuate it in a way similar to the displayed individuation of 3.) We can make a similar point for expression types. When we have indicated the condition for a token to be an instance of the type, we have done all that is required and possible in the way of individuating that type. The same is true of modes of presentation, or concepts, and their possession conditions.

The position for which I am arguing is plausibly committed to the view that any given concept or mode of presentation is essentially a concept or mode of presentation. This does not seem to me any more objectionable than the claim that any given natural number is essentially a natural number. If it does seem more objectionable, that may possibly be a result of a misapprehension about the consequences of saying that a mode of presentation is essentially a mode of presentation. To say that a mode of presentation is essentially the mode of presentation it is, is not to say that it features in any actual thinker's propositional attitudes. It is to say only that a condition exists that states what it would be for it to feature in the content of a thinker's thoughts, and that it is an essential property of the mode of presentation that this condition is the condition for it so to feature. Perhaps this position will still be thought problematic on the ground that modal notions or such constitutive notions as "what it is for such and such to be the case" should not enter a statement of what individuates an object. If this were a good objection, it would apply to the apparently legitimate individuation of the number 3 above. There are indeed many good questions about the still ill-understood notion of necessity and how it can feature in the individuation of an object. But however these matters are eventually resolved, it is hard to believe that it will not leave us endorsing the view that the above individuation of the number 3 is correct, however necessity is elucidated. My view is that the same is true of the way in which a possession condition individuates a concept or a mode of presentation.

On the present conception, then, we should be very skeptical of arguments that take the following form.[12] First they explore various candidate identifications of concepts with entities of some other kind, then they find each such candidate defective in some respect or other, and finally they conclude that there are then no such things as concepts or modes of presentation. Such arguments are unsound if concepts do not have to be identified with entities of some other kind.

4.6 Summary and the Role of Legitimation by Application

I have been arguing that the conceptual content of a belief encodes a complex relational property. The complex relational property is the property a state must have to be a belief with the given conceptual content. The property is systematically determined from the possession conditions of the concepts that comprise the conceptual content, together with the way in which they are combined. Reference to denizens of Frege's third realm, thoughts and their constituents, serves as a means of encoding these relational properties.

This conception raises many more questions than have been addressed in this chapter. One of the most immediate is this: what is the relation between the complex relational properties discussed in this chapter and the ordinary concept of belief we employ in folk psychology? I turn to this question in chapter 6.

As far as the theory of abstract objects in general is concerned, there are several paths leading from the point we have reached so far. One such path aims to evaluate fictionalism about abstract objects. With one exception, the views endorsed in this chapter are in themselves neutral on whether domains of abstract objects in general will yield to a fictionalist treatment. The exception is the unassuming view in the case of concepts. If the unassuming view is correct, then the application statements for concepts are themselves committed to the existence of concepts. So the fictionalist cannot appeal to them, at least in his positive account, and there are no obvious alternative means available. But if the bold view is correct, then there is no obstacle at least of that kind to proceeding with a fictionalist program. That metaphysical dispute will continue.

Another path from our present location moves into the territory of the epistemology of abstract objects. Though much of what I have said is in itself neutral on the question of fictionalism, it may nevertheless be that the general idea of legitimation by application, when it is properly developed, can provide responses to the epistemological arguments that have been offered in favor of fictionalist treatments. When discourse about a certain kind of abstract object is legitimized wholly by reference to its role in applications that make no reference to abstract objects, it is much less tempting to suppose that the agreed causal inertness of abstract objects makes them epistemologically problematic. The proper epistemology of a domain of abstract objects should rather make reference to their role in applications. But I have to leave the complexities of that topic here. In the particular domain of concepts and contents built up from concepts, I want to conclude by emphasizing that something like this account of how the pure theory of concepts is applied will be needed by both the fictionalist and his opponent. The opponent will need the account of applications if he is to justify the ontology by any general model of legitimation by application. The fictionalist too will need the account of applications precisely in explaining the instrumental utility of the pure theory of concepts. Eliminating the objects is very far from eliminating the applications.[13]

5 Concepts and Norms in a Natural World

5.1 The Challenge

Is it consistent for a theory to mention concepts in describing mental phenomena while also adhering to a naturalistic worldview? That is the question I will be addressing in this chapter.

Why should anyone think that there is prima facie a problem in reconciling the use of concepts in the description of mental phenomena with a naturalistic worldview? One reason lies in the ontology of concepts itself. The reference of a concept need not be naturalistically problematic, nor need some mental representation with that concept in its content. But what, naturalistically, are these *ways* in which the referent is thought about? And if there is a problem about concepts as entities from a naturalistic point of view, there is all the more of a problem about the relation of grasping a concept, relied upon by Fregean theorists.

The earlier chapters of this book attempted to provide the materials for answering these sorts of naturalistic concerns about a theory of concepts. In the immediately preceding chapter I attempted to show how the description of a belief by mentioning its conceptual content is a way of characterizing a complex, empirical, relational property of that state. In chapter 2, I also tried to explain ways in which a thinker's satisfaction of a possession condition—his "grasping the sense," as Frege would say—can be explanatory. What I have said so far is not even a sketch of a complete answer to these concerns. To mention just one issue that will recur later, the properties of a mental state in virtue of which it has a particular conceptual content involve a complex of relations to other mental states and, arguably, to the subject's environment. It is certainly a live issue how, if at all, these highly relational properties can themselves be explanatory. Nonetheless, we have made a start on the concerns raised by the ontology of concepts. What I want to address in this chapter is another source of concern, one that has so far not been addressed at all.

This second source of concern about reconciling naturalism with the mention of concepts in describing mental phenomena lies in the essentially normative character of concepts. These normative characteristics fall into two sorts. Those of the first sort are not specific to concepts but rather are present for any notion of content. Any notion of content will somehow or other, perhaps with various relativizations and qualifications, bring with it a distinction between correctness and incorrectness. This property of correctness depends upon the way the world is. It is a normative property: we aim at such correctness in forming beliefs. This property is one that applies as much to propositions built to Russell's specifications, with objects and properties as constituents, as to those built to Frege's. The question of how normative properties of this first sort are naturalistically possible obviously has to be addressed. But the problems in answering it are ones that arise even if the notion of a concept is rejected.[1]

The second sort of normative property covers those specific to concepts. These include what I call the "normative liaisons" of a specific concept or type of concepts. Certain circumstances in which a thinker may find himself can give him good reasons for taking particular attitudes to thoughts built up from given constituent concepts. In some cases the status of the reasons as good reasons is dependent upon the identity of one of the constituents of the complete content in question. When it is, we can count the triple of circumstance, attitude, and thought as among the normative liaisons of the constituent in question. Descartes could plausibly halt the progress of doubt with the thought "I think"; he could hardly have done so with "Descartes thinks." Again, seeing a man to be bald can give a thinker good reason to judge the perceptual-demonstrative thought "That man is bald"; it gives no such reason to judge "The spy is bald."

For many theorists, the notion of rationality plays a crucial role in explaining the nature of content-involving psychological explanation. For these theorists, normative liaisons must be taken as equally essential to content-involving psychological explanation. As all the examples above illustrate, rationality requirements on what attitudes should be taken in given circumstances are requirements that operate at the level of concepts (as I am using the term), rather than at the level of reference. It seems that one cannot formulate such requirements without use of a notion of a concept, with its normative dimension.

These two reasons—one relating to the ontology of concepts, the other to norms—do not exhaust the reasons why concepts might be thought to be naturalistically problematic. Another is the nature of the distinction between those liaisons that are supposed to be constitutive of a concept and those that depend upon collateral information. Yet another is the notion, apparently essential to content-involving, personal-level psychological explanation, of acting for a reason. But the issue of normative characteristics seems to be fundamental. If we had a naturalistic resolution of that issue, these others would fall into place.

What, then, is naturalism? The doctrine I mean has two parts, one about explanation and one about truth. The naturalistic claim about explanation is that any explanation of an event or temporal state of affairs is a causal explanation. Here the underlying intuition is that a treatment of an area is naturalistic only if it counts explanations within that area as fundamentally of the same kind as those that apply to the natural world, namely as causal explanations. This is compatible with acknowledging that there are many distinctions to be drawn within the class of causal explanations.[2] A conception that violates this first component of naturalism is found in Descartes. He appears to have held that when a person makes a judgement, this is sometimes a free act of the will that cannot be explained causally at all.[3]

The naturalistic doctrine about truth is that any truth is supervenient on purely descriptive truths. We can distinguish a moderate from a radical form of the doctrine. The moderate form allows that the supervenience of any truth upon descriptive truths may in some cases hold only when we take into account other possible worlds as well as the actual world. For purposes of the moderate version, these other worlds may be what David Lewis calls ersatz worlds: they do not have to be concrete, nonactual objects. This moderate naturalism about truth opposes, for instance, the claim that there are evaluative truths not supervenient on descriptive truths about this and other worlds.

The radical form of the naturalistic doctrine about truth holds that all truths supervene on descriptive truths about the actual world. Hume, on the reading that was until recently standard, was a radical naturalist about truths involving the relation of causation (as it is in this world). Radical naturalism is manifestly a challenging and controversial doctrine. There is, for instance, a question of whether it is consistent with any plausible account of truths involving necessity. The radical naturalist may either reject discourse about necessity as unintelligible or attempt some positive account of it consistent with his doctrine. If he rejects it as unintelligible, he should not, of course, formulate his position with use of the notion of supervenience, which is normally elucidated using modal terms. This radical naturalist would do better to characterize his position in terms of the reducibility of all truths to descriptive truths about the actual world, and to try to state the requirements on reduction in nonmodal terms. It is also an issue whether there can be a coherent rationale for being a radical naturalist about some kinds of truths but not about others.

In this general characterization of naturalism, neither the component about explanation nor the component about truth, whether moderate or radical, seems dispensable in favor of the other. If we omit the part about explanation and leave only the part about truth, we are left with a position that could more appropriately be called descriptivism, actualist descriptivism in the case of the radical position. Descriptivism alone would not rule our Descartes's views on the explanation of human thought, or indeed anything, however bizarre, provided it was regarded as captured by descriptive truths. On the other hand, if we omit the naturalism about truth and leave only that about explanation, we leave entirely open the nature of causation (and many other relations). Such a position would not exclude radically nonnaturalistic views of causation itself, or of any other relation.

Even if the doctrine about truth is endorsed only in its moderate form, this specification of naturalism leaves the challenge of reconciling naturalism with the mention of concepts firmly in place. The naturalistic claim about truth implies that there can be no concepts with normative dimensions unless the norms are supervenient on descriptive truths. The naturalist has at a minimum to show how this is possible.

Though the homeland of concepts is folk psychology, it is not only folk psychology that makes use of the notion. In one way or another it features frequently and essentially in theories in cognitive psychology. Any connectionist model given a "conceptual" interpretation in Paul Smolensky's (1986) terminology will be one in which concepts or hypotheses built up using concepts are assigned to nodes or assemblies. If the assignments were merely at the level of reference, these models could not explain the phenomena they set out to explain, for instance, the perception of an array not just as a shape but as falling under a concept, as an instance of a certain word type. For similar reasons, the labeling of nodes in a network of the sort employed in "spreading activation" models of memory (Anderson 1983) has to be taken as a labeling with concepts. The point also holds for cognitive-psychological models of the processes underlying understanding a perceived utterance.

It has become common recently to compare the relation between folk psychology and cognitive psychology to that between folk physics and a serious scientific physics. Suppose that we accept this analogy. Then to hold that the notion of a concept is unsound or irremediably confused because it is coeval with a questionable folk psychology is analogous to holding that we can expect a scientific physics to contain no refined versions of folk ideas of force, momentum, or friction. No doubt there is indeed much in folk psychology that is confused, erroneous, or inconsistent. But the challenge of reconciling the notion of a concept with a naturalistic worldview will disappear only if a scientific psychology makes no use at all of the idea of the way in which an object or property is represented in thought. It seems to me that there is little prospect of the challenge evaporating from such a cause.

5.2   A Teleological Solution?

Among the many things done by a state or a device, we can pick out some as its *natural function(s)*. These are the things it does that, when done by similar states or devices in ancestors containing them, contribute to the survival and proliferation of the ancestors. Thus the heart does many things, but its natural function is, by this test, to pump the blood (Wright 1976). More generally, we can classify states and what they do into types. Even if a state occurs for the first time ever in the history of a species, perhaps it has a certain function if it is a member of a more general type that includes states having a suitably corresponding natural function by this criterion. The idea is that for an attitude to have a certain content is for it to have a certain natural function in this sense. This idea has been in the air for some time and has been developed in detail by Ruth Millikan (1984, 1986) and David Papineau (1987, chapter 4). Millikan writes, "The entities that folk psychology postulates are indeed defined by their proper function [natural functions, in my terminology]" (1986, 57). I will call such theories of content "teleological theories." Can teleological theories reconcile mentioning concepts with naturalism?

In two respects, teleological theories are initially promising for accomplishing this task. They clearly use notions that are as naturalistic as the concept of explanation they employ. They also introduce, and in a naturalistic fashion, a simple normative notion: that of something performing properly or not, according to whether it is performing its natural function or not. So it is important to see whether the initial promise is fulfilled.

Millikan develops the idea that "apparently beliefs are named or described (typed) in accordance with certain of their Normal conditions for functioning properly" (1986, 69). A Normal condition for a device or state functioning properly is, in outline, a condition that is part of full explanations of the sort that historically accounted for the existence of such a device or state in organisms. More specifically, Millikan suggests, "Presumably it is a proper function of the belief-manufacturing mechanisms in John to produce beliefs-that-p only if and when p" (1986, 69).[4] Similarly, Papineau's formulation, later qualified in his text, is that "the truth condition of the belief is the 'normal' circumstance in which, given the learning process, it is biologically supposed to be present" (1987, 67). The difficulty I want to raise for this idea I will call the "problem of reduced content."

What explains the proliferation and survival of the belief-producing mechanisms and the organisms containing them when p is believed, p is true, and all is working properly is the truth of all the (logical) consequences of p that have a causal impact on the organism.[5] Now the truth of all such consequences in some cases falls short of the truth of p. Take universal quantification, for instance, the belief that all Londoners are under seven feet tall. It is only the truth of instances of this quantification for objects that come into some sort of causal contact with the thinker that contribute to the explanation of the persistence of the belief-producing mechanisms and organisms containing them. In a nutshell, the problem of reduced content is this: how is the teleological theorist to block an incorrect assignment of content to beliefs, namely one that requires for its truth merely the truth of all the logical consequences of p that have a causal impact on the thinker, rather than the stronger condition of the truth of p itself?

How might the teleological theorist respond? One reply is this: She may say, "The truth of all the consequences of p that have a causal impact on the thinker is itself explained by the truth of p. So there is no real gap here. The explanation of the persistence of the belief-producing mechanisms when all is working properly is that the belief that p is produced only when p is the case." But it is not true for every type of content that the truth of all its consequences that have a causal impact on the thinker is explained by the truth of p. Maybe that is so for certain observational contents, but it is not so for all universal quantifications. This seems particularly clear for accidental, contingent generalizations. If it is true that all Londoners are under seven feet tall, that fact does not *explain* the singular instance about some particular Londoner (whether the thinker has causal contact with the particular Londoner or not).

By way of another reply the teleological theorist may say, "The commitments incurred in believing a content, including commitments about objects that have no causal impact on the thinker, are reflected in his inferential dispositions involving the content. These inferential dispositions are produced by his belief-manufacturing mechanisms and are subject to testing by natural selection, like everything else." All this is true, but the truth (if they are true) of the commitments of a content that have no causal impact on the thinker remain unabsorbed into its content on the teleological theory as currently formulated. They do not contribute in the appropriate way to the explanation of the survival of the mechanisms and of members of the species. We should perhaps recall that in the case of absolutely unrestricted universal generalizations over space and time, these commitments will include those about objects outside the thinker's light cone, objects that could not have any causal impact on him. In discussing the correct characterization of the biological purposes of a particular ability, theorists like Millikan have very properly insisted that we should be careful not to include anything as a biological purpose that has not contributed in the required way to the explanation of the proliferation of organisms that exercise the ability: "A complexity that can simply be dropped from the explanans without affecting the tightness of the relation of explanans to explanandum is not a *functioning* part of the explanation" (Millikan 1990, 334). The objector who presses the problem of reduced content will emphasize that his objection rests precisely on this requirement.

The teleological theorist might try simply to incorporate such commitments as manifested in inferential dispositions, into the truth conditions. The theory would not then be a purely teleological one, since the notion of a commitment is not teleological. But more important, this modification also seems to make the teleological apparatus redundant. For the appeal to commitments can be used to capture the right truth conditions even in cases where the consequences of p do have a causal impact on the thinker (for further discussion, see Peacocke 1986b, chapter 3).

I have made the point with universal quantification, but other examples are available too. We could develop similar arguments for undecidable contents about the past. What explains the persistence of the belief-producing mechanisms concerned with past-tense contents is the truth of those consequences of believed past-tense contents that have a causal impact on the thinker. What is undetectably the case can have no such effects.

It is no accident that in developing the problem of reduced content, I consider contents for which a realistic, verification-transcendent account of meaning is most plausible. In these cases we always have the clearest divergence between the truth of a content and the truth of its consequences that have a causal impact on an individual. There is a certain irony here. Some teleological theorists like Millikan have aimed to use their ideas in support for forms for realism.[6] The problem of reduced content suggests that teleological theories of content will support only contents of a more constructivist stripe.[7]

To reject teleological theories because of the problem of reduced content is compatible with insisting that we build theories of why it is adaptive for organisms to have states with representational contents concerning the world. All that we are rejecting is teleology as a *constitutive* account of what it is to enjoy content-involving states. There is much that can be explained in terms of natural selection without it being the case that what is to be explained can itself be elucidated only in teleological terms. Natural selection can plausibly explain why we have eyes sensitive to just a certain range of wavelengths. What it is for eyes to be sensitive to that range should not itself be elucidated in teleological terms.[8]

5.3   Norms and the World

Earlier I gave some familiar examples to illustrate the fact that norms operate at the level of concepts—different concepts, different norms. But when one attempts to give a naturalistic theory of the normative dimension of concepts, there are at least two connections with the level of reference that one has to respect. The first concerns the normative distinction between correctness and incorrectness, present for any notion of content. Whether a content is correct depends on properties of the references of any concepts it contains. Any naturalistic theory that captures this normative dimension will have to concern itself at some point with the level of reference. The second family of connections involves the normative liaisons I mentioned. Again, though these are links of concepts, a theory that explains them is constrained by certain facts concerning references. Judgement aims at truth. So we need to show how judging in conformity with the normative links is consistent with aiming at truth. Once again, the truth of the content judged depends upon properties of the referents of its component concepts. Respecting the normative links unfolds into a constraint at the level of reference.

When we consider concepts as expressed in a language, senses in a strict sense, there are other normative aspects too, but I will not consider them here. These other aspects come in when we consider language and the intention that a word have a certain sense. There is a correctness/incorrectness distinction internal to the notion of intention. There is also a notion of justification for an assertion expressed in language that involves factors going beyond justification at the level of thought. I bracket these notions here and confine my attention to the level of thought. My reason for this is partly that on the account I will offer, the level of thought is more fundamental. On the theory I offer, an account of the normative notions specific to language has to draw upon materials in a positive theory of the normative notions involved in thought.

The challenge, then, is to answer these questions:

1.   How are the normative liaisons of concepts determined by naturalistic facts?

2.   How do these norms at the level of concepts succeed in constrain-
ing the level of reference?

3.   Can we say something informative and general about the answers
to questions 1 and 2 for all domains of concepts and objects?

To break up the task of answering these questions into pieces of
manageable size, I first take a particular example. Since it has received
a justly famous treatment by Saul Kripke (1982), I take the case of the
concept *plus*. I will approach the issues a little obliquely by asking,
what makes something the semantic value of *plus*? Here I am asking
a question about the semantic value of a certain concept, a concept
that intuitively has a certain function on the natural numbers as its
semantic value.

In our everyday use of arithmetic, we take certain identities for
granted. For instance, we use the identity $12 \times 9 = 108$ without
reflection, having learned it long ago by rote. But we can make sense
of the idea that what we take for granted might be wrong; we can
check it for ourselves, ultimately relying on counting. Suppose that
we want to find the sum of 18 and 65 by counting up 65 steps from
18. We find this procedure acceptable in part because its individual
steps involve compelling transitions like the following (where s refers
to the successor function):

$$\frac{(18 \; plus \; 64) \; is \; n}{\text{So } (18 \; plus \; s(64)) \; is \; s(n)} \tag{T}$$

The special respect in which such a transition is compelling is that
there does not seem to be anything standing to our ordinary acceptance
of this transition as counting stands to something learned by rote. The
transition is not specifically answerable to something else in the way
that (nondefinitional) arithmetical identities are answerable to counting. The transition is primitively compelling, in the sense in which I
used this phrase early on in section 1.2.[9]

Even though a transition is primitively compelling, we can still raise
the philosophical question of whether what we find primitively compelling can also be justified. Frege and Russell were raising precisely
such questions in discussing the foundations of arithmetic. The question of possible justifications is often likely to be more intriguing for
transitions and principles that *are* primitively compelling than for those

that are *not*. To say that a principle or transition is primitively compelling is to commit oneself to the view that the unreflective master of the concepts it contains is not required, as a condition of mastery, to treat it as answerable to anything else. The reflective master of the concepts may still want to understand the nature of truths involving them.

When we find such transitions as (T) compelling, we do so because they have a certain *form*. It is not as if there were a list of such transitions each of which we find compelling independently of their common form. It also matters here that someone can find a transition compelling because of its form without his having the ability, or even the conceptual apparatus, to make explicit that general form. Such is the situation of a nine-year-old who, after counting up from 18 and finding that $18 + 3$ is 21, moves from that to the conclusion that $18 + 4$ is 22.

More generally, it cannot always be the case that we characterize possession of a given concept (in the present case, *plus*) only by relating it to other conceptual capacities of the thinker. If we were to do so, we would have no fully adequate answer to questions of the type, What is it for the thinker to possess concept C rather than concept D? It cannot always be satisfactory to answer this question only by saying that to possess C is to possess a concept that stands in certain relations to the thinker's conceptual capacities involving the distinct concepts $C_1, \ldots, C_n$, while to possess D is correspondingly to possess a concept that stands in certain relations to his conceptual capacities involving the distinct concepts $D_1, \ldots, D_n$. For the same question can be raised in turn about possession of each of the C_i as contrasted with possession of the D_i. At some point a good account of conceptual mastery must tie the mastery to abilities and relations that do not require conceptualization by the thinker. For any concept not explicitly defined in terms of others, there must be a nonconceptual component in an account of mastery of it. This suggestion, in relating grasp of *plus* to the causal influence of a form of transition not necessarily conceptualized, provides just one example of a way in which a nonconceptual element may enter. There will, of course, be many other ways; chapter 3 investigated some of the other ways involving perception.

Consistently with these points, we as theorists can make explicit the causally influential form:

$$\frac{(m \; plus \; k) \; is \; n}{So \; (m \; plus \; s(k)) \; is \; s(n)} \quad \text{(R)}$$

This general form is equivalent to the recursive clause in the inductive definition of "plus" in the standard axiomatizations of first-order arithmetic. By similar considerations we can also make explicit another general form whose instances are primitively compelling and are found compelling because they are of this form:

$$(m \; plus \; 0) \; is \; m \quad \text{(B)}$$

With some oversimplifications to be removed in a minute, the core of the suggestion I have to make is this:

SV/*plus* The semantic value of *plus* is the function on the natural numbers that makes the general transition (R) always truth-preserving and makes principle (B) always true.

The semantic value that meets the condition given in SV/*plus* is the addition function (a familiar arithmetical fact).

Before discussing this proposal, I remove a few oversimplifications. First, I have been taking for granted the fact that the (senses of) numerals have certain references. An account of what makes this so would have to advert to their use in numerical quantifications, i.e., their use in applications. So while my first formulation may make it seem that we can give an "atomistic" account of what makes *plus* have a certain semantic value, an account that does not mention constraints on the semantic values of other senses, this is in fact not so.

Second, nothing is found compelling in every circumstance. There are hardly any contents at all, if any, that a person may not be brought to reject if there are carefully placed distractors or suitably chosen drugs in operation. A sufficiently devious psychologist might, if he ran trials on a subject long enough, make a subject reject contents that, in other circumstances, are primitively compelling for him. I will take it that propositional-attitude psychology, the home of concepts, gets a grip only in certain normal circumstances (whose nature may need empirical investigation). Only what is found primitively compelling in the normal circumstances on which propositional-attitude psychology relies should be mentioned in a full statement of SV/*plus*.

Does SV/*plus* ratify as the reference of the concept *plus* the classical addition function defined on all natural numbers? Or does it ratify as the reference merely a function defined only on accessible ("survey-able") natural numbers? It will ratify the classical addition function as the reference in a nonarbitrary way only if we can give philosophically adequate reasons for saying, of two inference forms that disagree only on (concepts of) the inaccessible numbers, that one rather than the other is causally influential in the accessible cases. It would take me much too far afield to discuss this complex and fascinating question here. Along one dimension, it is in fact orthogonal to the concerns of this chapter. For, one who holds that the concepts we employ can be defined only over accessible domains has to address the problem of the normative dimension of concepts no less than his more realistically inclined colleague (such as myself). In this chapter I will be offering something that could be employed to explain the normative dimension of concepts even by someone who doubts that our concepts could have determinate extensions beyond the accessible.[10]

We are now in a position to offer a reconciliation of naturalism with norms, at least for the concept *plus,* if we accept one additional premise. The additional premise is that finding instances of (R) and (B) primitively compelling and doing so because they are of the forms we discussed are constitutive of a grasp of *plus.* This additional premise seems plausible. In normal circumstances of the sort on which propositional-attitude psychology relies, it seems that a thinker is not thinking of the addition function in the way of *plus* unless he finds those instances compelling and does so in part because of their form. If this is so, we can then rewrite the account of a grasp of *plus* in the $\mathcal{A}(C)$ form:

Possession Condition for *Plus* *Plus* is that concept C to possess which a thinker must find transitions of the form

$$\frac{(m \; C \; k) \; is \; n}{(m \; C \; s(k)) \; is \; s(n)}$$

primitively compelling (where *m, n, k* are senses that obviously refer to natural numbers), and he must find them compelling because they are of that form. Similarly for the principle (*m C 0*) *is m.*

That a thinker finds certain transitions and principles primitively compelling and does so from certain causes is a naturalistically kosher claim. At least it is so if the notion of explanation is naturalistically acceptable. In any case, the claim is not normative. Suppose too that SV/*plus* is true. Then instances of (R) and (B) will actually be *correct* for the arithmetic function that is the referent of *plus*. That is, an account of what makes something the referent of *plus* shows those instances to have a normative status. In short, certain reasons for judging contents containing *plus* are certified by this account as being good reasons. For the special case of *plus* we have an account of how the normative liaisons of a concept can be determined by naturalistic facts, a preliminary answer to the earlier question 1.

We can also begin to see how respecting the norms for a concept in one's judgements cannot conflict with aiming at truth (question 2). The truth value of a content is determined by the semantic values (referents) of its constituents. In particular, the semantic value of *plus* is whatever makes the transition (or principle) that constitutes those norms truth-preserving (or true). So it is in the nature of the case that respecting the norms cannot conflict with the goal of aiming at the truth and at truth-preservation. Since aiming at the truth of one's judgements is part of rationality, judging in accordance with the possession conditions has an internal connection with rationality.

I should emphasize that I am here claiming correctness not merely for the arithmetic fact that the addition function conforms to (R) and (B). That is not news. The point is rather the following conditional. Suppose that all the following conditions are met: we are concerned with a concept of a binary function over the natural numbers; mastery of the concept requires that instances of certain principles be found primitively compelling because they are of the forms given in the principles; and the semantic value of the concept is whatever makes those principles always truth-preserving. Given all this, then instances of that principle will be correct for the concept in question. This whole conditional is not a truth about numbers but is rather something that should be formulated with a variable over concepts.[11]

The present treatment of *plus* is strictly a naturalistic one, provided that there are naturalistic treatments of the concepts whose mastery by the thinker is presupposed in the above account of grasp of *plus* (concepts of individual natural numbers, of succession, of identity). I chose Kripke's example of *plus* because he has made the issues so well known. *Plus* is located several steps up a hierarchy of concepts. But my treatment of *plus* exemplifies a general model that can be instantiated for a family of concepts at a fundamental level, at which an account of possession of them would not presuppose possession of concepts outside that family. Let us consider the general form of the proposed reconciliation in the abstract.

The general model for reconciling naturalism with the norms for any given sense will have three elements. The first element in the reconciliation of naturalism with the normative character of concepts is the provision, for any given concept, of an acceptable, nonnormative possession condition for it.

The second element we need for a reconciliation is a determination theory of the sort mentioned in chapter 1. A determination theory is a theory that says how the semantic value of a concept is determined from its possession condition (and the way the world is, in empirical cases). SV/*plus* is a determination theory. In effect it says how the semantic value of *plus* is determined from its possession condition. A theory playing a similar role is needed for every other possession condition we endorse.

The third element in the general form of the reconciliation is an explanation of how a possession condition together with a determination theory can give normative status to certain principles about judgements (or other attitudes) involving the concept. In the case of *plus*, we have seen how a plausible determination theory results in the transition and principle mentioned in the possession condition being counted as *correct*. The semantic value determined necessarily makes those transitions and principles truth-preserving and true, respectively. More generally, the correct determination theory for a given possession condition will validate as correct the judgemental and inferential practices mentioned in the possession condition. So those practices do have the status of correct practices, even though the possession condition itself does not employ normative notions. The general model then also ensures a general, internal link between possession of a particular concept and the rationality of certain core practices of belief formation involving that concept.

Not all the norms validated by possession conditions and determination theories need to be explicitly reflected in the possession conditions. There need not, for instance, be any such direct reflection when a norm results from the interaction of several possession conditions. But if a reconciliation of the sort in question is to be successful for a particular concept, what is required is this: each normative liaison specific to that concept must be explicable by reference to the possession condition and determination theory for the concept, together with the possession conditions and determination theories for the other concepts involved in the statement of the normative liaison.

This general model of reconciliation prompts several observations. First, not only naturalists should be interested in the possibility of such a reconciliation. An opponent of naturalism still has to answer the question of how a possession condition not itself stated in explicitly normative terms can individuate a concept with an essentially normative dimension.

Second, when we are giving a possession condition for a concept that is itself normative, the possession condition too may well contain normative material. It may well be that we cannot explain what it is to possess the concept *just*, predicable of institutional arrangements, without using the concept of justice. In such a case the naturalist will rely on the transitivity of supervenience to establish that the case is in accord with the principle that all truths supervene on descriptive truths. Content-involving normative features of a normative concept supervene on properties of its possession condition, and for the naturalist, whether this possession condition is met by a given thinker supervenes in turn on descriptive truths about the thinker.

Third, there is also a connection between the underlying motivation of the framework of possession conditions and a more limited kind of supervenience. It too is arguably a connection that can be acknowledged by anyone endorsing that framework and its motivation, even if such a person is not a naturalist. To make clear the more limited supervenience in question, I need to draw a distinction. Part of the possession condition of a concept can contain a normative notion without stating any of the normative liaisons of the concept. A normative liaison specifies good reasons for the thinker to take particular attitudes in given circumstances to certain contents containing the concept. But the above remarks about the concept *just* should remind us that part of its possession condition might state that the thinker who possesses it is willing to judge of certain manifestly unjust arrangements that they are unjust. This part states a requirement on possession of the concept *just* by itself making use of the normative concept of justice. Yet it does not itself *say* of any reasons that they are good reasons for making certain judgements about justice. Thus the more limited supervenience in question is the supervenience of the normative liaisons of a concept on those of its properties that do not specify its normative liaisons. These supervened-on properties may still be normative in some other way.

Finally in this section, I turn to consider the bearing of the position I have so far developed on a closely related issue about the supervenience of the normative characteristics of concepts. If we adopt the framework of possession conditions, we will hold that for every concept, there is an account of what makes it the case that someone is employing it rather than any other concept. This account will be formulated in terms of conditions relating to grasp of the concept in question. Derivatively, for each judgeable propositional content, we will also be committed to the existence of an account, similarly formulated, of what it is for a thinker to be judging it rather than any other content. Now suppose that the normative liaisons of contents fail to supervene on their other properties. Then there could be two distinct concepts C and C' that do not differ in respect of the conditions required for grasp of them. So far as grasp of them is concerned, the same conditions, if any, relating to the circumstances under which contents containing them are accepted, to their commitments, to the social and environmental explanation of judgements containing them, to inferential principles containing them, and to all remaining matters other than their normative liaisons have to be given for both C and for C'. So if supervenience fails, there could be two thinkers who have exactly the same nonnormative relations, actual and counterfactual, to concepts they each employ, and *ex hypothesi* have exactly the same dispositions to make corresponding judgements involving their respective concepts, for the same reasons, and yet their respective concepts are distinct.[12] If the more limited form of supervenience fails, if the normative liaisons of a concept fail to supervene on its nonnormative properties, the case just described is possible because their normative liaisons could differ without anything else differing. It is highly unintuitive that this is a genuine possibility. But there is also a theoretically motivated objection.

The theoretical objection to the alleged possibility is its incompatibility with the principle that there can be no more to the identity of a concept than is given by an account of what it is to possess the concept (the Principle of Dependence of chapter 1). It would violate the intent of that principle to suppose that we could have two legitimate possession conditions for alleged concepts C and C' of the following sort. The two possession conditions contain exactly the same requirements for matters other than normative liaisons. They differ, though, in that one has some clauses tacked on specifying circumstances in which judgements containing the concept would be made for good reasons, while the other has different clauses of this sort for the other concept. It is also, of course, part of the description of the case that these tacked-on clauses about normative liaisons cannot be eliminated by further expanding the other part of the possession condition. In such a case these tacked-on clauses represent additional requirements that make the alleged concepts ungraspable. They are ungraspable because the accounts have not explained how the alleged normative liaisons of the alleged concept in question are reflected in facts about what it is to possess the concept. The ungraspable addition can apparently make no difference to the role of the alleged concept in an explanatory propositional-attitude psychology. Derivatively, it would also be unknowable in principle whether a thinker was employing C rather than C' in his judgements. The case would not be one of merely inductive uncertainty, as can arise when a content involves an open-ended set of commitments. No amount of evidence could settle whether it is C rather than C' that is in the content of the thinker's thoughts. In short, if we accept that the nature of a concept is to be explained in terms of what it is to possess it, no amount of evidence could settle the question, because the question itself presupposes a spurious distinction between these alleged concepts.[13]

The general position for which I have been arguing can be compared with that of Quine. In "Ontological Relativity" Quine writes, "For naturalism, the question whether two expressions are alike or unlike in meaning has no determinate answer, known or unknown, except insofar as the answer is settled in principle by people's speech dispositions, known or unknown" (1969b, 29). If we replace "people's speech dispositions" here with "naturalistically specifiable facts about people's relations to the expressions," the resulting claim would be accepted on the position for which I have been arguing. The claim is still an important one when the behaviorist streak in Quine's formulation is removed. Quine would say that one who denies his quoted principle about sameness of meaning is committed to "the museum myth." I have been arguing for a theory of concepts committed to endorsing a behaviorism-free version of Quine's claim. A good theory of concepts is committed not to embracing, but rather to rejecting, the museum myth.

5.4 Kripkean Requirements

Does a naturalistic attitude to concepts and content face other difficulties of principle? It is high time to face the meaning skepticism developed by Kripke (1982). Kripke insists that an account of meaning one thing rather than another must capture the normative dimensions of meaning. I have been trying to respect this point. Insofar as the dispositional theories he criticizes fail even to address this requirement, my account is not one of them. I have brought in causally explanatory notions, but within a framework supposed to account for the determination of the norms associated with a concept. Still the question can be raised, do Kripke's more specific objections to dispositional theories apply equally to my account?

One of Kripke's objections to dispositional accounts is this: there is a danger that any disposition will determine *some* function or other, at least on the accessible numbers, and so a dispositional theory cannot make sense of the possibility that someone is under an illusion that he means something by a given expression. Yet such illusions are possible in several ways on my account. Suppose that a thinker is using expression **f** putatively for some unary function on the natural numbers.[14] Here are three ways, on my account, in which he can be wrong in thinking that **f** has any such meaning: (1) There may be no transitions or principles that he finds primitively compelling because of their form and to which some particular assertion containing **f** is answerable.

(2) Even if there are such principles or transitions, it may be that for assertions of different sentences containing it, the principles and transitions to which they are answerable are not mutually consistent. (3) For a given sentence containing f, asserted on different occasions, it may not be the same principles or transitions to which the thinker takes his judgements as answerable.

Possibilities 1 to 3 allow that the thinker may mean nothing at all. The account also allows for cases in which something *is* meant but the thinker has a false belief containing the concept. Some ways in which this can happen are these: (4) The thinker's judgement is not in accord with the primitively compelling transitions or principles to which contents containing the sense are answerable. This would be the case with incorrect identities learned by rote. (5) The content judged may concern a number under a mode of presentation other than that mentioned in the account of grasp of the arithmetical sense in question. In this case, even in totally normal circumstances, my theory allows for error. (6) When the circumstances are not the normal ones on which content-involving psychology relies, errors may occur concerning the contents mentioned in the account of grasp of the sense in question. (7) Finally, if the account of grasp adverts to the commitments of certain contents containing the sense in question, we can make sense of the possibility that the content is judged yet false because not all the commitments incurred are correct. This seems to be the case relevant to certain natural-kind concepts, such as *horse,* as opposed to *horse-like* (having a horsey gestalt). "That's a horse" judged on the basis of perception may be false because the commitment to its being of the same natural kind as certain other encountered animals may turn out to be false. In sum, a proponent of the present account can endorse Kripke's remark that "nothing is more contrary to our ordinary view—or Wittgenstein's—than is the supposition that 'whatever is going to seem right to me is right'" (1982, 23–24).

Kripke's skeptic also raises objections against other suggestions. A natural response to the skeptic, when the meaning of "plus" is the target, is to appeal to the answerability of judgements containing *plus* to the results of counting. Kripke replies on behalf of the skeptic to this response (1982, 15–17). Kripke's objection on behalf of the skeptic is that appeal to the results of counting won't help, because it does not exclude the possibility that the judgements are answerable rather to *quounting,* where quounting agrees with counting on numbers so far considered by the thinker and disagrees elsewhere. Kripke's skeptic does not consider the response that it is the *form* of the transitions and principles relied upon in counting that explains their compellingness and to which the antiskeptic should appeal. Kripke's skeptic does consider an objector who appeals to the recursion equations for addition, and again he says that they are applied in only finitely many instances (1982, 16–17). I have been emphasizing that what explains why certain transitions and principles are found compelling is a form that extends beyond instances that have been considered. (On the question of how the form can be explanatory, see section 7.1.) Kripke also emphasizes that an appeal to the recursion equations is overly sophisticated, because many of us who use *plus* are ignorant of them. I agree that any theory that says we must explicitly know the recursion equations to have grasped *plus* is wrong. But I have been offering a theory on which a certain form can be causally explanatory and can help to determine the recursion equations (and thereby the correct arithmetical function) without the ordinary thinker's having explicitly to know the recursion equations. My theory can acknowledge that to someone who has already grasped *plus,* his first study of Peano arithmetic can come as an illumination.

5.5 Summary and Disclaimer

In this chapter I considered some of the essential normative characteristics of concepts and tried to account for them within a theory of possession conditions. The account, which is broadly naturalistic, turned crucially on the relation between a possession condition for a concept and the semantic value of the concept. Like the case of recombinability discussed in chapter 2, this is another case in which we have to mention the level of reference and its relation to possession conditions to explain the phenomena.

There are still some normative aspects in the intuitive notion of a concept with which I have not yet grappled. I have yet to deal with the idea that when someone possesses a concept, there are facts about him that determine whether it would be correct for him to apply it to an as yet unencountered object, facts given in advance of any judgement he actually makes about the new case. I will return to this crux in the penultimate chapter of this book.

The reconciliation I have been offering of the normative dimension of concepts with a broadly naturalistic view is not committed to any strongly reductive version of naturalism. The descriptive possession conditions upon which the reconciliation is based employ such notions as belief and forming a belief for a particular reason, notions distinctive of propositional-attitude psychology. The reconciliation I offered is quite neutral on whether there can be any reduction of these notions to concepts that have a life outside of propositional-attitude psychology. What I have said could indeed be used by such a reductive naturalist as a first stage in his reductive project. It could also be accepted by someone who believes that, for one reason or another, such reductive projects are impossible to carry out.

This point about neutrality in respect of any reduction of the notions of propositional-attitude psychology applies more generally to the approach developed in this book. I am engaged in attempting to explain various concept-involving phenomena by appeal to particular possession conditions, to more general types of possession condition, or to structural constraints on possession conditions in general. Since possession conditions contain notions distinctive of propositional-attitude psychology, these proposed explanations operate at a level above that at which the question of reduction, naturalistic or not, arises. Explanatory philosophy does not require strong naturalistic reductions.

6 The Concept of Belief: Self Knowledge and Referential Coherence

6.1 The Issues

What is it to possess the concept of belief, to be capable of ascribing beliefs to oneself and to others? This is the question that I will be addressing and to which I will be returning a partial answer. While the question has some intrinsic interest, my motivation for considering it is more general. As with any question about the possession of a particular concept, a convincing answer must appeal to a general theory of concept possession. The desire to investigate the powers and responsibilities of a general theory of concepts, as shown in a proper treatment of the concept of belief, motivates this discussion.

Belief as a propositional attitude is also of particular interest in the account of concepts under development in this book. We would expect one who attributes a propositional attitude with a particular content to another to be required to be sensitive in some way to the other's satisfaction of the possession conditions for the concepts in the content attributed. What is the required sensitivity?

Consideration of the concept of belief brings several interrelated theoretical issues to front stage. It is a responsibility of any theory of a given concept to explain the epistemological and more generally the cognitive phenomena distinctive of that concept. If it is held, as I hold, that a concept is individuated by the condition for a thinker's possessing that concept, then this responsibility unfolds into one of explaining the distinctive epistemological and cognitive phenomena by reference to the concept's possession condition.

The first task, then, is actually to provide these explanations in the case of the concept of belief. The most natural way of carrying out the task raises a cluster of theoretical issues. It is very natural to propose for the concept of belief a possession condition that has two clauses: one clause for cases in which it is combined with the first person in the present tense and one clause for cases of other kinds. Such an approach would seek to explain the distinctive properties of first-person, present-tense ascriptions of belief by reference to properties of the clause dealing with just that case. Yet to give a possession condition with two clauses is to make a substantial choice, and this choice raises some of the theoretical issues.

It is certainly plausible that there are other examples of concepts whose possession conditions have multiple clauses dealing with different types of concepts with which they may be combined. Relatively observational concepts provide probably the least controversial example. A possession condition for a relatively observational concept will have two clauses (see, for instance, the discussion of the concept *square* in section 4.3). One clause will deal with the case in which the concept is perceptibly instantiated for the thinker by the object thought about, and the other clause will deal with the case in which it is not so instantiated. But reflection on the case of observational concepts serves only to emphasize the responsibilities of a theory that offers possession conditions with such multiple clauses. It is a condition of adequacy on a multiple-clause account of an observational concept F that there exist a property meeting both of these conditions:

· It is the property that the account requires an object to have if a judgement that an object is F, made when the object is perceptually presented, is to be correct.

· It is the property the account requires an object to have if a judgement that it is F, made when the object is not perceptually presented, is to be correct.

A corresponding condition of adequacy applies to the first- and third-person parts of a multiple-clause treatment of the concept of belief. As we will see later, it is not difficult to write out spurious "possession conditions" with multiple clauses that fail to meet such a condition of adequacy. So we will have to consider the question, which is a general one for any theory of concepts, of what is substantively required for a proposed multiple-clause possession condition to be coherent.

As is implicit in these remarks, I will also understand that a distinction is to be drawn between the property or state of believing a given content and the concept of believing the same content. The distinction between states and concepts of those states is analogous to the distinction between objects and concepts of those objects. A theory of the state of having a certain belief can indeed provide important constraints on a theory of the concept of belief. Indeed, wanting to have some account of the relation between the concept of belief and the state of belief is one motivation for the discussion of this chapter. But it remains that providing a theory of the concept is a distinct task from that of providing a theory of the state.

It is true that a theory of the state of having a particular belief will identify the state in a certain way. The account I offered in chapter 4 was a positive account of the state of believing a given content. That account said that someone who believes that p, is in a state with relational properties systematically determined from the possession conditions for the constituent concepts composing p, together with their mode of composition. It requires philosophical reflection to formulate the possession condition for a concept. It requires further philosophical reflection to reach an account of how the possession conditions for the constituent concepts of a content determine the complex property that amounts to belief in it. These points make it quite implausible that the way in which a good account identifies the state of believing a given content can be identified with the concept of belief we employ in everyday life. To have a theory of the state is not yet to have a theory of the concept.

Alternatively, it may be said that the conditions for a state to be a belief that p have to be merely tacitly known to anyone who possesses the concept of belief. Maybe some would find this objectionable on the ground that tacit knowledge must be irrelevant to possession conditions, which, for any concept, including the concept of belief, have to concern the thinker's conscious states at the personal level. If it is stated with that generality, the objection overshoots. Possession conditions do indeed concern the states of the thinker at the personal level, but tacit knowledge may be required to account for those personal-level states mentioned in the possession condition. This is precisely the situation for the most convincing cases of tacit knowledge. A subject's perceiving an uttered sentence as having a certain structure and sense, a conscious state, is explained by his tacit knowledge of a grammar for the fragment of a language. Again, ordinary speakers are notoriously unsuccessful if asked to offer an explicit definition of the concept *chair*. But these subjects' correct responses when asked of particular examples whether or not they are chairs can make it quite clear that they have tacitly mastered a quite specific definition; tacit knowledge of the definition explains the immediate impression for some example of a clear case of whether it is or is not a chair.

Suppose that we were to postulate tacit knowledge of the possession conditions of various concepts with a view to explaining a thinker's judgements about another person's beliefs. The supposition here involves postulation of various pieces of tacit knowledge with contents of the form "Concept F is the unique concept C to possess which a thinker must meet condition $\mathcal{A}(C)$" (or its appropriate variant where there is a local holism or indexicality). The content of this postulation must be distinguished from the proposition that a thinker's satisfaction of condition $\mathcal{A}(C)$ itself is a form of tacit knowledge (a supposition to which I am sympathetic). The postulation here is postulation of tacit knowledge of the whole possession condition, which consists of an identity claim about the concept F. Now suppose also that the thinker is given facts, not stated using the concept of belief, that, together with the possession conditions for various concepts, entail that the other person believes that such and such. That the other person believes this need not be immediately obvious to the thinker in these circumstances, even to one who possesses the concept of belief. The point can be illustrated with material from the discussion of chapter 4. There toward the end of section 4.3, I formulated a complex relational property obtained by multiplying out the possession conditions for the recognitional concept *Lincoln Plaza* and the observational concept *square*. That this complex property is the one required of a subject if he is to have the relevant belief that Lincoln Plaza is square does not have to be immediately obvious to anyone who possesses the concept of belief. So the case is not like that in which the plausible postulation of tacit knowledge of the definition of *chair* explains someone's classification of examples into chairs and nonchairs. Rather, presented with the complex relational property I identified in chapter 4, the thinker has to engage in a process of reasoning and reflection.

Part of what we have to capture in the possession condition for belief is something that fixes the goals and constraints under which this process of reasoning and reflection has to proceed if it is aimed at establishing whether the other person has a certain belief. We need a possession condition for the concept of belief, an account of a thinker's knowledge of when a state is a state of belief, one that accounts for that reasoning and reflection in which the thinker has to engage. Later on, I will be suggesting for incorporation into the possession condition for the concept of belief a species of tacit knowledge that fixes the goals and constraints on such reasoning, rather than tacit knowledge of the possession conditions for the concepts in the attributed belief content.

Accepting the distinction between the state and the concept of belief has a second consequence: it affects the targeting of points and one's general view of the commitments of a theory of the concept of belief. Objections that would be well taken if directed against a theory of the concept need not be so well taken against theories of the state of belief. Several writers have commented that functionalist theories of belief will be highly complex, and, they say, it is not plausible that young children who exercise the concept of belief in ascriptions to themselves and others know these complex functional characterizations.[1] A complex characterization may, of course, be tacitly known. But the important point here is that a functionalist theory of belief should be understood as a theory of belief *states*. It is an open question of what theory of the *concept* of belief a functionalist should accept. Indeed, the account of belief states I gave in chapter 4 is in some very broad sense functionalist, if experiences and externalist features can be accommodated within some form of functionalism. That account does not foreclose the possibility of a plausible account of the concept of belief. By the same token, someone who thinks he already has a good account of the state of belief should still be interested in addressing the questions asked here about the concept of belief.

So much by way of setting the stage. I now turn to consider a possession condition for the concept of belief.

6.2   The First-Person Clause

Here is a naive first-person, present-tense clause, the core of which I will defend:

Possession Condition for *Believes*, **First-Person Clause**   A relational concept R is that of belief only if the following condition is met:

(F)   the thinker finds the first-person content that he stands in R to the content p primitively compelling whenever he has the conscious belief that p, and he finds it compelling because he has that conscious belief.

Clause (F) offers a necessary condition for a concept R to be the concept of belief. It does so by giving a sufficient condition for a thinker's finding a certain first-person content primitively compelling. The clause uses the concept of belief in giving a part of the possession condition for the concept of belief. As always, this is consistent with the general requirements on possession conditions, provided that the concept of belief is not mentioned as the concept of belief within the scope of the thinker's propositional attitudes. The clause can be improved by taking account of the point that the thinker is required to find the first-person content primitively compelling only when the question of whether he believes that p has arisen in his mind. We can do this without importing circularity into the putative clause of the possession condition. We just replace the phrase "whenever he has the conscious belief that p" with the phrase "whenever he has the conscious belief that p and the question of whether he stands in R to p arises in his thought." By using the variable over the relational concept for a second time, I avoid using the concept of belief within the scope of the thinker's propositional attitudes.

A major question is whether it is legitimate to use the notion of a conscious belief in the possession condition. If having a conscious belief involves the subject in believing he has the belief, having a conscious belief requires the subject to possess the concept of belief. Any proposed possession condition that incorporates (F) would then be circular. However, I dispute the view that consciousness of a belief consists in some kind of belief that one has the belief.[2]

Rather, I would argue that a conscious belief, in suitable conditions, will surface in conscious thought, and conscious thought is something that can occupy the attention of the thinker. What events and states in conscious thought are manifestations of a conscious belief? It is important not to make the requirements for this too restrictive. It seems that there are two conditions that must be met for a state or event in conscious thought to be a manifestation of a conscious belief. The first requirement is the very general condition that the event or state represent in conscious thought a certain content as holding. Conscious judgement of a content is just one, rather sophisticated member of this broad generic type. There are other members of the type for which the notion of judgement may be inappropriate. In conscious, image-involving, spatial thought about how to maneuver an object through a narrow opening or how to arrange and use objects to reach a place on the ceiling, a thinker, even a nonlinguistic creature, understands that certain spatial relations hold between objects in his environment. These may include some objects he does not currently perceive. The spatial reasoner is in a state that represents in conscious thought certain relation's holding between the things of his immediate environment.

This first condition for an event or state of conscious thought to be a manifestation of a conscious belief is not in fact sufficient. Suppose that someone meets Anthony Blunt, that expert on art history and sometime Surveyor of the Queen's Pictures, and finds it overwhelmingly plausible that he is not a spy. We underdescribe the contents of his consciousness if we omit the fact that he is in a state that represents the content "This man is no spy" as being correct. Nonetheless, this overwhelming impression that he is not a spy can coexist with the conscious belief and knowledge that all the same he *is* a spy. In short, for a state to have a phenomenology of representing in conscious thought something as being the case is not yet for it to be a belief. In the example just given, the subject will indeed judge that the man is a spy, but we have already seen that it may be thought problematic to require the possibility of conscious judgement whenever there is conscious belief. A better second condition to add is this: the state that represents a certain content as holding must involve the subject's *accepting* the content. In the Blunt example the state representing "This man is no spy" as correct fails this test. But the test is not so strong as to exclude cases of conscious, image-involving spatial reasoning.

On this sketchy characterization of conscious belief, the consciousness of a belief should not be regarded as consisting in some form of higher-order belief that one has the belief. The characterization above of what is involved in a belief's being conscious can be fulfilled by a creature who does not even possess the concept of belief. What is true is that if a thinker does have the concept of belief and has a certain conscious belief, then he will be willing to judge that he has the belief. Indeed, this is precisely what one would expect if clause (F) is part of the possession condition for the concept of belief. But the point lends no support to the view that consciousness of a belief *consists* in having a second-order belief.

For what it is worth, believing that one believes that *p* does not seem to be sufficient for having a conscious belief that *p* either. The second-order belief may be unconscious. When it is, there need not be any obstacle to the first-order belief that *p* being unconscious too.

Suppose a person reads a piece of misinformation to the effect that anyone who has a certain belief has an increased risk of developing a particular illness. Suppose that he systematically avoids other circumstances known to lead to that illness and systematically seeks out circumstances that tend to reduce the chance of contracting it. On each particular occasion he offers some other rationalization for his behavior. We can fill out this story so that the best explanation of his actions is that he has an unconscious second-order belief to the effect that he has a certain first-order belief, the belief alleged to increase the risk of contracting the illness. But that first-order belief is not a conscious one. So there appears to be a two-way independence of conscious belief from believing one believes. Indeed, even when one has a conscious second-order belief that one has a certain first-order belief, that does not suffice to make the first-order belief into a conscious belief. Certainly in the example just given, when the subject comes to discover his unconscious belief that he has the first-order belief, that need in no way make him willing to make a conscious judgement that he has the illness. He may still regard such a judgement as quite irrational.

It is consistent with this approach to conscious belief to acknowledge an internal connection between the linguistic expression of a belief and its status as conscious. In particular, we have this datum:

Datum on Conscious Belief   A linguistically expressed belief is a conscious belief.

There are two attitudes toward this datum. One attitude is that a sufficient, noncircular condition for the consciousness of a belief can be given in terms of linguistic expression, and that is why the datum holds. I call accounts that endorse this claim "expression-based accounts." A second, rival attitude to the datum is that the notion of linguistic expression itself cannot be elucidated without reference to the consciousness of what is expressed, and that is why the datum holds. Each of these competing attitudes is consistent with the point that for language users, many beliefs are present in conscious thought in linguistic form. Each of these attitudes toward the datum is also consistent with clause (F) of the possession condition for belief, as long as their respective uses of the notions of expression and consciousness can be elucidated without presuming that the subject possesses the concept of belief.

The second attitude to the datum, and not any expression-based account, seems to me correct. Something is an *expression* of belief in a sense that makes the datum correct only if it is under the conscious intentional control of the subject. Even if there are syntactically structured external physical states or events in which the subject participates, ones that are systematically caused by the subject's beliefs, they are not expressions of those beliefs unless they are under the subject's conscious, intentional control. The conscious intentions that control expression will have access only to what is consciously accepted as being the case, that is, access to only the conscious beliefs among the thinker's beliefs. If this explanation is correct, expression-based accounts are incorrect. The consciousness of a belief cannot be given a noncircular sufficient condition by appeal to expression, because the notion of expression implicitly relies upon that of conscious attitudes.

The necessary condition (F) can incorporate some of the insights of Evans's Wittgenstein-inspired treatment of the self-ascription of belief. Evans wrote, "I get myself in a position to answer the question whether I believe that *p* by putting into operation whatever procedure I have for answering the question whether *p*" (1982, 225). Suppose that a thinker has the concept of belief and that his procedures for answering the question of whether *p* lead him to make a conscious judgement that *p*. Then on Evans's account, he will judge that he believes that *p*. According to a possession condition that incorporates (F), he will find it primitively compelling that he believes that *p*. One who defends such a possession condition will agree that in this sort of case, in making judgements about his own beliefs, a thinker considers the way the world is; he considers whatever bears on the truth of *p*. He does not have to reflect on his own mental states or behavior. However, if we allow unconscious beliefs, Evans's principle needs qualification.[3] We cannot then accept that if an application of my procedure for answering the question of whether *p* generates a negative answer or no answer at all, then I do not believe that *p*. A negative answer and no answer at all are equally consistent with my having an unconscious belief that *p*. Of course, an account that makes use of clause (F) must equally explain how our concept of belief leaves room for the possibility of unconscious belief.

I now turn to the epistemological obligations of an account of the concept of belief as they arise for first-person thought involving the concept. When a thinker judges something of the form "I believe that *p*" without relying on any evidence that he believes that *p,* in ordinary cases his judgement constitutes knowledge. The epistemological obligation is to explain how and why it can constitute knowledge.

In his well-known paper "Individualism and Self-Knowledge" (1988), Tyler Burge has emphasized the self-verifying character of some psychological self-ascriptions. (Burge's aim there is different from mine here: he is there concerned to reconcile the nonindividualistic character of content with the existence of authoritative knowledge of some of one's own content-involving mental states.) Burge takes as his starting point such Cartesian thoughts as "I think (with this very thought) that writing requires concentration" and "I judge that water is more common than mercury." These judgements are indeed self-verifying. But as Burge notes, a range of cases of self-knowledge go beyond the self-verifying cases (1988, 658 and n. 11, 663).[4] The important point for my purposes, though, is that self-verification cannot be the source of the usual epistemic status of the judgement that one believes that *p,* because judgements of the form "I believe that *p*" are not self-verifying just in virtue of being made and having the content they do. A thinker could falsely make such a judgement on the basis of poor or misinterpreted evidence that he has an unconscious belief that *p.* Unless an explanation is provided of the normal first-person knowledge of one's own beliefs that applies even when there is no self-verification, the epistemological obligations of a theory of the concept of belief will not have been met.[5]

What are the circumstances that make an ordinary judgement "I believe that *p*" into a case of knowledge and that are special to such first-person ascriptions? The circumstances are that the thinker finds the content *I believe that p* primitively compelling and does so because he has a conscious belief that *p.* Necessarily, if it is made in these circumstances, a judgement "I believe that *p*" will be true. But this fact does not by itself suffice to explain why such a judgement is knowledge. After all, there are many other cases in which we can correctly say something of the form "Necessarily, if the judgement that p is made in such and such circumstances, it is true," yet not all such judgements made in those circumstances are knowledge. Necessarily, if a judgement "That's H_2O" is made with demonstrative reference to water, it is true, but such a judgement may be far from knowledge (it may, for instance, be inferred from a false premise). A similar point could be made for mathematical beliefs that are not knowledge, even if the requirement of necessity is strengthened to the demand that the conditional be a priori. What differentiates the first-person ascriptions of belief from these others is that the circumstances of ordinary self-ascriptions of belief are those mentioned in a clause of the possession condition for the concept of belief as sufficient for finding it primitively compelling that one has the belief in question.

This differentiating feature is a special case of a quite general link between possession conditions and epistemology.[6] At an intermediate level of generality, the link can be formulated thus:

Link between Possession Conditions and Knowledge   Take any mental state of the thinker that a possession condition for a concept says is sufficient for the thinker finding primitively compelling a given content containing the concept. Then when a thinker judges that content and for the reason that he is in that state, his judgement constitutes knowledge.[7]

This link can be explained. It is explained if two principles hold. The first principle is that a semantic value is attributed to a concept so that a content is true in circumstances in which, according its possession condition, the content is found primitively compelling. This first principle is a consequence of the approach defended in the preceding chapter, under which semantic values are assigned so as to make the practices of belief formation mentioned in the possession condition always correct.

Suppose that a thinker judges a certain content that he finds primitively compelling, and he does so for certain reasons in certain circumstances. Suppose too that the possession conditions for the constituent concepts of the judged content, together with the first principle, entail that the content is true when it is judged for those reasons in those circumstances. The second principle then states that in such a case, the judgement is knowledge. This second principle is highly intuitive. If your reasons for a belief ensure its truth and do so as a consequence of the nature of the concepts it contains, you are in the best possible epistemic position with respect to the content of the belief. On this approach, a thinker's knowledge of his own conscious beliefs is a special case of this more general phenomenon.[8]

Can there be illusions of conscious belief? Can a thinker subjectively be just as if he had a conscious belief without in fact having it? From the earlier characterization of what is required for consciousness of a belief, for a thinker subjectively to be as if he had a conscious belief, two conditions must be met. First, he must be in a conscious state that represents the content as correct. Second, this state must be a state of conscious acceptance (rather than something of the sort exemplified in the Blunt example). But it is very plausible that these conditions are also sufficient for having a conscious belief. If so, an illusion of conscious belief is not possible. Let us say that a state is *Cartesian* if whenever a person subjectively is as if he is in that state, then he is in that state. These remarks support the view that conscious belief is Cartesian, and they generate a limited form of infallibility: if a subject is as if he has a conscious belief that p and he then judges that he believes that p, then he will be correct.

Is a theory in which a thinker's beliefs about his beliefs are caused by those beliefs committed to the objectionable consequence that there are infallible causal connections? The account I have been offering is one in which the thinker's beliefs about his own beliefs are, in the usual case, caused by those beliefs, but I dispute that there is any commitment to infallible causal connections. I dispute this even in the special case in which a thinker judges that he believes that p because he has the conscious belief that p. What is true is that, necessarily and a priori, if a thinker possesses the concept of belief, then when he has a conscious belief that p, he finds it primitively compelling that he believes that p, and he does so because he has that conscious belief that p. That conditional is necessary and a priori if the first-person clause of the possession condition is necessary and a priori. But anyone who thinks that this must involve a fundamental level at which there are infallible causal connections should be given pause by the fact that there are corresponding necessary and a priori principles for any other concept. It is necessary and a priori that if a thinker has the concept of conjunction and makes the supposition that p and the supposition that q with no compartmentalization, he is willing to infer the conjunction p *and* q. If we say this, are we thereby committed to the subject's possessing an infallible detector of whether a supposition has the content that p, and thereby to certain infallible causal connections? It seems to me that we are not. In the case of conjunction, the necessary and a priori conditional is ensured because it is partially definitive of what is involved in a conclusion's having a conjunctive content. If no subpersonal state stands in the relation given in the necessary and a priori conditional to states of supposing that p and supposing that q, then the thinker does not possess the concept of conjunction. This is consistent with the absence of any kind of infallible causal connection at the realizing level.

The same is true of the first-person case. If there is no state that a thinker is willing to enter whenever and because he has a conscious belief, then he does not possess the concept of belief. This equally applies in nonactual possible circumstances. Take a thinker who in fact possesses the concept of belief. On this account, there do not need to be fundamentally infallible causal relations. If there are no such relations, there will be possible circumstances in which the state that realizes this thinker's judging that he believes that p is not caused by his conscious belief that p. All that follows is that in these possible circumstances, if nothing else realizes his judging that he believes that p, then he does not have the concept of belief.

I am giving an account of the concept of belief on the theory of the state of belief that emerged from the description I gave in chapter 4 of how the apparatus of concepts and thoughts is applied empirically. Because of all the constraints this enterprise must meet, we are not yet halfway through. But it should be clear from the ground I have already covered that an enterprise of this sort stands squarely opposed to some recent views of Crispin Wright, according to whom "knowing of one's own beliefs, desires and intentions is not really a matter of 'access to'—being in cognitive touch with—a state of affairs at all" (1989a, 631–632). Wright's view is that first-person authority "is not a by-product of the nature of those states, and an associated epistemologically privileged relation in which the subject stands to them"; rather, according to Wright, first-person authority "enters primitively into the conditions of identification of what a subject believes, hopes and intends" (1989a, 632).

The account in chapter 4 offered a statement of the way in which the relational properties required of a state, if it is to be a belief that p, are fixed from the conceptual constituents of the content p together with their mode of combination. Though the details of the account are no doubt open to many arguments, it is questionable whether there is any alternative to an approach that tries to determine those relational properties from the conceptual constituents of the content (at least for anyone who countenances the idea of conceptual content at all). For it is not clear that there is anything else from which the relational properties might be determined. There is, though, nothing about avowals or first-person authority in the possession conditions for simple concepts of objects in, and properties of, the world around the thinker. Consequently, there will be nothing about avowals or first-person authority in the relational properties required of a state if it is to have contents built up from such simple concepts. The whole approach I have been developing is, then, in tension with Wright's view that first-person authority "enters primitively into the conditions of identification of what a subject believes, hopes and intends." A Wright-like account would certainly need to offer an alternative story about the functioning of conceptual content in the classification of mental states. Theories mentioning radical interpretation or ascription procedures do not supply an alternative answer. As I argued in chapter 1, the constraints respected in a good radical-interpretation procedure must actually incorporate the possession conditions for the concepts ascribed. An interpretation approach provides not a different story but only a different way of looking at the role of conceptual content in the classification of mental states.

The other problem I would raise for Wright's approach concerns the epistemology of self-ascriptions. I take it as given that a vast range of self-ascriptions that we make are in fact knowledge. What is the difference between a self-ascription that is merely true and one that constitutes knowledge? My own suggestion was that when a self-ascription is made in the circumstances given in clause (F) of the possession condition for the concept of belief, the self-ascription is knowledge. Part of the rationale for this is that in those circumstances it is guaranteed that the subject is in the state of having the relevant first-order belief. But Wright's proposal is committed to denying that there is any such substantial state to which a self-ascription may stand in distinctive relations.[9]

It may help in locating my position if I contrast my treatment of present-tense, first-person ascriptions of belief also with the early stance of Daniel Dennett on infallibility, as outlined in his first book *Content and Consciousness* (1969). (Dennett's and Wright's positions in fact have certain affinities.) Dennett was discussing the output of an analyzer that receives inputs from two television cameras and performs complex computations on these inputs. The analyzer's output is sent to a speech center. So we have three stages—cameras, analyzer, and speech center—and we are concerned with the outputs of the latter two stages. Dennett argued that the output states of the analyzer have a certain kind of infallibility. He wrote, "The infallibility, barring verbal slips of the 'reports' of the analyzer output, is due to the criterion of identity for such output states. What makes an output the output it is is what it goes on to produce in the speech centre, barring correctible speech centre errors, so an output is precisely what it is 'taken to be' by the speech centre, regardless of its qualities and characteristics in any physical realization" (1969, 110).

What this would explain, if correct, is the infallibility of certain tokens. It would explain why (subject to the qualifications Dennett notes) a token produced by the analyzer is infallibly true. If, though, we want to explain infallible knowledge or registration *that* such and such is the case, we have to say more. The further explanation, on Dennett's approach, would presumably have to employ at least the additional premise that the output produced by the speech center has a certain content. But what gives it the content it has? On my approach, in the case of sentences about one's own beliefs, the answer to the corresponding question should mention the content of conscious beliefs that give reasons for uttering the sentence. That is, the nature of the earlier psychological state is not determined by what judgements it gives rise to; rather, the determination of content is the other way around. I would say the same of the visual case that was Dennett's immediate concern. If we do not say this in both the case of belief and the visual example, the question "What gives the resulting judgements or tokens their contents?" becomes unanswerable.

Treating the matter in the way I advocate does not just shift the unanswerability. The question "What gives the belief states their contents?" is in turn answered by appeal to a theory of possession conditions for the concepts in the contents of the belief states, together with an account of the way in which these fix the relational properties required of a state for it to be a belief with a given conceptual content. Having a positive account of the *state* of belief gives us the anchor we need to hold the structure containing the *concept* of belief in place.

6.3   The Third-Person Clause

It is now a very familiar point that a thinker's concept of water can be of a kind instantiated by some samples he encounters and also by anything else of the same internal composition as these samples. Despite the generally acknowledged differences between natural-kind concepts and psychological concepts, I think the concept of belief exhibits certain limited structural parallels with such a concept of water. (On the equally important structural differences, see McGinn 1991.)

Consider a thinker's third-person attribution "*a* believes that *p*." This is true if the attributee is in a state with the same content-dependent role in making the attributee intelligible as the thinker's belief that *p* would have in making the thinker intelligible. According to me, this content-dependent role is precisely the relational property identified in chapter 4 as required for a given state to be a belief with a particular content. Early chemists might misidentify the composition of water while continuing to think about the natural kind water, as is essential if the case is to be one of *mis*identification. Equally, we may misidentify the content-dependent role of a belief that *p* in making a thinker intelligible. We may incorrectly include in that role properties only contingently possessed by a belief that *p*. In the other direction, we may omit essential components of the role. We may make these errors not just in philosophical reflection, but in everyday attribution of attitudes to others. Everyday practice and possession of the concept of belief presuppose just that there is a content-dependent role, rather than any particular specification of what it is.

The proviso that the role be content-dependent is important. If we were to rely rather on the de facto role of the belief that *p* in the thinker's own psychology, we would end up with the wrong conditions for attributing the belief that p. The concept of a belief with a given content allows for the possibility, prima facie often realized, of two thinkers with the same belief but who differ in many other respects: in respect of the strength of evidence they require before forming the belief, in respect of their creativity in constructing theories leading to acceptance of the belief, and much else. Only that part of the total role of a belief that p essential to its having the content p is covered by the phrase "content-dependent role." To insist on this point is not at all to deny that conceptual contents are individuated by their roles in a content-using psychology. It is just to require that the individuating role be sufficiently finely discriminated. It was the aim of chapters 1 and 4 to start in effecting this discrimination.

A first attempt to formulate a third-person clause that takes account of these points is this:

Possession Condition for *Believes*, Third-Person Clause   A relational concept R is that of belief only if, in judging a thought of the third-person form aRp, the thinker thereby incurs a commitment to a being in a state that has the same content-dependent role in making a intelligible as the content-dependent role of his own belief that p, were he to believe that p.

This is plausible as a truth, but it is not quite yet in the canonical $\mathcal{A}(C)$ form for possession conditions (section 1.2). I am trying to give part of a possession condition for the concept of belief. Yet within the scope of "incurs a commitment to," there occurs the phrase "his own belief that p." Still, we are almost home. The crucial point is that this reference to belief within the scope of the thinker's commitments is a reference to the thinker's own beliefs, and for the first-person case we have already formulated a clause. This allows us to replace the illegitimate occurrence of the concept of belief with a variable R, where the value of that variable is constrained by the first-person clause already formulated. The full result is as follows:

Possession Condition for the Concept of Belief   A relational concept R is the concept of belief only if

(F)   the thinker finds the first-person content that he stands in R to p primitively compelling whenever he has the conscious belief that p, and he finds it compelling because he has that conscious belief; and

(T)   in judging a thought of the third person form aRp, the thinker thereby incurs a commitment to a's being in a state that has the same content-dependent role in making a intelligible as the role of his own state of standing in R to p in making him intelligible, were he to be in that state.

For a thinker to satisfy this third-person clause (T), it is not required that he be able to give an explicit formulation of what this commitment is. Rather, he tacitly knows that this is the commitment of a third-person belief ascription. His tacit knowledge will be reflected in the circumstances in which he accepts or rejects contents of the third-person form aRp, together with the factors that explain his judgements. This content for the tacit knowledge can explain the reflection and reasoning involved in making third-person attributions without requiring the thinker actually to have tacit knowledge of the possession conditions for the concepts of the content in question.

By clause (T), there is a sense in which the concept of belief is a first-person concept. The sense is not that there is something it is like to have a belief—there is not. Nor is it merely that one clause of the possession condition for belief treats the combination with the first person separately. It is rather the stronger condition that the clause of the possession condition not expressly treating first-person predications nevertheless requires the thinker to have the capacity to ascribe beliefs to himself and relates mastery of third-person predications to that capacity to ascribe beliefs to himself. This sense in which the concept of belief is first-personal is analogous to that in which a natural two-clause treatment of an observational concept can be said to exhibit the perceptual character of a concept so treated. The clause dealing with predications of an object not so perceptually presented relates mastery of such predications to the circumstances mentioned in the clause dealing with the case in which the concept is applied to a perceptually presented object. The clause dealing with the case in which the object is not perceptually presented may state, for instance, that, in judging "Such and such is F" the thinker will be incurring a commitment to the object's being the same shape as something meeting the conditions given in the clause for judging "*That* is *F*," where the demonstrative is perceptual.

A first-person character is here being attributed to the concept of belief, and not to the state. Additional argument would be necessary to establish the subjective character of the state or property picked out by the concept of belief, that is, to establish the subjectivity of the reality itself, as opposed to one way of thinking of it. A shape concept can be perceptual in the sense just discussed. It does not follow that there is anything mental or perceptual about shape properties themselves.

It is also a consistent position to acknowledge the first-person character of the concept of belief while rejecting the subjectivity of belief states in the sense discussed by John McDowell. McDowell (1986) argues that propositional attitudes in general must make their subjects intelligible, and that there is no use for the distinction between what is really intelligible and what we could come to find intelligible. As I noted in chapter 1, a theorist might reject this on the grounds that there are concepts we could never possess with our actual intellectual capacities. He might hold that there is no substantial sense in which *we* could find fully intelligible the actions and attitudes of beings who are capable of employing these concepts. But this theorist could still also acknowledge that when those concepts are employed in the contents of attitudes that such intellectually superior beings attribute to one another, the concept of belief exercised in their third-person attributions has the indicated first-person character.[10]

The above possession condition for the concept of belief covers only the case in which a specific content is attributed as the content of the belief, a content that the thinker ascribing the belief can himself grasp. The concept of belief certainly extends beyond such cases, as is shown in our understanding of attributions in which the content is existentially quantified. We may, for instance, truly think or say of one of the superior beings just envisaged that he believes something that we cannot grasp and that explains his writing down what he did. The intelligibility of such thoughts requires a theorist to supply more than just the displayed possession condition incorporating (F) and (T). If a theorist were to try to include contents we cannot grasp within the treatment given by the displayed possession condition for belief, in applying clause (T), he would end up with counterfactuals with impossible antecedents concerning what would be the case if we were to believe things that we are not capable of grasping. The resulting account would be incorrect. Rather, I have to add something to the displayed partial possession condition to account for the general conception *x believes that p* when the variable *p* ranges over contents including some we cannot grasp. To have this general conception, the thinker has to form the general idea of content-dependent roles that cannot be roles of any of his states, because the roles require the ability to be in states that, for one reason or another, he cannot enjoy. The thinker must also conceive of these roles as roles of belief states, states that aim at truth. To have the idea of beliefs with contents one cannot oneself grasp is to have the idea of states that aim at truth and have content-dependent roles that cannot be the roles of any of one's own states. The required extension of the possession condition displayed above would have to elaborate these points, which, of course, draw upon the materials already present in (F) and (T).

I close this section by returning to an issue about the first-person clause that could not properly be addressed without a formulation of the third-person clause. A theory that endorses the first-person clause (F) traces the distinctive epistemological and cognitive properties of thoughts of the form "I believe that *p*" to a particular clause of the possession condition for the concept of belief. It is always a substantive issue whether cognitive properties of complete thoughts are to be traced to the possession conditions of one constituent of the thought rather than another, or indeed whether they are to be traced to the interaction of the several possession conditions of the several constituents. In fact, for some other phenomena displayed by first-person thoughts, it is quite implausible that the explanation involves the predicative concept. Consider immunity to error through misidentification, discussed by Shoemaker (1968, 1970) and Evans (1982, section 6.6). Take, for instance, the thought "That tower is in front of me," judged on the basis of perception of the tower. In these circumstances the thought is immune to error through misidentification of the person in front of whom the tower is located. It is not at all tempting to argue that to account for this cognitive phenomenon, we need multiple clauses in the possession condition for the relational concept *x is in front of y,* one dealing with thoughts involving the predicative concept *x is in front of me* and one dealing with other-person cases. Rather, the thinker has an undivided mastery of the concept of one thing's being in front of another, which can be applied to himself when he has a conception of himself as possessing a location and orientation in the world. The plausible explanation of the immunity to error through misidentification is rather that developed by Evans. That explanation traces the matter back to specific properties of the first person. There is a constitutive sensitivity of first-person spatial predications to non-conceptual spatial information received by the thinker in perception. So the question now arises, why have I opted for a different kind of account in the explanation of the phenomena involving the concept of belief?

I would give two reasons. First, if we try to give a single clause for the concept of belief, what is the undivided understanding of the relational concept *x believes that p* that involves no special treatment of the first person? I have been arguing that a correct third-person clause actually makes reference to first-person judgements involving the concept of belief. If this is so, then the enterprise of trying to eliminate special treatment of the first person by somehow applying the third-person clause to all cases is doomed to failure. (How first-person authority would then be secured in that enterprise I do not know.) Perhaps the idea of undivided understanding is not that, but rather some more fundamental characterization from which both the third- and the first-person clauses can be derived, but I confess that I do not know how this bare possibility of a possibility could be fleshed out.

The second reason for tracing the cognitive phenomena involving belief to the predicative concept rather than to the first-person concept would also rule out that bare possibility of a possibility. Suppose that we were to write into the possession condition for the first-person concept itself a requirement with the consequence that the subject is willing to judge that he believes that p when he has a conscious belief that p. That would make it impossible for a subject to be capable of conscious first-person attitudes without having the concept of belief. Yet this does seem possible. In fact, it seems positively desirable to have an account of what is involved in a subject's making the transition from having only attitudes about his nonpsychological properties—his location in the world, his past, his nonpsychological relations to the world around him—to possessing psychological concepts too. I agree that the phrase "richer and richer conceptions of the self" picks out something real, but we had better have a theory that underwrites the claim that it is one and the same way of thinking of oneself associated with the richer and richer conceptions.

6.4 The Possession Condition and Simulation Accounts

If the third-person clause (T) is correct, then attribution of belief to others will require some imagination in the basic case. The attributor will need to imagine what would be the causes and effects of he himself believing that p, and he must make some effort to identify those causes and effects that are content-dependent. In an ideal case the thinker's imagination will be guided by his own satisfaction of the possession conditions for the concepts in p. If, say, the possession condition demands that the thinker judges a particular content p if certain conditions hold, then the categorical basis of that conditional should cause the thinker to imagine that in those conditions he would judge that p. Imagination does not serve up this result as an unexplained datum. Rather, one imagines that one would form the belief in question for certain reasons. Hypothetical self-attributions made by this method are ensured a certain intelligibility for the thinker.

As a result, the third-person clause (T) can give a limited rationale for the practice of ascribing attitudes by simulation. Let us say that an attribution of a belief that p is reached by simulation when two conditions are met. Condition 1 is that the attribution results from an inference of the following form:

Person a is in such and such circumstances.
In such and such circumstances I would believe that p.
_____
So a believes that p.

Condition 2 is that the second premise of the inference results from the attributor imagining what he himself would believe in such and such circumstances, and in doing so, aiming to be guided by the factors that would influence his beliefs in those circumstances.

The limited rationale that the account earlier in this chapter provides for attribution by simulation is that the attributor's own hypothetical beliefs reached by simulation are intelligible and the conclusion is meant to reflect only these intelligible influences. Because someone who accepts the third-person clause (T) can acknowledge that simulation inferences will play a large part in the attribution of attitudes, he can to that extent at least agree with the tradition of thought that goes back through Collingwood and was inspired, in outline if not in detail, by Vico.[11]

It is important that on the present account the simulation inferences have a rationale derived from a more fundamental conception, a conception that also shows the limits of the validity of simulation. Simulation inferences do not have the same primitive, underived status for the concept of belief that certain primitive inferential principles arguably have for the logical constants. Simulation inferences are subject to kinds of fallibility that cannot be explained by a theory that treats them as primitively valid.

A theory that treats simulation inferences as primitively valid might run as follows. It could say in its treatment of third-person attributions that belief is a concept R such that inferences of this form are valid:

Person a is in such and such circumstances.
In such and such circumstances I would believe that p.
So aRp.

Here as before the second premise is meant to be accepted as a result of imaginative simulation. If the first-person attributions of belief relied upon in the second premise are treated separately, this could be a component of a noncircular account of what makes a relation the concept of belief. Indeed, the account could instantiate the canonical $\mathcal{A}(C)$ form for possession conditions.[12] Such a theory can acknowledge that a thinker's belief in the second premise may be false. Falsity here is falsity only of a counterfactual involving a first-person attribution. So again there is no circularity in acknowledging this source of fallibility.

The kind of fallibility damaging to an account that treats simulation inferences as primitively valid arises rather in cases in which the second premise is true. It may be true that the attributor would believe that p in such and such circumstances, even though to do so is in no way required by the possession conditions for the concepts from which content p is constructed. To take a simple case, p might be a universal generalization, and the circumstances those of knowing of a finite number of positive instances. In these circumstances, the attributor, let us suppose, accepts the universal generalization. But if the attributee thought of in the third-person way a is not so bold in generalizing, the conclusion of the simulation inference will be false.

One might seek to modify the criticized account so that the second premise is strengthened by adding that the first-person belief that p held in such and such circumstances is required by the possession conditions for its constituent concepts. This would not be a pure simulation theory, and indeed, once some appeal is made to possession conditions, it is not clear that we need to make any reference to simulation theories at all. But in any case, this modified version suffers from a converse problem. The inference with the premise so strengthened will indeed count as true those third-person attributions of beliefs that must be held if the attributee possesses the constituent concepts. But it fails to capture the many cases of true third-person attributions of beliefs where those beliefs are held in circumstances that in no way constitutively require them to be held. Yet in these cases the condition required by clause (T) is met. The attributee will be in a state with the same content-dependent role in making him intelligible as the same belief in the attributor would have in making him intelligible. I conjecture that what is right in the desire of those who are attracted by the essentially first-person character of theories that count simulation inferences as primitively valid is already captured by the sense noted in which clause (T) treats belief as a first-person concept. This is a sense true of the concept itself, and so it applies even when simulation inferences are fallacious or fail to cover the ground.

In response to these points, someone who wants to write simulation inferences into mastery of the concept of belief may ask, "Is it not a sufficient account of third-person attribution that we make attributions by simulation, and when our expectations about actions are falsified, we adjust our attributions accordingly?" I do not think that this is an adequate account. An attribution may be reached by simulation and still be false, even though it does not, as it happens, have false consequences about the attributee's actions in the actual world. If we try to neutralize this objection by saying that the attribution will be true if it is reached by simulation and it has no false consequences about actions in this or certain other possible worlds, we say something that is both too strong and too weak. It is too strong a requirement because in some counterfactually specified circumstances the attributee will lose the belief in question. It is too weak because a subject may not actually have the belief attributed by simulation but may gain it in the counterfactually specified circumstances. These possibilities cannot be excluded except by appealing to actual states not characterizable solely in terms of the simulation procedure and true predictions of actions.[13]

6.5   Referential Coherence

It would be hard to contest the validity of the following inference:

I believe that the earth moves.
I am John.

So John believes that the earth moves.

It would be equally hard to query the validity of this inference:

That building is round.
That (same) building is the Sheraton Hotel.

So the Sheraton Hotel is round.

To reject the validity of these inferences would be to abandon the idea that "believes that the earth moves" and "is round" are predicates true or false of objects. A condition of adequacy on a statement of the possession conditions for the contained concepts is that they ensure the validity of these inferences when taken together with a theory of how semantic value is determined from the possession conditions (together with the way the world is). Let us say that a possession condition for a concept F and a theory of how it contributes to the determination of semantic value are jointly *referentially coherent* if they ensure the validity of inferences of the following form:

s is F
$s = t$

So t is F

I have just introduced referential coherence by considering inferences in the thought of one individual thinker, but I could also intro-

duce it by considering the requirements on the thoughts of two different thinkers. If John thinks "I am F" and Peter thinks "John is
F," a theory of the concept F had better ensure that John's thought is
correct if and only if Peter's is. Referential coherence could also be
defined for concepts of other categories.

The requirement of referential coherence bites hardest when there
are good reasons for writing a possession condition with more than
one clause and each clause treats grasp of the predicational combination of the given concept F with a different kind of singular mode
of presentation. Such multiple clauses can be called "partnership
clauses." Not all multiple clauses of a possession condition are partnership clauses. Consider, for instance, the multiple clauses of a possession condition for a logical constant. In dealing with the different
primitive, constitutive forms of inference in which the constant features, they deal with different ways of moving to and from a given
kind of thought involving the constant. They do not deal with different
types of modes of presentation (in this case, thoughts or predicative
concepts) with which the constant may be combined. Suppose, though,
that we are concerned with a case in which there are partnership
clauses and in which the codenoting singular modes of presentation s
and t are of the different sorts dealt with in distinct clauses of the
possession condition for the concept F. Then the requirement of referential coherence demands that the account of how the possession
condition contributes to the determination of semantic value should
ensure that when the thought "s is F" is true, so too is the thought "t
is F."

Can we give some informative account of what is required for referential coherence? It may be tempting to suggest that it requires that
each clause of the possession condition individually determines (together with the world) the same semantic value. But though that would
be sufficient for referential coherence, it is certainly not necessary,
and the condition is not met by some concepts. Actually, it is not met
by the various clauses of the possession condition for a logical constant. The semantic value of the constant is determined only by the
clauses taken collectively. More pertinently, the suggested condition
is not met in some cases where the multiple clauses are partnership
clauses. Consider the concept red*, which a thinker can truly apply

to an object at a given time in the present tense if the thinker himself perceives the object to be red at that time. This can be set up so that the clause of the possession condition for *red** that deals with visually demonstratively presented objects is exactly the same as the corresponding clause in the possession condition for the concept *red*. But *red** and *red* have different semantic values. Their extensions differ on objects not currently perceived by the thinker.

What is required for referential coherence would be better formulated thus: there is an extension (or relation) that, taken as the semantic value of the concept, makes *correct* each of the practices of judgement, inference, or rejection mentioned in the several clauses. What this means is that if a clause gives an outright sufficient condition for judging a content, the content with the assigned semantic values comes out true under those sufficient conditions; if a clause mentions an inferential transition that a thinker must be prepared to make, the inference must be truth-preserving under the assigned semantic values; if the clause gives sufficient conditions for rejecting a content, the content must come out false under those conditions. This requirement for referential coherence is in the spirit of a general thesis of chapter 5 to the effect that the appropriate determination theory for a given possession condition should make the judgemental practices mentioned in the possession condition correct. The requirement that there be a semantic value for which all the clauses are correct can be met without that value being uniquely determined by any one clause (together with the world).

One can make up at will clauses that, taken together, fail to determine a concept because they are not referentially coherent on a plausible theory of how a possession condition helps to fix a semantic value. Here is a specification of a spurious concept:

"Possession Condition" for a Spurious Concept   Concept Z is that unique concept to possess which a thinker must meet these conditions: (1) for an object perceptually presented under a perceptual-demonstrative mode of presentation m, when the thinker is taking his perceptions at face value, he finds the thought "m is Z" primitively compelling when and only when the object is perceived as square, and (2) for an object thought about under some other singular mode of presentation k, the thinker finds the thought "k is Z" primitively compelling iff it is round.

There is no such concept as Z, for these clauses are not referentially coherent in the presence of the natural account of how semantic value is fixed. When the thinker perceives a particular garden to be square, from the first clause one would expect the thought "That garden is Z" to be true; from the second clause one would expect the thought "John's garden is Z" to be true iff John's garden is round. But that perceived garden may be John's garden. So is this particular garden in the extension of this alleged concept or not? Neither a positive nor a negative answer is acceptable. Either answer, if accepted, will violate, for one clause or the other, the only plausible account of the relation between clauses of the possession condition and the semantic value. The clauses are not referentially coherent.

A genuine perceptual concept C avoids this by having a special kind of clause dealing with the case in which the object is not perceptually presented. In this case the clause will say that the thinker is committed to the object in question being the same in some specified respect as objects that, when perceptually presented, meet the correctness condition for the perceptual-demonstrative thought "That's C." The specified respect may be that of sameness of shape, for instance, for observational-shape concepts. Possession conditions of this form are guaranteed to be referentially coherent, because even when a perceptual-demonstrative, singular mode of presentation and a nondemonstrative mode of presentation refer to the same object, the condition for the object to be in the extension of the concept will be the same, whichever of the two singular modes ·of presentation are combined with the observational concept.

Structurally, the same point applies to the concept of belief if its possession condition incorporates clauses (F) and (T). In accordance with the general view developed in sections 1.3 and 5.3, let us understand that the condition given in (F) as sufficient for finding "I believe that p" primitively compelling also suffices for the truth of the subject's first-person belief that he believes that p. Similarly, we can also understand that fulfillment of the commitment mentioned in the third-person clause (T) is sufficient for the truth of the corresponding third-person content "a believes that p." Clauses (F) and (T) can then jointly contribute to a referentially coherent possession condition. This is so because the third-person clause (T) requires for correctness of a third-person judgement "a believes that p" that the attributee be in a state that has the same content-dependent role as the state required of the subject for the correctness of the first-person judgement. If a state has the same content-dependent role as a belief that p, it is itself a belief that p. The form of clauses (T) and (F) thus guarantee that the concept of belief is referentially coherent.

6.6 Summary and the Need for More

This chapter has been an attempt to build a possession condition for the concept of belief. The construction has aimed to give a certain primacy to first-person ascriptions while respecting the need to build a referentially coherent possession condition. I have also argued that the approach helps to explain why a simulation approach should seem attractive and also explains why that approach does not give a correct account of all cases.

I said at the outset, though, that I would be offering only a partial answer to the question of what it is to possess the concept of belief. The conjunction of (F) with (T) does not amount to a full possession condition. We can see this when we ask whether the concept in question is the concept of conscious belief or that of belief more generally, whether conscious or not. To treat conscious belief, it would have to be made clear that in the third-person clause, sameness of content-dependent role is to be taken without restriction, so that it includes the conscious status of the putatively self-ascribed beliefs by which it identifies a role. The naturalness of this unrestricted construal may indeed explain why the possibility of unconscious belief may come as a surprise to us when we are first aware of it. (In a treatment of conscious belief, the first-person clause would also have to be expanded to cover judgements of "It's not the case that I believe that p," so that their truth merely requires the subject to have no conscious belief that p.) To treat unconscious belief, we would correspondingly have to have a restricted construal of sameness of role in the third-person clause and to allow for the correctness of ascriptions of unconscious belief in the first-person clause. It is noteworthy here that possession of the concept of beliefs that may be unconscious seems to require some tacit grasp of the notion of consciousness, since that notion has to be used in restricting the sameness of role in question. We have here one of many points at which it seems clear that we will not have a full understanding of content until we have a better understanding of consciousness.[14]

7 Concepts, Psychology, and Explanation

What should be the relation between a philosophical theory of concepts of the sort outlined in the preceding chapters and a psychological theory of concept possession? In this chapter I aim to identify one of the relations that ought to hold between such philosophical and psychological theories. I will go on to trace out some of the consequences of the conception I will be endorsing for some fundamental issues about the nature of content, meaning, and understanding. The conception I will be developing is consonant with the vision of a broadly mechanical and computational explanation of human mental capacities.[1] A computational conception would hardly be compelling if it had to exclude from its scope the capacity for conceptual thought. In fact, the approach I will be developing suggests a general agenda for psychological and computational studies.

7.1 Insularity Rejected: The Simple Account

One view of this territory is that philosophical and psychological theories of concepts should be relatively independent of one another. According to this view, philosophers and psychologists have no professional reasons, beyond such incidental matters as intellectual stimulation, for reading each others' journals. A holder of this view will urge the distinctness of the goals of the philosopher and the psychologist when each theorizes about concepts. The possession conditions supplied by the philosopher have a relatively a priori character. The psychologist, by contrast, will give empirical accounts of such matters as the acquisition of a concept, how attitudes involving the concept are formed, the influence of desires and emotions on attitudes, and so forth. Like any other theories we accept, we will want our philosophical and psychological theories of concepts to be jointly consistent. But, according to this view of their relative independence, there is no closer connection between the two theories. In particular, the goals of each theory do not need to make use of the results of the other theory.

I will be disputing that account. Here is a competing conception of one of the relations that should hold between a philosophical theory of a particular concept and a psychological theory of the same concept:

Simple Account   When a thinker possesses a particular concept, an adequate psychology should explain why the thinker meets the concept's possession condition.

On the Simple Account, one of the goals of a psychological theory makes reference to something that is the concern of a philosophical theory, namely the possession condition of a concept. So the Simple Account denies the relative independence of philosophical and psychological theories of concepts. I endorse this Simple Account.

A defence of the Simple Account must distinguish sharply between explaining why a thinker meets the possession condition for a concept and explaining how the thinker came to acquire the concept. We can compare the case with explaining why some object is a reflector of light. An explanation of why an object is a reflector will proceed by stating that light consists of a stream of photons and how the physical properties of the surface of the object affect the behavior of photons that strike it. Such an explanation of why the object reflects light is neutral on how the object came to acquire the surface properties that make it a reflector. Many different explanations of its acquisition of this property are consistent with the correctness of this explanation of why it now reflects light. Of course, the identity of a concept may place some restrictions on possible routes to its acquisition. But even in the (probably hypothetical) extreme case in which only one subpersonal explanation of acquisition is possible, it is still important to distinguish between the psychological explanation of acquisition and the psychological explanation of how the subject is able, after acquisition, to fulfill the possession condition. They are different explananda.

Though the case of the reflector lacks many of the complexities of psychological cases, one further similarity of structure exists. An explanation of an object's being a reflector has to explain its participation in a certain kind of transition, the transition from light hitting it at a certain angle to light leaving it in a certain direction. Similarly, when a thinker meets the possession condition for a concept, in given circumstances there will be specified transitions he makes between mental states, some of which involve the concept. It is equally a task for an explanatory psychology to say why he now makes those transitions in the given circumstances.

The Simple Account must face the charge that it illegitimately attempts to place a priori constraints on the outcome of empirical psychological research. In the context of a discussion of some other relations between philosophy and psychology, Stephen Stich writes,

"Philosophy has a long history of trying to issue a priori ultimatums to science, decreeing what must be the case or what could not possibly be the case. And those a priori decrees have a dismal track record" (1990, 11). Patricia Churchland and Terence Sejnowski equally complain of philosophy that purports to "set the bounds for science" (1989, 17). It would be disingenuous of me to reply that possession conditions for concepts do not have an a priori status. All the possession conditions I have mentioned are relatively a priori. As with other a priori truths, philosophers and other theorists concerned with content are not infallible in identifying them, but it is quite true that the appropriate methods are not empirical. What is important in answering the objection, though, is that in formulating a possession condition, we aim to formulate a *true* principle about a concept. Incorrect formulations should not, of course, be allowed to constrain anything, and no doubt philosophy, like other disciplines, has produced a goodly share of incorrect formulations. But if we do succeed in formulating a true principle, it is hard to see anything objectionable in the requirement that a psychological theory should explain how we are capable of satisfying the principle. The requirement is no more objectionable than the principle that a good micro theory of gases should explain the macro truth that pressure increases with temperature for a given volume. A possession condition may be regarded as formulating a large-scale, high-level constraint on a system to which a given concept is attributed. Churchland and Sejnowski write, "Without the constraints from psychology, ethology and linguistics to specify more exactly the parameters of the large-scale capacities of nervous systems, our conception of the functions for which we need explanation will be so woolly and tangled as effectively to smother progress" (1989, 45). On the conception for which I am arguing, philosophy, insofar as it can supply possession conditions for particular concepts, should be added to their list of subjects from which constraints should be drawn.

A proposed psychological explanation has to meet certain requirements if it is to explain why a thinker meets the possession condition for a given concept. The most fundamental requirement is that the states mentioned in the proposed explanation are subrational.

Definition   A state is *subrational* if (1) it is not individuated in part by what gives the subject good reasons for being in that state, nor by the reasons it gives for being in other states—in short, it is not individuated in reason-involving terms—and (2) the state is not individuated by reference to states that are themselves individuated in reason-involving terms.

The states mentioned in the explanation of a thinker's meeting a possession condition must be subrational because, according to the theory developed in this book, the reason-giving characteristics of states themselves depend on features of possession conditions. The explanation of a thinker's fulfillment of a possession condition must cut below the level of states with reason-giving characteristics. If a state is subpersonal in Dennett's sense, that is sufficient for it to be subrational. But being subpersonal is not obviously a necessary condition for a state to be subrational. A state, say one identified by a computational psychology, may require various relations to hold between the subpersonal systems that are constituents of a mind. The state will then have to be taken as a property of the whole system. Such a state may nevertheless be subrational. I can now redeem a promise made back in section 2.4 by noting that the class of subrational states does not coincide with the class of states that are subdoxastic in Stich's sense. Indeed, the very state of fulfilling a given possession condition is not subrational, for it fails part 2 of the definition. But this state, as I noted in note 11 of chapter 2, is subdoxastic on Stich's definition.

Another requirement on a psychological explanation of a thinker's fulfillment of the possession condition for a concept is that the states mentioned in the explanation do not presuppose that the thinker possesses the concept in question. If any state involved in the proposed explanation does presuppose such possession, the proposed explanation is circular. In addition to being intuitive in itself, this requirement is a consequence of the fundamental requirement that the explanatory states be subrational. If a state presupposes that the thinker possesses a certain concept, then it will be individuated in part by reference to the possession condition for that concept. According to the theory of this book, that possession condition will involve states individuated in terms of their reason-giving relations. The original state that presupposes possession of the concept will then fail clause 2 of the definition of a subrational state.

This requirement that there be no presupposition of possession of the concept in question is by no means a general requirement on psychological explanations, not even on explanation by subpersonal states. On the contrary, when, for example, we are considering the different topic of the psychological explanation of linguistic understanding, it is important to mention states that *do* presuppose that the thinker has the concepts expressed in the language. Consider those theories that explain a thinker's understanding of an utterance by citing subpersonal mechanisms that draw on information about the semantic properties of the constituent words of the utterance (Davies 1987, 1989; Peacocke 1989d). On these theories, the meaning of the utterance is computed from subpersonal information about the meaning of its parts. It is essential for such theories that at least some of the constituents of the information drawn upon be concepts possessed by the thinker at the personal level. The subpersonal information that an object satisfies the predicate "is square" just in case it is square must involve the same concept *square* as is used in giving the meaning of sentences containing the public predicate "is square." If it did not, the mechanisms would not be computing the right meaning for an utterance containing "is square." This presupposition of concept possession by the explanatory subpersonal states is in order as long as what we are out to explain is why the thinker understands sentences in a particular way. For that purpose we can take for granted his possession of the concepts in question. We cannot do so, however, when our concern is with the explanation of concept mastery itself.

It is probably true that there is no concept for which we know the full subpersonal psychological explanation of why humans meet its possession condition. But we do have partial subpersonal explanations of how humans can be in some of the states mentioned in some possession conditions, explanations that are of the right form for incorporation into an explanation of the thinker's fulfillment of the possession condition. We also have accounts of hypothetical subpersonal mechanisms that could explain a thinker's meeting a possession condition. I will consider two examples, one of each of these sorts.

As an example of the first sort, consider the concept possessed by the mature English speaker-hearer of the (spoken) word "vat." The speaker-hearer can recognize utterances of the word on particular occasions and has such beliefs as that "vat" means a certain kind of container in English. As is well known, there is no straightforward correlation of the acoustic properties over time with the way an utterance is heard. No acoustic property is common to the middle of one-syllable words we perceive as containing a short "a" vowel sound. It is not a temporal sequence of three acoustic properties of an utterance that causes it to be heard as an utterance of the word "vat." At any given time in an utterance of the word, several properties, which contribute to the identification of more than one of the constituent phonemes, may be instantiated (Lieberman and Studdert-Kennedy 1978).

The possession condition for this concept of the word "vat" will mention the sensitivity of the thinker's judgements that an utterance falls under this concept to his perceptions of it. A subpersonal psychology must explain how the subject is able to perceive the word in this way. One empirical hypothesis is that devices in the subject subpersonally compute the sequence of three sets of phonological features of the acoustic event:

$$
\begin{bmatrix}
+ \text{ consonant} \\
- \text{ stop} \\
+ \text{ voiced} \\
- \text{ nasal} \\
\text{ labial}
\end{bmatrix}
\quad
\begin{bmatrix}
- \text{ consonant} \\
- \text{ high} \\
+ \text{ front} \\
- \text{ round}
\end{bmatrix}
\quad
\begin{bmatrix}
+ \text{ consonant} \\
- \text{ stop} \\
+ \text{ voiced} \\
- \text{ nasal} \\
\text{ dental}
\end{bmatrix}
$$

This is certainly the beginning of an explanation. But it is only the beginning, because we also need an account of how these features are computed and a more philosophical or constitutive account of what it is for these features, rather than some others, to be computed. It is also important to note that it is the assigned phonological features themselves that contribute to the explanation of the way in which the utterance is heard. Had the feature of being unvoiced been assigned in the first segment, all else remaining the same, then the utterance would have been heard as the word "fat" instead.

The phonological features computed in the perception of the word "vat" do not presuppose that the subject has the concept *the word* "*vat.*" The subpersonal account can contribute to an explanation of the thinker's meeting the possession condition for the relevant concept of the spoken word. It should also be emphasized that the subpersonal contents—the phonological features—that the subpersonal account here relies on are not to be taken as themselves concepts possessed by the thinker. A final point about this example is that it illustrates that a subpersonal explanation contributing to an account of why a thinker meets a possession condition is not necessarily exclusively "internalist." It may invoke states that are individuated in part by their relations to matters outside the subject. What makes the content of a given state involve the labial feature rather than something else is presumably a complex function of its relation to perceived utterances in which the lips are used in a certain way.

To say something about the way in which an experiential state—hearing something as an utterance of the word "vat"—may be subpersonally realized is not yet to explain a thinker's fulfillment of a possession condition that mentions that experiential state. But it is a necessary first step. To give an explanation of the thinker's fulfillment of the possession condition, we will need subpersonal characterizations of the other components of the possession condition, including judgements that an event is an utterance of this word. We would then have to explain the fulfillment of the relations given in the possession condition by accounting for some appropriate subpersonal states by reference to features of other subpersonal realizing states.

I have chosen the concept *the word "vat"* to give some variety in my examples. Corresponding points, with correspondingly different subpersonal states invoked, could be made about the explanation of the subject's meeting the perceptual clauses of the possession conditions for the relatively observational concepts *square* and *red*.

The second example I want to consider illustrates the possibility of hypothetical explanations. Consider the possession condition given in section 1.2 for the concept of conjunction. That possession condition contains the requirement that the thinker find inferences of certain forms compelling in part *because* they are of those forms. Similarly, the possession condition for *plus* of section 5.3 speaks of the thinker finding certain transitions compelling because of their form. What could explain the thinker's meeting such conditions on the form of the transitions? How is it possible at all? After all, what is here called a "form" is a form of transition between contents. Whether these contents are Fregean Thoughts or neo-Russellian propositions, it is far from clear how the form of such a thing can causally influence a thinker. This implies that it is unclear how one part of the possession condition for conjunction can be true of a thinker.

There is a familiar type of subpersonal psychology that could explain how and why this part of the possession condition can hold of a thinker. (There is no commitment here to the claim that it is the only type of theory capable of such explanations.) First, the psychology gives a description of how the state of finding something primitively compelling is subpersonally realized. It will do this in tandem with whatever notion of mental representation it employs. It will say, for a given thinker, what property has to be possessed by a mental representation with a certain content for the thinker to find that content primitively compelling. Second, the theory states that there are types of mental representation that correspond to particular concepts and can be combined in some subpersonal functional analogue of concatenation to form mental representations of complex contents. That is, it endorses the hypothesis of a language of thought. If the theory meets these two conditions, then a mental representation of an inference will involve a mental representation of its premise and a mental representation of its conclusion. Such a theory can postulate a mechanism ensuring that the mental representation of an inference is assigned the subpersonal property that realizes the property of being found primitively compelling if the mental representations of premises and conclusion are themselves of certain forms. Since the latter forms are forms of token representations, rather than forms of abstract objects or something in Frege's third realm, there is no principled problem of how they can causally influence a thinker's mental states.

As a hypothetical explanation of how and why the possession condition holds, this description presumes, of course, the correctness of several philosophical accounts underwriting its assignment of particular contents to mental representations. Nonetheless, it does seem that if a psychological theory of this sort were correct, it would offer a genuine empirical explanation of why the thinker fulfills one part of the possession condition for conjunction. Again, the explanation does not presuppose that the thinker already has the concept of conjunction.[2]

Having some subrational realization (in the thinker) of the property of finding a given content primitively compelling is an essential part of this account. We would lose explanatory power if there were mental representations of the premise and conclusion of the inference, but no subrational realization of the property of finding something primitively compelling. For in these circumstances there would be no subrational explanation of why the thinker finds inferences mentally represented in a certain way primitively compelling. It would be a brute fact, and we would be without any explanation of why the thinker goes on one way rather than another when presented with a new inference with one of the forms in question. The point is not special to this particular example but rather generalizes to all possession conditions that employ the notion of finding something primitively compelling. An adequate psychological explanation of a thinker's meeting such a possession condition must give some subrational account of what is involved in his finding a content primitively compelling. When a theory does give such an account, I call it *response-absorbent*.

A subrational account of a thinker's state of finding something primitively compelling must involve describing that state in other, non-folk-psychological ways. Of course, both connectionist models and nonconnectionist versions of language-of-thought models are potential sources of such non-folk-psychological characterizations.

For a subrationally characterized state to realize a content-involving personal-level state, stringent conditions must be met. Suppose that it is constitutively required for something to be a particular personal-level content-involving state that it stand in a network of actual and possible causal relations to certain other personal-level states and external events. Then any subrational realization of that state must stand in the same network of actual and possible causal relations to those other states and events.[3] So, for example, a subrational realization of the belief discussed in chapter 4, that Lincoln Plaza is square, must stand in the network of relations identified in that chapter as necessary for a belief to have that content. The requirement that subrational realizations preserve such actual and possible causal relations allows the Simple Account to respect an important distinction. The distinction is that between explaining why a certain transition takes place between two merely subpersonally characterized states, and explaining why some component of a possession condition holds. The latter is the target, and it is achieved only if the subrational states stand in the network of relations required to realize the personal-level content-involving states mentioned in the component of the possession condition.

Does the claim that a subrational state realizes the property of a thinker's finding a content primitively compelling commit us to the possibility of some subrational reduction of any concept involved in the primitively compelling content? Far from it. Finding some content primitively compelling involves judging that content. The possession conditions for the concepts in that content will determine what in turn is involved in something's being a judgement with that content. In general, those possession conditions may require that something is a judgement involving the concept of *fairness,* for instance, only if it displays some specified sensitivity to whether decisions or institutions are fair. Such a requirement applies a fortiori to a primitively compelling judgement that something is fair. A subrational realization of some state described at the personal level must stand in the same actual and counterfactual relations as the state it realizes. It would follow that we cannot even say what it is for something to be a subrational realization of a primitively compelling judgement that something is fair without including conditions which relate that state to what *is* fair (compare the remarks in section 5.3 on the concept of justice). Subrational reductions of concepts are thus not in the offing here. They are not required for present purposes.

Non-folk-psychological characterizations of a state need not be completely free of any use of a notion of content. The characterization I offered in the phonological example involves some notion of content. The question now arises, if a fully explanatory psychology is to be possible, must transitions between content-involving states ultimately be explained by transitions not characterized in content-involving terms? I will argue that there are reasons for answering this question in the affirmative for any notion of the content of a state whose individuation makes some reference to the state's relational properties, that is, any intelligible notion of content, whether conceptual or nonconceptual, personal or subpersonal.

Consider the following two suppositions. The first supposition is that event α with content A explains the occurrence of event β with content B. The second supposition is that there is no further explanation of why this holds. This combination of suppositions is highly problematic. Event α will have the content A because of a complex network of relations in which it stands. The event β will similarly have content B because of some different network of relations in which it stands. These relational properties may, for example, have to do with the causal antecedents of α if α is an event in a subpersonal visual computation. Or they may have to do with the inferential or computational behavior of some type of representation in α, within transitions other than the one presently in question. In general, it seems that whatever the relevant relational properties of α are, they are not the ones that produce event β (except in the hypothetical or rare case in which a device actually scans to detect what relations a state stands in, and does so for all content-involving states it detects). It should be emphasized that this point continues to apply with full force if content A is narrow (not involving matters outside the subject's head) rather than broad. (See Jackson and Pettit 1988, 392.) The conceptual component *or*, for instance, is narrow if anything is. But what makes it the case that a belief state has content A *or* B is in part that in suitable circumstances the subject would move into it from the belief that A alone and equally from the belief that B alone. These are relational facts about this narrow component of the content. Indeed, even for the relational property of being implicated in a single type of transition, this relational property itself does not causally explain instances of the transition.

Yet (overdetermination and preemption aside) the description of the case involving α and β still commits us to the counterfactual that if there had not been an event with content A, there would not have been an event with content B. Like any other counterfactual, it is not plausible that this one can be barely true, i.e, true but not true in virtue of any feature of the actual world (Dummett 1976, 94 ff.). One way for it not to be barely true is for there to be some locally causally influential property of the event α, a property that, in the organism, represents content A. It is this locally causally influential property that, in the context, causally explains the occurrence of β. Event β will also have some local property, instantiation of which is caused by the local property of α and that, in the organism, represents content B. But to say this is to admit that there is after all some further explanation of why events with content A produce events with content B in the organism. So it seems that anyone who denies that such further explanations must be possible has either to admit barely true counterfactuals or at least to offer some alternative account of why they are not barely true.[4]

A rather different approach to explanation by content-involving states has been urged by Jackson and Pettit (1988). They argue that a content-bearing event can causally explain an effect if the effect occurs under all the ways (or all but very unlikely ways) in which the content-bearing event can be realized. It seems to me, though, that it is not a necessary condition of explaining by reference to an event with content that the effect would occur under all the ways in which the content-bearing event can (easily) be realized. Suppose that a person has a visual perception as of an elephant and that its occurrence causally explains his judgement that an elephant is passing by. The experience is realized by some subpersonal state with a complex representational content. We can also suppose that there are two different ways in which visual experiences can be realized in this subject. Perhaps various subpersonal decisions on allocating resources determine that now one, now the other, system of states is put on-line to the visual system for the production of visual experiences. These two systems may not have, for instance, the same associative connections to other psychological states. We can write into the example that one of the systems, when activated, makes the subject much more cautious in accepting the veridicality of certain experiences, such as one of an elephant passing by, than he is when the other system is activated. In this example, then, it is not true that had the actual visual experience been differently realized, the subject would still have judged that an elephant is passing by. He would not. This does not seem to me to undermine the point that, as things actually are, his having a visual experience with a certain content causally explains his judgement. The counter-factual "If he had not had the experience, he would not have made the judgement" can also remain true in this example. Actually, the point made in this example seems to apply not just to content-based explanation but to explanation by higher-level or relational states quite generally. We explain the plane crash by saying that its wing was vulnerable to disintegration at high speeds. The basis of this disposition was, let us say, cracks in its wing. The disposition to disintegrate at high speeds could also have had the looseness of bolts as its basis. It may be that this and alternative bases would not have led to a crash, because they are factors that are checked before the aircraft is permitted to take off. But this does not undermine the explanation of the crash that cites vulnerability to disintegration at high speeds.

To these objections it may be replied that I have not fixed upon the right property as explanatory. In the example of the visual experience as of an elephant, it may be said, the explanatory property is more complex: it is having an experience as of an elephant, where the experience is one the subject is not disposed to question. The problem with this response, though, is that it characterizes the explanatory state in such a way that it is a priori that the explanandum will occur. An experience the subject is not disposed to question is one whose content he endorses in judgement or belief; the empirical character of the consequence is lost. This problem with the response to the above objection is generalizable. If the explaining state is characterized as a priori sufficient for the consequence in question, the empirical character is lost. But if it is not so characterized, it will always be possible to set up examples in which alternative realizations of the explaining state do not have the consequence that, in the actual world, the explaining state does have.

So far I have been arguing that a subpersonal psychology can explain why a thinker meets a possession condition. The question arises of whether there *must* be an explanation of why a thinker meets a possession condition, when in fact he does. I note very briefly that the reasoning so far seems to contain the materials for constructing such an a priori argument. In general, possession conditions mention judgements made in certain specified circumstances. These circumstances always comprise other content-involving states, including sometimes the nonconceptual representational content of experience. Possession conditions should also be understood as requiring that the relevant judgements are made *because* the subject is in these other content-involving states. (The possession conditions would not be sufficient otherwise.) Now the same problem raised for explanation by subpersonal mental representations with content can be raised here too at the personal level. The relational properties in virtue of which a state has its content are not normally causally efficacious in producing the judgements mentioned in the possession condition. So again the question arises of how the content-involving states can be explanatory of the judgements mentioned in the possession condition. And again we can give an answer in terms of subpersonal representational properties that are locally causally efficacious.[5]

On the conception I have been defending, a subrational psychological explanation of why a thinker meets a certain possession condition is not precisely analogous to an advanced physical explanation of some phenomenon characterized in folk physics. According to my account, the ultimate subrational psychological explanation of the fulfillment of a possession condition must not use notions of content. In this respect, we have a radical discontinuity with the folk psychology in which talk of concepts is embedded, for there mention of content is pervasive. By contrast, a serious scientific physics can be seen as reached by a series of improvements in attaining the same kinds of goal as those of folk physics. There is no requirement in advance that a scientific physics make less use than does folk physics of a certain notion in the way that such a requirement holds for subrational psychology.[6]

An agenda for psychology suggested by the general approach I have been advocating is, then, this: for each type of thinker and for each concept possessed by a thinker of that type, to provide a subpersonal explanation of why the thinker meets the possession condition for that concept. While some psychological work already carried out is relevant to this agenda, there is surely an immense amount we do not understand at present. Carrying out this agenda is also in its very nature an interdisciplinary enterprise. For any particular concept, the task for the psychologist is not fully formulated until the philosopher has supplied an adequate possession condition for it.

7.2 Explanation, Rule Following, and Objectivity

I now turn to address the bearing of what I have said on some fundamental issues about meaning, content, and understanding.

Wittgenstein's arguments about rule following have sometimes been taken to exclude the possibility of giving a psychological explanation of why a thinker meets a possession condition. In section 1.2, I have already said that Wittgenstein's insight seems to me to be consistent with the Simple Account on one central issue—that of the need to mention what is found primitively compelling, how we "naturally go on," in the possession condition. But the fact is that Wittgenstein's rule-following considerations comprise a battery of arguments, some of them independent of others. It would be quite wrong to represent all these arguments as equally consistent with the Simple Account. Let me start by considering the arguments that are consistent with the Simple Account.

The Wittgensteinian points summarized by saying that rule following has "no essential inner epistemology" (Wright 1989b) are consistent with the Simple Account. The fact that my justifications when following a rule or applying a concept come to an end does not imply that the explanation of my reaction to a case comes to an end at the same point. The subrational states and computations that explain the thinker's fulfillment of the possession condition are unconscious. They lie below the bedrock at the bottom of reason-giving explanation.

For some philosophers, these comments will serve only to increase the tension between the Simple Account and Wittgenstein's insights. It is, they will say, internal to the nature of a concept that it involves a distinction between correct and incorrect applications. The norms somehow grasped in possessing a concept must surely have to do with the conscious level, at which the notion of justification can get a grip (thus Baker and Hacker 1984, 297, 309). These are entirely correct observations. They do not, however, undermine the Simple Account. The normative dimensions of a concept should be accounted for by citing various properties and relations of its possession condition, which involves notions at a level that is reason-involving, personal, and conscious. It would be quite inappropriate to try to explain the normative dimension of concepts at the subrational level. Certainly, the normative aspects I considered in chapter 5 all emerge from the personal-level possession condition.

The general point, though, does not depend on the correctness of the details of the account of the normative dimension in chapter 5. We already have the resources for making the point if we accept the following minimal claims: concepts are individuated by their possession conditions; concepts, together with the world, determine reference (perhaps relative to a context); and a truth value is determined by reference of the components of a thought. Under these minimal claims, the truth value of a thought is determined by the possession conditions for its various constituents, together with the world. But we surely have the materials for building an account of one fundamental normative dimension of a concept when we can elucidate what is involved in aiming at the truth of thoughts containing it. It is the possession condition, rather than the empirical subrational explanation of a particular thinker's meeting it, that supplies these materials. Properly understood, the normative dimension of concepts is no obstacle to the Simple Account. If the normative is elucidated with materials at the conscious, reason-involving level, we can still give an explanation at the subrational level of why the thinker meets the possession condition.[7]

What Wittgenstein's rule-following arguments do exclude is a certain kind of platonism, characterized by Crispin Wright as "the view that the correctness of a rule-informed judgement is a matter quite independent of any opinion of ours" (1989b, 257). On one understanding of the phrase "quite independent," the general framework within which I am working here is not platonistic in Wright's sense. Whether a rule-informed judgement is correct depends on the semantic values of its conceptual constituents. In the framework I am using, the account of what makes one object, function, or whatever the semantic value of a concept will show how it is fixed from the possession condition for the concept (together with the world). Since the possession condition in turn mentions what thinkers find primitively compelling, there is one clear sense in which correctness is not in the present framework "quite independent of any opinion of ours."

Making this point does not commit one to verificationism, nor to any kind of subjectivism. Universal quantification over the natural numbers can illustrate the point. As I noted back in chapter 1, a plausible possession condition for such universal quantification will state that the thinker finds the transition from such a quantification to an arbitrary instance primitively compelling and does so because the transition is of that form. (This form can also be instantiated for inaccessibly large numbers.) Such a possession condition manifestly mentions what is found primitively compelling. I also noted that the natural way to fix a semantic value from this possession condition is to say that the quantification (*for all n*) *Fn* is true just in case all its commitments are true, where its commitments are the instances *Fi*. This truth condition can obtain without our being able to know that it does. In general, a possession condition can mention a response without our being able to respond affirmatively and reliably to the question of its truth in every case in which the concept applies. Similarly, an explanation of a thinker's meeting a possession condition can respect this aspect of Wittgenstein's rule-following arguments without any commitment to verificationism as long as its subrational explanation of concept possession is response-absorbent.

There is, however, a second, more radical way of understanding the doctrine that the correctness of a rule-informed judgement is not independent of our opinions. On this reading, the doctrine is taken to be what I call the Ratification Thesis.[8]

Ratification Thesis When someone possesses a particular concept, the correctness of his judgement of whether a given object falls under the concept is not determined by any of the circumstances surrounding his judgements of whether other objects fall under it.

The thesis gets its name because if it is true, there is a sense in which the correctness of a judgement in which a concept is applied to a previously unencountered object involves some ratification on the thinker's part, a ratification not settled by anything in the circumstances of his previous judgements involving the concept. The Ratification Thesis is to be distinguished from the claim that from the fact that all the objects in a given set each fall under a concept, it does not follow that some new object outside the set also falls under the concept. That claim should command unhestitating assent, since it would be generally agreed that for any set of examples, we can find two concepts that agree on objects in that set but diverge on an object outside it. What distinguishes the Ratification Thesis is its claim about a failure of determination of correctness in a new case by anything in the circumstances surrounding the thinker's application of the concept in question in previous cases.

The Ratification Thesis is a denial of a certain kind of objectivity of meaning and content. It clearly undermines the idea that new judgements are responsible to a meaning already grasped. It was in fact the consequences of this idea for the notion of a proof in mathematics which provoked Turing's reported opposition at Wittgenstein's lectures (Diamond 1976, 62–67).

We ordinarily think that it can be determinately true or determinately false whether some unencountered object falls under a given concept.

That is, we think of the concept as "investigation-independent" in Crispin Wright's sense (1980, 206). As Wright emphasized, anyone who believes in the possibility of such investigation-independent concepts is committed to rejecting the Ratification Thesis. Conversely, belief in the Ratification Thesis for a particular concept provides a major motivation for those who wish to deny that the concept is investigation-independent. In fact, we have here one of several points at which a metaphysical problem turns on issues in the philosophical theory of concepts.

On the theory of concepts presented in this book, the Ratification Thesis is false. Suppose that the explanation of a subject's judging something to fall under a given concept is that certain conditions hold, and that part of the possession condition for the concept is that those conditions should explain the subject's judgement. Suppose also that the account of how the semantic value of the concept is determined from the possession condition entails that the object does fall under the concept in such circumstances. Then, first, we should expect the same conditions to explain a corresponding judgement for a new object if the subject continues to possess the concept. This much generality is implicit in the idea of a nonprobabilistic explanation.[9] Second, given the supposition about how the semantic value of the concept is fixed, the judgement about the new object will also be correct. Contrary to the Ratification Thesis, the correctness of his judgement about whether the object falls under the concept is determined by the circumstances surrounding his earlier judgements of whether other objects fall under it, for those circumstances include his satisfaction of the possession condition for the concept. This point continues to apply even if the new case is the first occasion on which the thinker judges in accord with one of the clauses of the possession condition, for instance, the first occasion on which he applies a certain shape concept in the present tense to an unperceived object. If the thinker was genuinely employing that concept in the earlier cases, it was still true of him then that he satisfied the clause dealing with the concept's application to objects not currently perceived. In the terminology of knowing-what-it-is-for (section 2.4), he still then knew what it was for a currently unperceived object to fall under the concept, even if he had not so far employed that knowledge in forming beliefs.

The role of the explanation for a thinker's judging a particular content is quite crucial in this rationale for rejecting the Ratification Thesis. If a possession condition for a concept treats a thinker's judgemental reactions to new individual examples case by case without making any reference to the explanation of the reactions, it is extremely difficult to avoid a commitment to accepting the Ratification Thesis in its full generality. There would be nothing, of the kind required for rejection of the Ratification Thesis, in common between the clauses of such a "possession condition" covering different instances to which the concept can be applied.[10]

It is also worth noting that on the present approach, one and the same feature of a possession condition, its reference to the explanation of certain of a thinker's judgements, both undermines the Ratification Thesis and allows that the concept has a determinate application to objects too distant, too large, or in other ways inaccessible to the thinker. It is indeed a myth that the possessor of a concept knows something that determines inferential reasons for the correctness of an application of the concept in both accessible and inaccessible cases. But the myth can be regarded as in part a mistaken way of incorporating a correct insight: that one and the same feature of mastery of a concept simultaneously allows a new application to be fixed as correct from the circumstances of previous applications and also permits there to be determinate facts about the extension of the concept in cases inaccessible to the thinker.

It is sometimes objected that anyone who rejects the Ratification Thesis must be attributing to a thinker some kind of first-person privileged knowledge of his meanings and concepts such that there is no more to an application of a concept being correct in a new case than its seeming so to the thinker. This line of thought is attributed because, once it is agreed that the fragment of the extension of a concept fixed by responses to previous examples by itself settles nothing about a new case, there may seem nothing else for knowledge of meaning and concepts to consist in (see Wright 1980, 216). On the account I have been developing, however, what makes it the case that someone is employing one concept rather than another is not constituted by his impressions of whether he is. Rather, it is constituted by complex facts about the explanation of certain of his primitively compelling judgements. This position leaves room for a major desideratum in the theory of content: an epistemology that makes possible first-person privileged knowledge of one's meaning and concepts without also making it vacuous and while also leaving the content of the knowledge accessible to others too.

Insofar as the Ratification Thesis is one strand in Wittgenstein's rule-following considerations, the account I have been developing is indeed incompatible with that part of them. This is not the place for detailed exegesis, but there are certainly some passages in Wittgenstein that are most naturally read as relying upon the Ratification Thesis. One example is his treatment of the statement "The sequence 770 occurs in the decimal expansion of π." He rejects the idea that this statement must have a determinate truth value, and his grounds appear to involve his views on rule following (1978, section V.9; see also Wright 1980, chapter 8). If Wittgenstein had held not the Ratification Thesis but only the weaker claim that the notion of what is found primitively compelling must enter the possession condition of any concept, then there would be no good reason for his denying determinacy of truth value to such statements. The statement in question can be taken as a universal quantification over natural numbers: for any natural number **n**, the **n**th, (**n** + 1)th, and (**n** + 2)th numerals in the decimal expansion of π are not the sequence 770. I have already noted that someone who holds that the notion of what is primitively compelling must enter any possession condition can consistently attribute to such a quantification a determinate truth value in advance of any ratification.

A second, closely related respect in which the views developed here are in tension with Wittgenstein's emerges from Wittgenstein's descriptions of what is involved in understanding an expression. Section 209 of his *Philosophical Investigations* starts,

"But then doesn't our understanding reach beyond all the examples?"—A very queer expression, and a quite natural one!

But is that *all*? Isn't there a deeper explanation; or mustn't at least the *understanding* of the explanation be deeper?—Well, have I myself a deeper understanding? Have I got more than I give in the explanation?

The theorist of possession conditions should answer yes to this last question. The "explanations" Wittgenstein is talking about here are those given to a pupil learning an expression, and they will consist fundamentally of giving examples. The understanding of the teacher will involve more than any examples he can give, because the teacher's own verdicts on examples have to have a certain kind of explanation if the teacher is to understand. The teacher's own verdicts on whether a presented object falls under, say, an observational-shape concept must be explained by the representational content of his experience, along the lines sketched in chapter 3. That the teacher's verdicts must have a certain explanation is not to imply that the teacher knows either what the required explanation is or that there is a required explanation. The requirement is one on the explanation itself, not on knowledge of the explanation.

These are not the only respects in which Wittgenstein would disagree with the position I have been outlining. His general distaste for causal accounts of psychological concepts would reinforce his rejection of the possession-condition account. As he said, his view was that use flows from meaning as behavior flows from character (1978, section I.13). It seems to me, however, that Wittgenstein's most powerful arguments—the rejection of the mythical and regressive accounts of understanding and concept mastery—are already taken on board once we recognize that possession conditions can mention what is found primitively compelling. My dispute with Wittgenstein is over the further step to the Ratification Thesis and its associated claims.

7.3 Summary

I have argued that an explanatory psychology should explain why a thinker meets the possession condition for a concept she possesses. A full explanation must involve only subrational states. The explanation must also give some account of the subrational realization of the thinker's finding a content compelling. An explanation that does so need not be in conflict with what is right in Wittgenstein's arguments about rule following, nor need it be committed to verificationism. The conception of possession conditions and their explanation endorsed here does, though, conflict with those parts of Wittgenstein's discussion that commit him to the Ratification Thesis. By endorsing a theory of concepts, possession, and explanation that rejects the Ratification Thesis, we restore a certain objectivity to conceptual content.

8 Illusions of Content: Thought

A thinker may suppose that there is a concept of a certain kind and that a particular hypothesis formulated using the concept makes sense even though there is in fact no such concept. The thinker is under an illusion of content. Some of these illusions form the subject of this chapter. The failure of the supposed hypothesis to make sense will be traceable to properties of the concepts, or purported concepts, it contains. One task of a theory of concepts is to explain why such hypotheses are unintelligible.

Unintelligible hypotheses have often been classified as such on verificationist grounds. These treatments pose a dilemma for many contemporary philosophers. We are not inclined elsewhere to verificationist theories of meaning and content, yet we have little doubt that some of the hypotheses classified as spurious by the verificationists were rightly so classified. I will be arguing that the approach to conceptual content developed in this book and the constraints to which it aims to conform allow us to find a way out of this dilemma. As it must if it is to merit the title of a way out of the dilemma, the proposal gives us a rationale for rejecting certain hypotheses as spurious without committing us to verificationism.

8.1 The Dilemma: Examples

I begin with three familiar examples of hypotheses that are likely to strike us as spurious. The first example is that of perfect fission of a person. It seems that we can coherently conceive of a person whose brain is more symmetrical than our own. We can conceive that this brain is extracted and divided, each half being placed in, and suitably connected with, a perfect replica of the original person's body. The two resulting people are perfect duplicates. Roderick Chisholm insisted of this case that there is always a fact of the matter as to which one of the resulting persons is identical with the original.

> The questions "Will I be Lefty" and "Will I be Righty?" have entirely definite answers. . . . What I want to insist upon . . . is that this will be the case even if all our normal criteria for personal identity should break down. . . . Even if there is no procedure or criterion whatever by means of which anyone could reasonably decide whether one or the other will be I, none the less, the questions "Will I be Lefty?" and "Will I be Righty?" do have definite answers. (Chisholm 1970, 188–189)

Many of us are, nevertheless, strongly inclined to regard as spurious
the hypothesis that just one of the resulting persons, and not the other,
is identical with the original.

The second example is the most extreme form of the inverted-
spectrum hypothesis. This extreme form asserts that another subject's
visual experience can be qualitatively different from your own when
you are both seeing the same object, even though your relevant brain
states are physically identical and so are your environmental conditions. The form of the hypothesis we are considering is extreme in
that it goes beyond the type of inversion that such writers as Shoemaker (1984) regard as intelligible. Shoemaker allows that such inversion is a possibility only if the physical realization of the experiential
state in the other is of a different kind from its realization in you. The
extreme theorist does not take this as a necessary condition. Again
there is an inclination, though not as strong as that produced by the
first example, to say that the hypothesis of extreme inversion is
spurious.

The third example is that of absolute space, in the sense in which
hypotheses about the relations of objects and events to absolute space
seem to be beyond all experimental confirmation. Our inclination is to
say that hypotheses committed to the existence of absolute location,
as opposed to hypotheses committed only to some form of relative
location, are spurious. Of course, many issues were at stake in the
dispute about absolute space, as Newton used the notion. In classifying hypotheses committed to absolute location as spurious, we need
not be committed to the eliminability of place-times, we need not be
rejecting the possibility of unoccupied place-times, nor do we need to
deny the possibility of picking out some distinguished frame of reference for empirical reasons. What we are rejecting is a conception of
space on which it always makes sense to suppose that the entire
material universe is moving undetectably at a particular uniform velocity with respect to absolute space.[1]

Many of us will want to declare the hypotheses in these three
examples to be spurious while not endorsing any general claim of the
form "All genuine contents must, it true, be verifiable in such and
such ways." Thomas Nagel, for instance, is one of our number. He is
certainly no verificationist, but of the view that the question "Will it
be *me*?" always has an all-or-nothing answer, he writes, "There must

be something wrong with this picture" (1986, 34). Many of those who agree with Nagel on that particular case would nevertheless want to allow that a thinker's thoughts about the past can be true without the thinker being able to verify them, and similarly for various unrestricted universal quantifications over material objects. Corresponding points could be made *pari passu* for falsificationism.

Early on in their writings, the logical positivists made a move to verifiability in principle (Ayer 1946, 38). For the moment we can take this as verifiability by someone somewhere (the details will not matter). Would a similar treatment of these three examples dissolve the dilemma? Certainly the notions admitted by one who finds the apparently spurious hypotheses intelligible do allow the framing of hypotheses that are in principle unverifiable. In a case of perfect fission, the hypothesis that one rather than the other of the resulting persons is identical with the preoperative person is unverifiable in principle in this sense, so too under the extreme inverted-spectrum theorist's conception is the statement that two subjects are having experiences of the same subjective type, and so are statements about location in absolute space. It would not be a good objection to reply, "The hypothesis in the personal identity case *is* verifiable. The person who survives the operation can tell whether he is viewing the world from the location of Lefty or from the location of Righty." This would be as unsatisfactory as saying, "You can verify whether an object is at rest in absolute space: you simply remain stationary in absolute space and determine whether the object is moving relative to you." Both answers must be counted as cheating. If the conditions under which the verification is to be carried out are not themselves verifiable in principle, the procedures are not ones available to one who requires verification in principle. So I do agree that there is an important sense in which the spurious hypotheses are unverifiable in principle. Nevertheless, the dilemma persists, for two reasons.

The first reason is that there are still some apparently intelligible contents excluded by verifiability in principle. Verifiability in principle seemingly counts as genuine, contents about arbitrary individual places and times that could be verified at those places and times.[2] But the truth value of an unrestricted universal quantification over places and times is determined by the truth values of infinitely many propositions about places and times. It need not be verifiable by anyone anywhere. So it is not clear how such a quantifier could consistently be admitted by one who accepts verification in principle as the test. These points seem to me to apply equally to Hilary Putnam's more recent view that to claim of any statement that it is true is, roughly, to claim that it could be justified were epistemic conditions good enough (1990, vii).

The second reason is more general and should move even someone prepared to reject such quantifiers. The second reason is that it is not clear how one could so much as explain what it is to understand quantification over not just nearby places and times but also arbitrary places and times, infinitely many of them inaccessible to the thinker, by using only the resources available to the verificationist. Perhaps verifiability in principle does count as genuine some otherwise excluded contents once one has the conception of arbitrary places and times. Once he has the conception of a suitable location in space and time, a thinker may perhaps go on to form the idea of a being located there who may verify propositions about it. But that does not help if one cannot explain within the limits of verificationism what it is to have the conception of the place and time. Though the point needs extensive independent argument, it seems to me that the most plausible accounts of what it is to have some conception of a particular past time make no reference to a thinker's ability now or subsequently to verify propositions about that time, nor do those accounts require that any such ability exist.[3] They rather suggest the beginnings of a nonverificationist account of thought about the past.

If there is indeed a problem for the verificationist over the possession of the conception of arbitrarily distant places and times, it also prevents the verificationist from attempting to save his view by appealing to what could be verified by one with greater powers. (The powers would have to be infinitely great to cover unrestricted universal quantification.) For such an appeal can solve his problem only if he has legitimate access to the conception of a range of places and times with respect to which the greater powers can be applied. But if a nonverificationist account of possession of the conception is to be given, will it allow back in the apparently spurious hypotheses? At this stage of the discussion, the question is still entirely open.

There is another problem with this type of appeal to beings with greater powers. The schematic idea of a being able to decide unrestricted empirical universal generalizations is entirely parasitic on our possession of a conception of what it is for those quantifications to be true. So the idea of such a being cannot be used to explain our understanding of these quantifications. Rather, it presupposes that understanding.

The result of this speedy trip through the history and problems of verificationism and epistemic theories of truth is that we have not extracted a good reason for declaring the hypotheses in the three examples to be spurious. We need a different approach.

8.2   The Discrimination Principle and Strategies of Application

I suggest that the principle to which we need to appeal is not verificationism but rather the Discrimination Principle.

Discrimination Principle   For each content a thinker may judge, there is an adequately individuating account of what makes it the case that he is judging that content rather than any other.

By "content" I mean the object of judgement and other propositional attitudes. I will continue to formulate the issues in a broadly Fregean framework. To say that an account of what is involved in judging a particular content is adequately individuating is to say that is gives a condition that states correctly and informatively what it is for the thinker to be judging that particular content, a condition that distinguishes judging that content from judging any other content. If there is any other content at all such that judging the given content has not been distinguished from judging this other content, then the account is at best incomplete. It will not have said what it is for a thinker to be judging the given content rather than this other content.[4]

Why should we believe the Discrimination Principle? We should believe it because of the general consideration that it is incorrect to attribute to a thinker propositional attitudes or other psychological relations to finely sliced things if the abilities possessed by the thinker that might be cited to justify such an attribution do not slice that finely. This general consideration applies not only to conceptual content but also to any other notions of content or reference applied to mental states or to a thinker's relations to a language. It is, for instance, a consideration we should invoke if we want to explain what is wrong with interpreting an ordinary thinker who is really just referring to the natural numbers as referring to the Zermelo numbers $\emptyset$, $\{\emptyset\}$, $\{\{\emptyset\}\}$, ...[5] If we allow violations of the Discrimination Principle, we admit the possibility that a thinker could be judging content C_1 rather than content C_2, even though we can say nothing nontrivial about what makes it the case that he is judging C_1 rather than C_2. Indeed, if a theorist admits this possibility with respect to C_1 and C_2, it is not clear what argument he would have against a third possibility consistent with the facts about the given thinker, namely, that it is indeterminate whether he is judging C_1 rather than C_2. Consider the boundaries among judging C_1 rather than C_2, judging C_2 rather than C_1, and indeterminacy. If we endorse the Discrimination Principle, we will be insisting that each of these boundaries can be drawn on the basis of facts about what is involved in judging the various contents in question.

A fully developed theory of possession conditions will automatically respect the Discrimination Principle. For each conceptual constituent of the content of a judgement, the theory will supply an account of what is involved in judging an arbitrary content containing the conceptual constituent. The account will distinguish that conceptual constituent from all other conceptual constituents. Taken together, the accounts for each of the constituents of a judged content jointly entail a resulting account of what it is to judge that content. This resulting account distinguishes judging that content from judging any other content. It is in this way that the theory of possession conditions respects the Discrimination Principle.

These points should make it clear that the Discrimination Principle is not merely "a special case of the general principle that if two things are different there must be a difference between them" (Craig 1990, 279). In the context of the theory of this book, it is equivalent to the principle, specific to conceptual content, that if two judgeable contents are different, there must be a difference in the possession conditions of some of their constituent concepts. The ultimate rationale for this principle is the Principle of Dependence of section 1.2, which is again something specific to the theory of concepts.

The Discrimination Principle is a claim at a different level from verificationism. The Discrimination Principle has the status of a (proposed) condition of adequacy on substantive theories of content. Unlike verificationism, it not by itself even an outline of what form a substantive theory of a given sort of content should take, nor does it specify the materials from which such a theory should be built. We can, though, still raise the question of whether verificationist theories are the *only* substantive theories of content which respect the Discrimination Principle. According to the discussion in this book, the answer to this question must be no. At the risk of emphasizing the obvious, I mention (for what I promise is the last time) the case of universal quantification over the natural numbers. The theory of possession conditions allowed us to formulate a natural treatment of grasp of such quantifications that explains how they can be true though unverifiable in any relevant sense (see sections 1.2 and 1.3). But the treatment certainly respects the Discrimination Principle.[6]

If distinct from verificationism about contents themselves, is the Discrimination Principle at least equivalent to verificationism about ascriptions of content? Here a middle course must be taken. One of the more extreme kinds of realist may be tempted simply to declare that if verificationism about content is incorrect, there is no reason to object to possession conditions that may be satisfied, unverifiably so, by thinkers. The problem with saying that and no more is that it leaves us without even a sketch of how such a position is to be squared with a plausible epistemology of content ascription. Our accounts of meaning, knowledge, and the transmission of information through language will all be crippled if we do not develop a theory of content on which it is possible to know what someone else means. Does this point mean that we must move to the other extreme and insist that in any case in which we can know that a possession condition is satisfied by a thinker, that condition must be verifiable whenever it is true? That is implausible on other grounds. For each of the concepts for which possession conditions have been outlined in this work, it is plausible that we often know that other thinkers possess those concepts. But all the possession conditions I have outlined in one way or another include, for instance, requirements on the explanations of certain judgements of a thinker. With the many commitments made by a true claim about the explanation of something, it seems to me unlikely that we can formulate a useful notion of verifying claims about explanation if that notion, when met, guarantees fulfillment of all the commitments of a claim about explanation.

The specification of the middle position we need is this: Though there is no working notion of conclusive verification for attribution of concepts, it should be possible to develop a good epistemology that nevertheless allows that such attributions can on occasion be knowledge. Such a combination of views seems independently desirable for many other kinds of content. It seems right to regard the issue about content ascription as a special case of this general epistemological issue. It should be squarely acknowledged, though, that the acceptability of the account of concepts given in this work depends upon the possibility of developing such an epistemology. I do not think that this reliance on an epistemology yet to be well developed should lead us to reject the views that produce this dependence. The other theoretical options seem unattractive. It is not tempting to dispense with the requirement of explanation, for instance, in the detailed possession conditions. It is even less tempting to reject the Discrimination Principle. I discuss further below the severe epistemological problems of content ascription for one who rejects the Discrimination Principle.

So much by way of discussion of the principle from which I wish to reason. The next task is to develop the argument that the Discrimination Principle excludes spurious hypotheses from the category of genuine contents. If the Discrimination Principle is correct, then it can play a regulative role in determining which putative contents are genuine. Suppose that we have reason to believe that no adequately individuating account can be given of what it is to judge a putative content. Then by the Discrimination Principle, we have reason to believe that the putative content is not genuine. There are two conceivable strategies that might be followed by a theorist attempting to exploit this regulative role so as to exclude the spurious hypotheses mentioned at the outset of this chapter.

One strategy I call the "enumerative strategy." It first lists the types of content that in fact feature in our propositional attitudes, and it supplies accounts of grasp of contents of those types. It then aims to show, in part by drawing on these accounts, that the kinds of alleged contents essential to formulating the spurious hypotheses are not among the types we actually employ.

This enumerative strategy can take one a certain distance. Consider, for instance, the hypothesis of extreme spectrum inversion. It does not fall within the various models of grasp of content that have been developed so far. The three-tier model of *Thoughts,* for instance, allows that a concept may apply to something inaccessible to the thinker if it has the same physical property that in a certain sense explains a thinker's applications of the concept in accessible cases.[7] But this model becomes irrelevant at just the point at which the defender of the intelligibility of extreme spectrum inversion needs help. For the extreme hypothesis we are considering is one on which experience may vary independently not only of any sort of functional role (individualistic or otherwise) but also of the physical realization of the state. So the three-tier model cannot help give sense to the extreme hypothesis.

The enumerative strategy suffers, however, from two drawbacks. One is that even if it were carried through to completion, it offers no answer to a determined defender of the apparently spurious hypotheses who agrees that the concepts they contain are not ones we ordinarily employ. He may just insist that they are nevertheless intelligible concepts in their own right. The other drawback results from our current lack of understanding of the concept and nature of consciousness. As long as we lack adequate philosophical theories of consciousness, we are in no position to show that the extreme hypothesis violates whatever is the correct model for grasp of contents concerning consciousness.

The different strategy I will follow proceeds by reductio. The first way of proceeding by reductio is to carry out the *switching tactic.* In applying this tactic, we aim to show that, for each spurious hypothesis, there is an alternative hypothesis. This alternative hypothesis is legitimate by the standards of the spurious hypothesis itself, but the spurious hypothesizer can give no account of what it is for a thinker to judge it rather than the original hypothesis. If the spurious hypothesis were genuine, there would then be a violation of the Discrimination Principle, so it is not genuine.

The other tactic I will consider within the reductio strategy is the *deflationary tactic.* Here we suppose that the spurious contents are genuine, and we raise the question of how judging them is distinct from judging certain other unproblematic contents. If no answer can be given, then again the Discrimination Principle excludes the spurious contents. The deflationary tactic differs from the switching tactic in that in applying it, we compare the initial spurious hypothesis not with another spurious content but with a genuine content.

The reductio strategy does not suffer from the first drawback of the enumerative strategy. The reductio strategy makes no assumption that the contents we normally employ are all possible contents. If it is used with care, it can also avoid the second drawback, which results from our meager current understanding of consciousness. We may simply grant to the spurious hypothesizer the notion of a conscious, experiential, subjective state and not question his right to it. What the reductio strategy presses is just the question of *which* concept applicable to conscious states the spurious hypothesizer is employing.

Is the reductio strategy self-defeating? It might be argued that if we know what a spurious hypothesizer is hypothesizing, his hypothesis must have some content. So any argument that concludes it does not must be unsound. I reply that we do not know what the spurious hypothesizer is hypothesizing. We know only certain properties that the hypothesizer asserts of his alleged notions. He supposes, for instance, that there is some notion of location with the property that truths about locations of that kind are not fixed by all the truths about relative locations. This occurrence of the existential quantifier "there is some notion of location" is inside the scope of "he supposes that"; the statement of what he supposes does not commit us to the existence of any such notion. If the spurious hypothesizer insists that he is using the ordinary notion of location, personal identity, or sameness of experience, we should not then declare his hypothesis to be unintelligible. Rather, it is false, but false for special reasons. By the arguments I am developing, there could not be concepts for which the spurious hypotheses are true.

8.3 Executing the Switching Tactic

In executing the switching tactic, we have to take three steps.

1. Identify an initial alleged content admitted by the spurious hypothesizer. (Henceforth I will often suppress the qualifier "alleged.")

2.   Identify a second alternative content, built up from the various notions admitted by the spurious hypothesizer.

3.   Argue that the spurious hypothesizer cannot by his lights adequately distinguish between judging the content chosen at step 1 and judging the content chosen at step 2.

That will then establish a violation of the Discrimination Principle. I will apply this treatment to the hypothesis of extreme spectrum inversion and to the case of absolute space.

Consider someone who claims to have a conception of what it is for another subject to have a different type of experience from his own even though this other subject is in the same physical and relevant functional states as he is. For simplicity, suppose too that we are concerned with a monochromatic spectrum ranging from pure white through shades of gray to pure black. For step 1 in the case of the inverted spectrum, I select the following content:

Content at Step 1   When the other is looking at things that look light gray to me, he has an experience of the same kind as I have when I see things that look dark gray to me, and he is then in the same relevant functional and physical states as I when I look at light gray things.

In the scheme I actually employ—a scheme distinct from that envisaged by the spurious hypothesizer, if the present argument succeeds— we can make sense of some limited inversions. We can make sense of the possibility that someone who is making experientially based, non-inferential discriminations of light gray objects is in fact seeing them as dark gray.[8] We can make sense of this if he is in brain states that in us realize experiences of objects as light gray. But as I have twice emphasized, the spurious hypothesizer's conception goes beyond this.

At step 2, I select a content just like that chosen at step 1 except that all occurrences of "dark gray" are replaced by "light gray":

Content at Step 2   When the other is looking at things that look light gray to me, he has an experience of the same kind as I have when I see things that look light gray to me, and he is then in the same relevant functional and physical states as I when I look at light gray things.

This content, of course, implies that things looking light gray to me also look light gray to the other.

At step 3, I have to argue that the spurious hypothesizer cannot distinguish between judging the content selected at step 1 from judging the content selected at step 2. The spurious hypothesizer will certainly want to hold that they are distinct. Indeed, taken as contents built up from our ordinary concepts, they *are* distinct. But I will argue that what allows us to distinguish judging one of the contents from judging the other is something unavailable to the spurious hypothesizer.

What is it for a thinker to employ the concept of an experience of an object as light gray? Suppose that the thinker and another person are both looking at an object that the thinker sees as light gray. Suppose that the thinker takes the other to have an experience of the sort implicated in the latter's experientially based, noninferential ability to discriminate what are in fact the light gray objects. Suppose also that the thinker does not doubt that relevantly similar brain states and functional states are produced in both of them by the object they both see. Finally, suppose that the thinker judges that the other's experience of the light gray object is not an experience of it as *F,* for some particular concept *F*. Then, prima facie, *F* should not be taken as the concept *light gray*.[9] This point is not concerned in the first instance with how the thinker verifies or confirms hypotheses. It is rather a constitutive point. The concept of an experience of something as light gray is the concept of an experience of a type that plays a certain role in the subject's experientially based, noninferential ability to discriminate light gray things. This condition in no way eliminates conscious experience; on the contrary, it twice makes reference to it. The constitutive point does leave several difficult issues unresolved, but it is all we need here in outlining the way in which the Discrimination Principle is in fact met for our actual concepts of color experience.

This constitutive point, as it applies indifferently to one's own experience or another's, anchors the concept of an experience's being an experience of an object as light gray. The anchor connects that concept with a property of objects, that of *being* light gray. But this anchor is one from which the believer in the possibility of extreme inversion has explicitly cut himself loose. In admitting the possibility of extreme inversion, he is prepared to judge that an experience can be of a type that allows its owner to discriminate the light gray things noninferentially on the basis of experience while simultaneously he accepts that the owner of the experience is in a physical state others are in when they see light gray things as light gray, and yet he holds that the experience in question may not be an experience of an object as light gray. So the anchor is apparently unavailable to the extreme theorist.[10] But I used the anchor in saying, on our actual conception, what is involved in a thinker's judging the content at step 1 rather than the content at step 2. Without the anchor, it is hard to see how the extreme inversion theorist can answer the challenge, based on the Discrimination Principle, to supply an account, acceptable by his own lights, of the difference between judging these two contents. In fact, I noted that the content at step 2 is equivalent to the content "The other sees light gray things as I do." So in fact, by the standards of the Discrimination Principle, the extreme theorist has not even distinguished his apparently extreme supposition from the supposition that all is normal, with no inversion whatsoever.[11]

There are at least two responses that the extreme theorist may make to this argument. The first response is to suggest an alternative anchor. The extreme theorist may say that our concept of an experience in which something looks light gray is the concept of an experience of a type implicated in the subject's experientially based ability to noninferentially discriminate those things that produce an experience in which they *look* light gray to him. This, though, is to attach the anchor not to the seabed but to the vessel from which it was dropped. It attempts to constrain the concept *looks light gray* by a condition involving not the concept *is light gray,* as did the original anchor, but the very same concept *looks light gray* again. This, of course, would not prevent the proposed constraint from stating a requirement on the concept *looks light gray.* For we can replace the occurrence of "look light gray" in the condition by a variable "C" over concepts, in a way now familiar from chapter 1. The requirement would then read as follows: the concept of an experience in which something looks light gray is the concept meeting the condition on concept C that experiences falling under it are of a type implicated in the subject's experientially based ability to noninferentially discriminate things producing in him experiences falling under C. This is true, but it is a condition met by any concept of an experience type whatsoever. It cannot provide an anchor specific to the concept *looks light gray.*

The second and more frequently encountered response of a determined defender of the possibility of extreme inversion is to accept the argument so far. He may simply go on to draw the conclusion that it was a mistake to suppose that the essentially incommunicable content of experience in which he believes can be adequately expressed by such words in the public language as "light gray" or "dark gray." We can at most use variables (i, i', . . .) in referring to them, he will say.

The switching tactic can, however, also be applied against this determined defender. To apply it, I select this content at step 1:

Alternative Content at Step 1   When the other sees things that produce a certain incommunicable quality i of experience in me, he has an experience of the same kind as I have when things produce incommunicable quality Inv(i) in me (where Inv(i) is the inversion of i), and he is then in the same relevant functional and physical states as I am in the former situation.

At step 2, I select a content that differs from this only in that it results from replacing the relation *is of the same kind as* by the relation *is of a kind that is the inversion of the kind of:*

Alternative Content at Step 2   When the other is looking at things that produce incommunicable quality i in me, he has an experience whose kind is an inversion of the kind of experience I have when things produce experiences with quality Inv(i) in me, and he is then in the same relevant functional and physical states as I am in the former situation.

As before, the two inversions cancel out. This alternative content at step 2 implies that the other's spectrum is not inverted relative to mine.

How is the determined defender to distinguish between judging these two contents? In effect, the question reduces to the question of what it is to mean the relation *is of the same subjective type as* rather than a relation involving inversion. More specifically, the question is what it is for the determined defender to mean *is of the same subjective type as* rather than the relation R, defined thus:

Definition   If e and e' are token experiences of the same person (the thinker or another) or if neither is an experience of the thinker,

Ree′ iff **e** and **e′** are of the same subjective type. If **e** is an experience of the thinker and **e′** of some distinct person (or conversely), **Ree′** iff **e** is of the type that is an inversion of that of **e′**.

It seems to me that the determined defender can give no satisfactory answer to this challenge prompted by the Discrimination Principle. For by the determined defender's standards, someone certainly could mean by "same" the relation **R**. The problem is that for any assignment, to a thinker, of attitudes with contents countenanced by the determined defender, there will be a variant assignment. Where on the original assignment the subject's beliefs have contents containing the component *is of the same type as,* on the variant assignment that component is replaced with the relation **R**. In addition, compensating beliefs are assigned to the subject about patterns of inversion holding between the incommunicable properties of different subjects' experiences. If we accept the Discrimination Principle, we will want to ask the determined defender what it is for one assignment rather than such a variant to be correct. The anchors have now become irrelevant to meeting this challenge, since we are concerned with incommunicable qualities. From the fact that the other is in a conscious state that enables him to discriminate objects that appear in a certain way to others, nothing whatsoever follows that helps to meet the challenge. I suggest that in moving to the alleged incommunciable properties, the determined defender loses touch with what allows him to mean one thing rather than another.

Am I denying that each of us can know directly whether, in his interpersonal and intrapersonal statements about experience, he means something uniform by the word "same"? Certainly not. In our actual scheme, with concepts properly anchored, nothing I have said excludes the possibility of such direct knowledge. But such knowledge is possible only if there is a good account to be given of what the knowledge is knowledge *of.* My position is that there is no such account for the notions that the determined defender claims to exercise.

This completes my remarks on the determined defender. The general challenge in the switching objection to the extreme inversion theorist has been made without any commitment to verificationism or to a reductionism about concepts we actually use. It would, of course, be surprising if the unknowability of the character of another's experience on the extreme theorist's conception were not playing some role in the argument; it is. There is no question, either for the extreme theorist or for us, of perceiving another's experience. Nor is there any other relatively direct way of coming to know its character for the extreme theorist either. So once he cuts loose from the genuine anchor, there is no other way for him to allow a thinker to be sensitive to features of another's experience in a way that might permit an answer to the challenge based on the Discrimination Principle.

A structurally analogous treatment can be given in applying the switching tactic to the case of absolute space. In outline, we would proceed as follows. We ask the believer in absolute space, What is it for a thinker to be exercising the concept of absolute location, rather than the concept of location relative to a frame of reference moving with a uniform velocity with respect to (alleged) absolute space? What, by his lights, would be wrong with reinterpreting such a believer's phrase "absolute location" to mean location with respect to a particular frame of reference moving at a uniform velocity with respect to absolute space? So the contents we select at steps 1 and 2 would be contents differing only in that one uses the alleged notion of absolute location, while the other uses the notion of location relative to a framework in uniform motion with respect to absolute space. As before, the third step consists in arguing that the believer in absolute space can give no account of what it is to judge the content selected at step 1 from judging the content selected at step 2.

If there were experimental setups that permitted the measurement of absolute velocity, a speaker's reaction to the outcome of the experiment might perhaps be used to help determine which he means. But it is problematic whether there can be any such experiment. Consider, for instance, the Michelson and Morley experiment. Its outcome shows that there is no ether. But suppose the experiment had had the opposite outcome. Would this show that the apparatus was moving in absolute space? No, since on the conception of absolute space in question, the ether itself could be moving uniformly with respect to absolute space.[12] This problem with using an alternative outcome to the Michelson and Morley experiment to claim that hypotheses about absolute space are confirmable, and so derivatively can meet the Discrimination Principle, seems to generalize. Take any hypothesis to the effect that a certain measurable physical magnitude is a particular function of absolute velocity. It seems clear that whatever measurements are made, they would equally be predicted by the physical magnitude being the same function of velocity relative to a frame in uniform motion with respect to absolute space.[13] In sum, it is in the nature of the way in which absolute space is conceived that it seems impossible to give a satisfactory answer to the question of what it is to mean absolute location rather than something else. So again, if the Discrimination Principle is correct, then the conception of space that allows the intelligibility of absolute location is illegitimate.

8.4   Executing the Deflationary Tactic

The other way of carrying out the reductio strategy is by executing the *deflationary tactic*. In executing it, I consider two competing descriptions of the nature of mastery of the spurious hypothesizer's problematic conception. The deflationary description characterizes the nature of mastery of the spurious hypothesizer's concepts without any use of the problematic conception that the hypothesizer claims to exercise. The challenge it presents to the spurious hypothesizer is to say why possession of his conception comes to anything more than is given in the deflationary description. The challenge once again relies on the Discrimination Principle. The spurious hypothesizer will be violating that principle if he cannot adequately distinguish between judging the contents he claims to grasp and judging a content whose possession can be described in deflationary terms.

The deflationary tactic can be applied to Chisholm's attitude to the fission of persons. Chisholm insists that he knows what it is for one postoperative person rather than the other to be the original person, even in a perfectly symmetrical case. Here the deflationary description is that Chisholm is simply someone who agrees with our judgements of identity in more normal cases and then additionally insists in the fission case on endorsing the content "It is determinately true or determinately false that Lefty is the original person; and the same holds for Righty." ("Determinately" is present to emphasize that this theorist takes truth to distribute over alternation.) There does not seem to be anything beyond such insistence to possessing the conception Chisholm claims to have. Chisholm would say, by contrast, that he knows what it is for Lefty rather than Righty to be the original person, even in the case of perfect symmetry, and that he draws on this knowledge in asserting, "It is determinately true or false that Lefty is the original person." According to the deflationary description of Chisholm's mastery, there is no such knowledge, for there is nothing to be known. The proponent of the deflationary description will find no feature of Chisholm's judgements containing the notion of personal identity that can be explained only on the supposition that he has such knowledge.

The deflationary description concerns the concepts a person exercises. In applying the deflationary form of the reductio strategy, we in no way exclude the possibility of mastery of concepts of irreducible properties and relations. For example, nothing in the present treatment of perfect fission excludes the coherence of agreeing that Chisholm's conception is illegitimate but insisting that the identity of persons is not reducible to any notions that do not tacitly presuppose the relation of personal identity. Concepts of irreducible properties and relations are not excluded, provided there exists an account of possession of these concepts that respects the Discrimination Principle. I have been arguing only that Chisholm's conception of personal identity does not meet this condition.

A similar deflationary tactic would be appropriately applied against a theorist who accepts both of these statements: (1) that current physical theory is true and genuinely indeterministic, and (2) that nevertheless the counterfactual "If that lump of uranium were placed on this tray, it would emit an alpha particle" is determinately true or false. The theorist in question insists on the determinate truth or falsehood of the counterfactual even when it is not actually on the tray and not actually emitting an alpha particle. This theorist's evaluation of counterfactuals can agree with ours in more ordinary cases. Again, it seems that there is no more to having the conception this theorist claims to possess than understanding counterfactuals in the same way as the rest of us in more normal cases, together with an additional willingness to assert, "It is determinately true or determinately false that if the uranium were placed on this tray, it would emit an alpha particle." So again, if this theorist insists that his conception goes beyond what is picked out by this deflationary description, he will be failing to respect the Discrimination Principle. I will return to counterfactuals in the last section of this chapter.

Though they both play a role in the reductio strategy, the contents and descriptions considered in executing the switching and deflationary tactics do not have the same status. The alleged contents considered in the switching case are framed in terms of notions, or presuppose particular conceptions, that are rejected if the *reductio* succeeds. So if it does succeed, they are no more genuine than their purported rivals. But a deflationary description draws only on our actual concepts.

The reductio strategy is concerned with constitutive questions that the spurious hypothesizer seems at a loss to answer. It is only fair to note, though, that the argument has an open-ended character and is not simply demonstrative. The open-ended character results from the negative existential that there is no way for the spurious hypothesizer to answer the question of what it is to be judging one of the two selected contents rather than the other. We may have seen that some answers are unavailable to him, but I have not strictly proved that he can give nothing better.

8.5   Indeterminacy and Internal Collapse

Many spurious hypotheses contain a term with a problematic reference. Some of them refer to absolute locations, others to persons or properties of experience conceived of in ways that, I have been arguing, violate the Discrimination Principle. However, not all spurious hypotheses involve a problematic subsentential reference: the counterfactual about the uranium has impeccable subsentential references. It is important that the Discrimination Principle is more general than any that confines its attention merely to subsentential reference. Nevertheless, in this section I want to consider in more detail the structure of the special cases in which the spuriousness of a hypothesis does derive from a problematic subsentential reference. This will also allow me to consider the relation between the Discrimination Principle and indeterminacy.

Certain alleged indeterminacies of reference result in a violation of the Discrimination Principle. The sort of alleged failure of determinacy in question is that in which all of the assertions a thinker is prepared to make involving the problematic expression, together with the relations of his uses of it to the world and to others' uses of it, fail to determine its reference, under his conception of possible referents. What this means is that we can draw on features of the thinker's (alleged) conception to construct an argument for such indeterminacy of reference. When there is this sort of indeterminacy, we can execute the switching tactic and argue that the Discrimination Principle is violated.

In at least some cases it is possible to give a sharper and more formal sense in which a spurious hypothesis is liable to internal collapse. In explaining this sense, I use Field's (1974) notion of partial denotation. When a term in a given language has no unique denotation (or extension), we can still say that it partially denotes each of the objects, properties, or magnitudes between which its denotation in the ordinary sense is indeterminate. Thus we can say that Newton's term "mass" partially denoted rest mass and partially denoted gravitational mass. A sentence is then said to be true (outright) if it comes out true under every assignment of legitimate partial denotations for its terms. Newton's statements of the form "Mass is thus and so" are true outright if both rest mass and gravitational mass are thus and so. There are further refinements that can be introduced, but this is all I need here.

Now consider an alleged language L that can be used to formulate sentences violating the Discrimination Principle, and suppose that these violations are all traceable to the presence of some problematic term T. Suppose, in particular, that on the conception of the objects, magnitudes, and properties that L is supposed to express, it is indeterminate what T denotes. In a partial-denotation semantics for sentences of L, suppose that we *allow* T to partially denote objects, properties, or magnitudes of the problematic kind. Consider those sentences of L that are free of logical constants and are true (outright) under the Field-style semantics, i.e., true under all partial denotations. Then in the cases I want to consider, all such sentences are necessarily equivalent to conditions making no reference to the problematic object, property, or magnitude.

An example of such a case would be that in which some relational term supposedly denotes absolute location in space. Take, for instance, the sentence **s**: "The distance between the locations of objects **a** and **b** is constant over the interval of time from t_1 to t_2." To simplify the discussion, I will also assume that our physics is Newtonian. As between different assignments of alleged absolute locations to objects, the assigned locations of **a** and **b** at any given time will vary. But if the distance between the locations of **a** and **b** is constant in the interval between t_1 and t_2 under any one such assignment, it is constant under all. Sentence **s** is equivalent to a condition mentioning only relative locations over time, not absolute location. So if **s** is true outright (or false outright), we can say what makes it true (or false) without mentioning the problematic absolute locations of objects. The point generalizes. Consider a language containing a term **T** for alleged absolute location, and fix on the sentences free of logical constants that are true outright under the Field-style semantics. Each such sentence is necessarily equivalent to contents mentioning only relative location, velocity, or acceleration. This gives a sense in which for these sentences, alleged absolute location drops out as irrelevant to their truth or falsity.[14] (We can "divide through" by absolute location.) It is fair to call this a case of internal collapse precisely because the alleged relation of absolute location was not excluded as one of the partial denotations of **T**. It would be a conjecture for further investigation that in every case in which the Discrimination Principle is violated because of some problematic subsentential term, there is internal collapse in this more precise sense.

Does the Discrimination Principle simply beg the question against the inscrutability of reference and against the indeterminacy of interpretation more generally? If there is inscrutability of reference, I follow that part of Field's argument that says that the response to apparent indeterminacy should be the development of a semantics using partial denotation. Consider a sentence containing a term whose reference is inscrutable. There is then nothing indeterminate about the condition that the sentence be true under all legitimate assignments of partial denotations. This is its absolute, unrelativized truth condition. This absolute truth condition may or may not have a simple equivalent free of semantical vocabulary. Whether it does or not, it is uniquely fixed once the range of partial denotations is fixed. We are not, contrary to the Discrimination Principle, left with some other condition from which it has not been adequately distinguished as the truth condition for the given sentence. Maybe we might be left with some such other condition if the range of legitimate partial denotations were itself indeterminate. But the examples and arguments for indeterminacy have not gone that far.[15]

There is a more charitable way of construing the objection that the Discrimination Principle begs the question against indeterminacy. Perhaps what the objector has in mind are treatments of semantic indeterminacy on which the theorist makes what is, as far as semantic constraints go, an arbitrary choice of one interpretation scheme over another. Davidson, for instance, favors this approach. He holds that where there is inscrutability of reference, an interpreter has the choice of regarding the speaker as speaking either one of at least two different languages (1984, 239–240). But, the objection may continue, if there are two equally good interpretation schemes attributing different contents to a given sentence, surely we cannot accept that the Discrimination Principle holds for those two contents. For could not anything that genuinely says what it is for one rather than the other to be the content of an attitude also be used to choose between the two interpretation schemes?

Presumably it could. But insofar as, for one practical reason or another, we make a semantically arbitrary choice between the competing schemes, we should not regard the content attributed by either one as giving that sentence's content. To make what is agreed to be a semantically arbitrary choice and then to complain that the Discrimination Principle is incompatible with the resulting attributions is somewhat similar to recognizing the physical arbitrariness of using degrees Farenheit rather than Centigrade and then complaining that zero degrees Farenheit does not express the complete absence of any physical quantity.

8.6 Links and Consequences

The Discrimination Principle is linked with several other doctrines in the theory of content. In some cases it is the ground of the other doctrine; in others it determines the range in which the doctrine applies. Again, I will consider three examples.

First, the principle is one of the grounds of the communicability of content. By "the communicability of content" I mean the possibility, for any particular content, of knowing that a subject is judging that content. Communicability in this (partially stipulative) sense is to be distinguished from a thinker's ability to judge the very same content as someone else. As we know from the theory of demonstrative thought, there is a relatively unproblematic sense in which you cannot judge what another does when he judges the first-person content "I am hungry." If you employ the first-person way of thinking, you will be referring to yourself, not to him. All the same, you can still know *what* he judges, even if you cannot judge it yourself.[16]

I have formulated and defended the Discrimination Principle quite independently of considerations relating to language and communication. But the principle, originally formulated simply in terms relating to the theory of content, seems to be a necessary condition for the communicability of content. This can be established by contraposition. Suppose that there is a judgeable content for which there is no account that respects the Discrimination Principle. Then there are distinct contents p and q for which there exists no adequately individuating account of what distinguishes judging that p from judging that q. How in these circumstances can the content p be communicable? A content is communicable only if one person can know that another is judging it. In the given circumstances, one could not come to know, for instance, that someone is judging p rather than q by discovering that his practice displays features constitutive of judging p but not of judging q. Ex hypothesi, there are no such distinguishing features. Could there then perhaps be something explained by someone's judging p that would not be explained by this judging q? Under the conditions we are supposing, this too seems problematic. Take what is allegedly explained by his judging p. Is it constitutive of judging p that it explain that consequence? If it is, it will equally be such a constitutive feature of judging q, so this case will not help toward knowing the difference. On the other hand, suppose the consequence is not constitutively linked with the identity of p. Then the explanation of the consequence will rely on some further empirical feature. For instance, let the consequence be that the subject believes that r, so that the further feature might be the subject's conditional belief "If p, r." But then the belief "If q, r" would equally explain the consequence that the subject believes that r. The general problem is that good reasons for distinguishing a psychological state involving the content that p from one involving the content that q always seem to trace back ultimately to constitutive differences between judging that p and judging that q. There are no such differences if p and q violate the Discrimination Principle. It seems, then, that if there were a content for which the Discrimination Principle fails, it would have to be incommunicable.

The argument just sketched has no commitment to verificationism. In Dummett's writings, communicability is often linked with verificationism or with falsificationism (see Dummett 1978b, 218–225). Dummett argued that communicability requires that meaning be determined by use and that no realistic truth-conditional theory of meaning could conform to the principle that use determines meaning. Of course, I disagree with Dummett about that second step. But this discussion of the first link of the Discrimination Principle should point up my agreement with something close to his first step. His first step is that communicability requires a form of the manifestation requirement for meaning. If the Discrimination Principle captures what is defensible in a manifestation requirement, the arguments I have given commit me to the correctness of a defensible version of Dummett's first step.

The Discrimination Principle is, secondly, linked with several forms of the private-language argument. This is to be expected. For any communicable content, there must be an account of it that respects the Discrimination Principle, and formulations of the private-language argument are characteristically concerned to attack the conception of incommunicable content the private linguist endorses. At first blush, however, the various strands of the private-language argument seem to appeal to diverse and not obviously related considerations. I suggest that they can each be taken as tracing out various consequences of a violation of the Discrimination Principle.

The private-language argument is sometimes elaborated by saying that there is no criterion for a correct application of the vocabulary distinctive of a private language. Here the link with the Discrimination Principle is that if there were such criteria, the supposed contents the private linguist introduces would not violate the principle.

Again, it is emphasized in the polemic against the private linguist that a mere impression that there is a rule one is trying to follow and that one is following it correctly does not suffice to ensure that these things are so. This point too will be endorsed if we accept the Discrimination Principle. An impression that there is a content that a form of words expresses and that it is correct to judge the content is far from ensuring that there really is a content fulfilling the requirements of the Discrimination Principle.

As another example, consider those readings that emphasize the preconceptual character of the private states and events in which the private linguist believes (Rorty 1980, McDowell 1989). The private linguist is reduced to inarticulacy:

What reason have we for calling "**S**" the sign for a *sensation*? For "sensation" is a word of our common language, not of one intelligible to me alone. So the use of this word stands in need of a justification which everybody understands.—And it would not help either to say that it need not be a *sensation;* that when he writes "**S**," he has *something*—and that is all that can be said. "Has" and "something" also belong to our common language.—So in the end when one is doing philosophy one gets to the point where one would like just to emit an inarticulate sound. (Wittgenstein 1958, 261)

If the Discrimination Principle is correct, all genuine contents and concepts must conform to it. The private linguist is reduced to inarticulacy because he cannot use any genuine concepts to characterize the crucial properties of what is designated in a private language.

The link between the principle and the private-language argument further emphasizes the fact that that argument need not be taken as a verificationist polemic. The Discrimination Principle rules out the possibility of a private language; the Discrimination Principle does not entail verificationism; so arguments against a private language need not commit one to verificationism.[17]

The third link of the Discrimination Principle is with Dummett's principle (C):

Dummett's Principle (C)   If a statement is true, there must be something in virtue of which it is true. (Dummett 1976, 89)

Contrary to first appearances, this does not mean that Dummett holds that each statement of whatever kind is true in virtue of statements of some other kind. Dummett acknowledges a category of barely true statements, those that are not true in virtue of statements of some other kind. His real position is that certain sorts of statements conform to (C).

In Dummett's thought, (C) is closely connected with principle (K):

Principle (K) If a statement is true, it must in principle be possible to know that it is true.

Indeed, he holds that statements conforming to (C) must conform to (K) (more strictly, he holds that those failing (K) must also fail (C)): "If it were in principle impossible to know the truth of some statement, how could there be anything which *made* that statement true?" (Dummett 1976, 99). I will argue that (C) does not in fact entail (K) and that in at least some cases the rationale for holding that a particular sort of statement conforms to (C) is given not by verificationism but by the Discrimination Principle. But first I need to sharpen a term of the discussion.

Dummett (1976, 94) gives the following definition:

Definition A class **M** of statements *reduces* to a class **R** just in case for any statement **A** in **M**, there is a family **A′** of sets of statements in **R** such that **A** is true iff all the members of some set in **A′** are true.[18]

Dummett says that knowledge of the truth condition of a statement is not problematic when the statement, if true, has a nontrivial reduction class.

That last statement about unproblematic grasp ought not to be Dummett's official position. The definition of reducibility allows the family **A′** of sets to be infinite and also allows members of the family to be infinite. So in the sense of the definition, both classical universal quantifications and classical existential quantification can be true in virtue of suitably chosen families formed from their instances, and thus reduced to their instances. Reflection on this also casts doubt on the argument that (C) entails (K). It suggests an answer to the question, "If it were in principle impossible to know the truth of some statement, how could there be anything that made that statement true?" The answer would be that what makes the statement true is the truth of all members of some set in a family of statements, where it is not possible, even in principle, that all members of the set can be known by just one person. That is the natural answer in the case of universal quantification. Of course, this may show only that Dummett's characterization of reducibility does not capture his intuitive notion of true-in-virtue-of. Perhaps on a different formal characterization (C) would entail (K). But what I want to consider, without altering the definition of reducibility, are nonverificationist principles to the effect that a given class of statements conforms to Dummett's (C).

Such nonverificationist principles are linked with the Discrimination Principle as follows. The Discrimination Principle helps to constrain the location of the boundary between contents that conform to (C) and those that do not, that is, those that can be barely true.

Definition   A statement is *barely true* if it is true but the only class of statements to which it can be reduced already contains it or trivial variants of it. (Dummett 1976, 94)

Consider counterfactuals. We can make sense of someone's judgement of a counterfactual being influenced by the categorical ground of the counterfactual, if he knows it to be such. His judgements may also be influenced by the evidence for a counterfactual. But if a counterfactual can be barely true, it can be true without being categorically grounded and without indirect evidence for it. What is it for a thinker to grasp a counterfactual content that can be true even in this case? It cannot involve his being rationally influenced in his judgements by the coun-terfactual's being true (which is arguably how he grasps barely true observational contents), for it seems that the truth of a counterfactual cannot itself cause anything to be the case. If we speak as if it could, that is only a *façon de parler* to cover the case in which its ground is causally influential. It is for just this collection of reasons that we were forced earlier into applying the deflationary strategy to the thinker who believes in the bare truth of the counterfactual about the uranium. A case could equally be made that true and suitably unrestricted univer-sal quantifications cannot themselves be causally influential either. But it does not matter if they cannot, since plausible accounts of mastery of them do not require them to be so. An account on which their truth conditions are determined by certain of their commitments, such as I gave earlier for arithmetical quantification, is necessarily one on which, when the quantification is true, it is not barely so, on Dum-mett's definition. But the believer in the bare truth of counterfactuals is committed to the *non*existence of any such reduction. No such analogy with the quantifiers can help him.

8.7 Summary and Prospect

In this chapter I have argued that various spurious hypotheses exceed the limits of intelligibility. By drawing on a theory of concepts that sustains the Discrimination Principle, we can argue, without any commitment to verificationism, that there cannot be concepts for which the spurious hypotheses are true. But it is not only in respect of the contents of thought that we can be subject to illusions. I believe that we can also be subject to philosophical illusions about the nature and content of subjective experience, and indeed much else. The argument of this chapter has proceeded by identifying constraints on legitimate contents of thought and employing them to explain why certain hypotheses are spurious. I hope that a comparable strategy of charting the limits of the intelligible by reference to a constitutive philosophical theory will prove equally effective in dispelling other illusions to which we may succumb.

Appendix A: Conceptual Role and Aiming at the Truth

In note 9 of chapter 4, I said that there is a connection between the relational property required of a belief state if it is to have a particular content and the fact that belief aims (no doubt among other things) at truth. The purpose of this appendix is to spell out the connection.

To that end I introduce the notion of a way in which a thought can have a truth value. More precisely, we ought to speak of ways in which, relative to a given thinker, a thought can have a truth value, but for brevity I will suppress this relativization. A *way in which a thought can have a truth value* is given by a series (or tree) of selections, one selection being made for each conceptual component of the thought. What is selected is a clause (or a set of clauses) of the possession condition for the given conceptual component. Strictly, it will become clear, we should say that one selection is to be made for each occurrence of a conceptual constituent in a thought. One and the same concept may have many occurrences in a thought, and in some cases different selections of clauses of its possession condition may be made for each of its separate occurrences in the thought.

The way in which a thought has its actual truth value is fixed as follows. Start with some innermost conceptual constituent of the thought. Let us suppose that it is a singular mode of presentation. Consider its possession condition. Does this possession condition have more than one clause or not? If it has only one, select it. If it has more than one, select the clause in virtue of which, as things actually are, the conceptual component has its semantic value. Here I am presupposing the account of how semantic value is determined from possession conditions given in chapters 1 and 5. For any given possession condition, a determination theory says how semantic value is fixed from that condition together with the world. So, for instance, suppose that the singular mode of presentation is a recognitionally based concept of an individual. Its possession condition will then come in two parts, one treating thoughts in which an object is presented to the thinker in the way required to activate the recognitional capacity at the time of the thought, the other treating the case of thoughts involving the singular concept when the object is not so presented at the time of the thought. If the referent of this singular recognitional concept is currently recognized, we select the clause of the possession condition dealing with that case; otherwise we select the other clause.

Now suppose that some monadic concept occurs in predicational combination with the singular concept in the given thought. In accordance with a determination theory, its possession condition will fix a function from objects to truth values. Consider in particular that component of the function that maps the referent of the singular concept onto a particular truth value. That the semantic value of the concept should map that object onto one truth value rather than another will again be grounded in a particular clause of the possession condition of the monadic concept. For that occurrence of the monadic concept, we then select that clause.

Now consider a logical constant, conjunction say. Suppose that it is applied to two thoughts that have the truth values true and false, respectively. The possession condition for conjunction contains three clauses, each corresponding to an instance of the standard introduction and elimination rules for conjunction that the thinker finds primitively compelling. A conjunction has the value false when the first of its constituents is true and the other false. This segment of the semantic value for conjunction is grounded in that clause of the possession condition that requires thinkers with the concept of conjunction to find inferences of the form

p and q
___
q

primitively compelling. For it is this clause that forces any conjunctive proposition for which conjunction is truth-preserving to have the value false when applied to two components which, taken in order, are true and false respectively. It is this clause because inferences of the displayed form can be truth-preserving only if the conjunction *p and q* takes the value false when *q* takes the value false.[1]

In a similar fashion, select for each constituent of the thought a clause (or set of clauses) of its possession condition.[2] The totality of such selections (formally, a tree of clauses, the tree corresponding to the tree structure of the thought) is the way in which the thought has its actual truth value. Generalizing once again, we can go on to form the idea of all the possible ways in which the thought may have a truth value, as determined from the possible semantic values of its constituents. Each of these ways will consist of a series or tree of clauses of possession conditions. If a thought has n constituents (in the sense of occurrences) and the number of clauses in the possession condition for the ith constituent is n_i, then an upper bound on the number of ways in which the thought can be true is the product of all the numbers n_i. (It may be less than this if concepts occur more than once or if we take into account the thought-theoretic analogue of Carnapian "meaning relations" between concepts.)

A fundamental commitment of this approach to content is that whenever a thought has a truth value, there is a way in which it does. If it appears that a thought could have a truth value without having it in one of these ways, that could only be because either the formulation of the possession conditions for its constituent concepts is inadequate or the determination theories have received an inadequate formulation. Allowing a thought to have a truth value without having it in one of these ways constitutes a violation of the Discrimination Principle, the principle that there must be an account that distinguishes what is involved in judging a given content from judging any other content. To allow an alleged thought to have a truth value but not in one of these ways is to admit a thought with the objectionable property that there is no way of distinguishing judging it from judging a pared-down version of it, one that coincides with the alleged thought only when there is a way in which it has a truth value.

I can now put these ways to work. I suggest that when we derive the conditions for a belief to have a certain content in the way given in chapter 4, the resulting conditions systematically reflect the ways in which the content may have a truth value. For each way in which a content may have a truth value, there is also a corresponding condition required for a state to be a belief with that content. When I discussed the content *Lincoln Plaza is square* in section 4.3, the cases I considered—(L1) with (S1), (L1) with (S2), and so forth—each corresponded to ways in which the content may have a truth value, and conversely. The significance of this correlation lies in the fact that it is a foundation for an identity claim. One and the same thought meets two conditions. Semantically individuated, it is the thought built up from components that have certain semantic values under certain states of the world. Psychologically individuated, it is the thought to judge which is to stand in certain complex psychological relations. The techniques of chapter 4 and this appendix give a uniform means of fixing the psychological properties from the ways in which the thought may have a truth value, and conversely. The semantic and the psychological properties of the content are integrated.

Appendix B: Evans's Derivation of the Generality Constraint: A Comparison

This second appendix deals with issues arising from chapter 2. It is placed here in part because it presupposes material from chapters 1 through 6. Where not otherwise specified, page references in this appendix are to Evans 1982.

Evans's account of "how our thinking can conform to the Generality Constraint" (p. 111) rests on his descriptions of mastery of predicative concepts and singular concepts. He explains both kinds of mastery using the notions of the fundamental ground of difference of an object, and of a fundamental Idea of an object. The *fundamental ground of difference* of an object is "a specific answer to the question 'What differentiates that object from others?', of the kind appropriate to objects of that sort" (p. 107). Evans's view is that for every kind of object, there is a general answer to the question "What makes it the case that there are two objects of this kind rather than one (or three rather than two)?" (p. 106). Following Wiggins, he says, for instance, that what distinguishes a spatial object from all others at a given time is its location at the time, together with the fact that it is of a certain kind (Evans cites Wiggins 1968; see also Wiggins 1980). Evans holds that "any object whatever" has a fundamental ground of difference (p. 107). Using this apparatus, he introduces a *fundamental Idea* of a particular object: when one employs a fundamental Idea, "one thinks of [the object] as the possessor of the fundamental ground of difference which it in fact possesses" (p. 107). I follow Evans in using "δ" and variants thereof as variables over fundamental Ideas.

Consider a concept F, applicable to things of kind G. Evans holds that to possess F is to have knowledge that, when conjoined with knowledge that constitutes possession of a fundamental Idea δ^* of a particular G, yields knowledge of what it is for the proposition "δ^* is F" to be true. He calls this, "slightly inaccurately," knowledge of what it is for an arbitrary proposition of the form "δ is F" to be true.[1] Thoughts of the form "δ is F" thus have for Evans a more basic status than other predications containing the concept F. In the case of spatiotemporal objects, these points are modified in the natural way to accommodate relativization to a time. Let δ_t be a fundamental Idea that gives the fundamental ground of difference at time t of a particular object, and let F_t be the concept of being F at time t. Then, says Evans, in the first instance, to possess the concept of being F_t is to know what it is for arbitrary propositions of the form "δ_t [is] F_t" to be true, where the square brackets indicate a tenseless predication (p. 110).

Possession of a nonfundamental singular Idea a of a G is identified with knowledge of what it is for an arbitrary proposition of the form "$\delta = a$" to be true (pp. 109–110). This is in the context of a general conception according to which any thought involving the idea of a G's being F is conceived to be true, when it is true, in virtue of the truth of some proposition of the form "δ is F" (p. 109).

These claims then allow Evans a straightforward derivation of a form of the Generality Constraint (pp. 111–112). Suppose that the thinker has a singular concept c of an object of kind G and also possesses the concept F, true or false of G's. We are required to establish that the thinker knows what it is for "c is F" to be true. If c is a fundamental Idea of a G, the required conclusion follows immediately, because, on Evans's account, to possess F is to know what it is for an arbitrary predication involving a fundamental Idea to be true. If c is not a fundamental Idea, then the thinker knows what it is for "c is F" to be true because (1) he knows that it is true, if it is, in virtue of the truth of some pair of propositions of the form "$\delta = c$" and "δ is F," and (2) it follows from his possession of the concepts c and F that he knows what it is for such propositions to be true.

What is the relation between Evans's derivation, with its presuppositions, and the treatment of concepts in this book? The fact that Evans nowhere in the derivation uses the idea of a possession condition and employs throughout the notion of knowing what it is for something to be true should not lead us to suppose that his approach and mine are necessarily incompatible theoretical options. For first, Evans is very clear that the notion of knowing what it is for something to be true is in urgent need of elaboration, particularly for those opposed to verificationism (p. 106). A theory making use of possession conditions may be just what is needed for such elaboration. And second, I have emphasized that a possession condition for a predicative concept must adequately ground the description of one who possesses it as knowing what it is for the concept to be true of an arbitrary object, and I have also tried to say how the notion of knowing what it is for something to be the case can be sustained in a theory of possession conditions. The general form and apparatus of the two approaches, then, leaves open the question of their compatibility. The issue needs to be considered at the level of the detailed content of each approach.

Some features of some of the possession conditions considered in this book can indeed be seen as elaborating Evans's conception. Some of the possession conditions presented earlier have a clause with the property that judging in accordance with that clause requires, in the most basic case, making a fundamental identification of the object of predication. This is true, for instance, of the initial, perceptual clause of the possession condition for a relatively observational shape concept (see chapters 3 and 4). Judging in accordance with that clause involves identifying the object of predication in a perceptual-demonstrative way. In the most basic case, this provides an egocentric identification of the location of the object at the time of the judgement.[2] I also emphasized in earlier chapters that the other clauses of these possession conditions ride on the back of the perceptual clause: these other clauses make reference to experiences of the sort mentioned in the perceptual clause, but not vice versa. This gives a relatively clear sense in which for a concept with such a possession condition, a central place is given to grasp of predicational combination of the concept with what Evans would classify as a fundamental identification of the object.

This apparent underwriting of Evans's approach can be extended by two observations. First, the points just made can be applied more specifically to temporally relativized predications. The fundamental identification of an object employed when the thinker judges in accordance with the initial clause of the possession condition for an observational concept identifies its object in relation to the same time as that at which the perceptual concept is judged to apply to it. Second, some generalization is possible to more theoretical, nonobservational concepts. Insofar as these involve thinking of a property in terms of some complex explanatory relation to properties picked out by observational concepts, perceptual-demonstrative identification, and its attendant fundamental identifications in the basic case, will again play a central role.

In the case of abstract objects, there are also many examples in which judging in accordance with the possession condition for a concept true or false of abstract objects will require identifying the abstract object in one of Evans's fundamental ways. Mastery of the concept *prime,* true or false of natural numbers, will consist in knowledge of a decision procedure that can be applied only when the natural number in question is given in a way that locates its position in the series of natural numbers.

There is also arguably some convergence on the treatment of "*a* is *F,*" where *a* is not fundamental and *F* is a relatively observational concept. Both accounts offer a treatment of this case that involves some articulation. Evans treats the case as one in which the thinker knows that the proposition, if true, is true in virtue of some pair of propositions of the forms "*a* = δ" and "δ is *F.*" I have said that in judging "*a* is *F,*" the thinker is committed in such a case to the referent having a property of some specified kind (shape in the case of shape concepts) that is the same as the property object is required to have if a thinker's judgement is to be correct in the circumstances of the perceptual clause of the possession condition (see chapters 4 and 6). At first sight these may seem to be very different and competing articulations, but such an impression is incorrect. On the one hand, a possession condition with two clauses of the sort proposed for perceptual concepts would hardly be tenable unless we can make some sense of the idea that the thing referred to by a nonfundamental singular mode of presentation can also be thought about by means of a fundamental Idea. (The discussion of referential coherence in chapter 6 relies on this fact.) On the other hand, it is questionable whether we can intelligibly attribute a nonfundamental Idea *a* of an object to a thinker unless on occasion he can reasonably judge or reject the proposition "*a* is *F,*" for concepts *F* he possesses.

So much for areas of agreement. There are other respects in which the account of this book is less demanding than that in *The Varieties of Reference.* Evans's treatment of concept possession relies on the general proposition that every object has some nontrivial fundamental ground of difference from all other objects. It also proposes particular grounds of difference for objects of particular kinds. His views on both matters could be disputed. Kripke and Johnston have suggested counterexamples to the view that a material object is individuated at any given time by its location and kind.[3] If they are right, Evans's views would need revision, though it is plausible that suitably modified versions of his doctrines could still be formulated. It would take us too far afield to pursue these fascinating issues, which lie mainly in metaphysics proper rather than in the theory of thought and content. What I do want to consider here very briefly is this question: if there are objects of a kind for which there are no significant fundamental grounds of difference, does that necessarily make thought about them problematic?

I suggest a negative answer to this question, and I will reason from the case of thought about particular times. It is plausible that there is no significant ground of difference for an individual moment of time. A time is indeed uniquely distinguished by its temporal relations to other times. But what is then the fundamental ground of difference for these other times? Our answers to these questions should not be circular when taken collectively. If we try to avoid circularity by not mentioning any individual time in the answers, it seems impossible to cite any fundamental ground of difference when we are concerned with an infinite series of times with no first and no last member. But this does not seem to make thought about, for instance, the present moment of time impossibly problematic. We can still give a possession condition for the present-tense way of thinking of a time. In combination with a possession condition for some particular concept F true or false of times, what will distinguish the present-tense way of thinking is that for any given time, the conditions for then judging or rejecting the content $F(now)$ as determined by the possession conditions concern the time at which the judgement is made. This condition can be met without there being any significant fundamental ground of difference for any particular time. This is as it should be for the purposes of the Generality Constraint. Even if there is no fundamental ground of difference for any particular time, it remains compelling that if a thinker knows what it is for "It is sunny" to be true and he possesses the concept *foggy,* then he knows what it is for "It is foggy" to be true. Absence of a fundamental ground of difference for times does not undermine such structural truths about conceptual content, nor would one expect it to do so under the Referential Explanation of chapter 2.

Notes

Chapter 1

1. For more discussion of properties, see Putnam 1970 and Wiggins 1984.

2. I am, though, committed to disagreeing with Jackendoff's further view that a mental representation can serve as the meaning of a linguistic expression (1989, 73 ff.). If "meaning" is used correlatively with "sense," meanings are the concepts expressed, not the mental representations of them. If it is used correlatively with "refer," we will want nonmental referents for concepts. On the relation between concepts and their referents, see section 2 below.

3. A relatively sophisticated thinker may find the principle of induction for natural numbers compelling. But I would argue that it does not need to be found primitively compelling for possession of the concept *all natural numbers*. Someone whose inferential practice is characterized by finding just the elimination inference primitively compelling, and nothing else essentially involving such quantification, may *work it out* that the principle of induction is correct for the notion he is employing. Here the considerations of section 3 below are relevant.

4. This treats only present-tense predications. A full account must deal with arbitrary modes of presentation of arbitrary moments of predication.

5. This is too simple in various respects, even if sensational properties are recognized. An object that emits ultraviolet light in which it looks red is not really red if it would not look so without the ultraviolet light. However, the complexities needed to take care of this (and other points) do not import circularity into the possession condition.

6. This rules out accounts in which $\mathcal{A}(C)$ contains "judges that . . . C . . . , and in fact C is the concept F."

7. These considerations in favor of a hierarchy of concepts are also connected with the applicability to mental states of a classification involving concepts considered abstract objects. See section 4.4, the second point.

8. When it is not a specific theory but a theory type that enters the possession condition for a concept, we will have an extra layer of quantification. For instance, in the possession condition for the concept *mechanical force,* it might be required only that there is some relation of a certain kind in which that magnitude is thought by the possessor of the concept to stand to the magnitudes of mass and acceleration. David Lewis's exposition of a functional definition provides a clear structural model for the treatment of the technicalities of individuating a particular concept when it is a member of a local holism. See Lewis 1980, 1983a.

9. For an excellent discussion of these cases and their consequences, see Sainsbury 1990.

10. For a penetrating discussion of Wittgenstein's insight, see particularly Pears 1988. This insight does not exhaust the positive content of Wittgenstein's claims about rule following. See further the discussion of the Ratification Thesis in chapter 7.

11. The main point of this paragraph seems to me to apply to part of the position developed by Philip Pettit in 1990. In a move highly congenial to the position I have been developing, he argues that which rule someone is following depends in part on his inclinations in favorable circumstances to go in a certain way from initial examples. But apparently not distinguishing there between a theory of concepts and a theory of properties, he concludes that properties in general display "a relativity to our species"; "properties are in a certain sense relative to our kind" (p. 17). I discuss below the relation of other aspects of Pettit's position to the one I am elaborating (see section 7.2). I should note that Pettit's views have altered (see Pettit 1991).

12. For a discussion of intrinsic properties, see Lewis 1986a.

13. For some necessary further discussion and refinements of this method of fixing the classical truth function, see my 1987 and 1991b papers. If it is held that the semantic values of complete thoughts are entities structured along the lines of Barwise and Perry 1983, the semantic value must correspond to the classical truth function in equally guaranteeing preservation of truth for the inferences.

14. Prior 1967. Elsewhere I have argued that only verificationists can object to *tonk* on the grounds that it nonconservatively extends a deducibility relation. See Peacocke 1987.

15. See in particular section 8.3, "Executing the Switching Tactic."

16. Dummett 1981, especially chapter 3. The conception is also in Dummett's earlier writings (see Dummett 1973, 229–240). Of course, Dummett is sympathetic to antirealistic conceptions of conceptual content. But as I emphasized above, the requirement that a determination theory exist for each concept applies to both realistic and antirealistic conceptions. When Dummett identifies grasping a sense with knowing the condition for something to be its semantic value and then gives that in turn an antirealistic construal, that should not be regarded as disputing the requirement that a determination theory exist for each concept. On the contrary, he accepts the requirement. My disagreement with Dummett is not over his first step in identifying grasping the sense but with the second step, which gives it an antirealistic elaboration.

17. Burge (1979) explicitly applies his argument to the case of misunderstanding the range of a color word on pp. 81–82.

18. For a relatively recent statement, see Putnam 1988, chapter 2, especially p. 29.

19. The whole topic of deference dependence merits extensive independent discussion.

20. "Suppose . . . one were concerned to construct a correspondence theory that required that there were *facts* that were language independent in just the way that propositions are supposed to be. Then one would take no comfort in the utterly pleonastic sense of 'fact' that enabled one to move back and forth between 'Michele is funny' and 'It's a fact that Michele is funny'" (Schiffer 1987, 51).

21. I have been arguing that there is a species of propositional attitudes that consist of relations to structured contents built up from concepts in my sense. I have also been saying that not all meaningful English words express concepts. The question then arises of how we succeed in attributing the species of propositional attitudes in question with English sentences. It would take us too far off the main course to pursue this here. For an attractive treatment whose main ideas mesh well with the approach offered here, see Crimmins and Perry 1989.

22. I do not pretend that the $\mathcal{A}(C)$ form gives us an adequate theory of our knowledge of what others mean by their words and of their propositional attitudes, and part of McDowell's objection to Dummett concerns the epistemology of meaning. The $\mathcal{A}(C)$ form and particular possession conditions are intended to address questions of the type, What is it to mean this rather than that? rather than those of the form, How is it possible to know what another person means? Certainly answers to questions of the first sort must not make impossible answers to those of the second, epistemological sort. But it does not seem plausible that the correct epistemology of meaning would undermine the possession condition for conjunction displayed earlier or the "commitment" account of universal quantification over natural numbers outlined above. As far as I know, no one at present has a satisfactory epistemology of meaning; one is urgently needed.

23. That McDowell understands his subjectivism in a way that excludes the apparent possibility discussed here is suggested by his criticism of Nagel for espousing a realism about subjective states that allows there to be subjective facts completely beyond our reach (1986, n. 26).

24. Of course, there could be accounts of possession conditions that impose restrictions relating to subjectivity analogous to those stated by McDowell. There would not then be a divergence between such a possession-condition theory and a subjectivist interpretational theory (or not for the reasons in question, anyway). But I would equally doubt whether such a restricted theory of possession conditions is reconcilable with a plausible realistic account of mathematical and scientific concepts and properties.

Chapter 2

1. It may be possible to regard this position as one in which tacit knowledge of the semantic significance of predicational combination is attributed to the thinker. The content of the tacit knowledge is this:

An arbitrary thought of the form Ft is true (or perhaps is mapped to *true* by the semantic value of F) just in case the referent of t falls under the concept F.

Attribution of such tacit knowledge would certainly allow the derivation of the Generality Constraint. Such an approach would need to respect the point that the content of tacit knowledge is not conceptualized in this instance. This is so for two reasons. First, any attribution of propositional knowledge, whether tacit or not, including that just displayed, will presuppose some grasp of the semantic significance of predicational combination. Since some grasp of it is presupposed in the very propositional content that is tacitly known, the attribution of a piece of propositional knowledge can never fully elucidate all grasp of predicational combination. However, if the content of what is tacitly known is not conceptualized by the thinker, there need not be any threat of infinite regress here. What is explained by the attributed tacit knowledge is grasp of the significance of predicational combination at the level of conceptual content. The second reason concerns the concept of reference. If the content of the tacit knowledge were conceptual, it would be highly problematic whether a possession condition for the concept of reference could ever be written. If grasping thoughts containing the concept of reference involves knowing what it is for them to be true and if this in turn involves the displayed propositional knowledge, which presupposes possession of the concept of reference, then we have a circle in the explanation of possession of the concept of reference. It is certainly not tempting to exempt the concept of reference from the demands of the $\mathcal{A}(C)$ form. For more on the relations between tacit knowledge and the absence of conceptualization, see Davies 1989.

2. Contrast the explanation given in Campbell 1986. For a comparison with Evans's explanation of the Generality Constraint, see appendix B at the end of this book.

3. On sortals, see Wiggins 1980. The restriction to sortals is necessary; otherwise the concept *object* would trivialize the criterion.

4. Dummett (1976, 94) defines "barely true" this way: "A statement is barely true if it is true but there is no class of statements, not containing it or trivial variants of it, to which any class containing it can be reduced." This criterion can be accepted whatever one takes the significant notions of reduction to be.

5. Fodor's view is that "it's about as empirical as anything can be whether [the minds of animals] are systematic" (1987, 153). But it is worth noting that elsewhere in *Psychosemantics* Fodor endorses views that nudge one in the direction of the necessity of the Generality Constraint. He insists that to grasp a content, one must possess its conceptual constituents (1987, 92, in discussion of Stich's views). He also links understanding a proposition with "having some idea of what it would be" for it to be true (1987, 55). It seems unlikely that this idea of "what it would be like" could be elucidated without relying on the element of generality in the concepts from which the content is built up.

6. If the Generality Constraint is necessary, that in no way preempts arguments that concept possession can be realized only in a creature that possesses a language of thought. Consistent with what I have said, Fodor's conclusions may be true, even if the Generality Constraint is not an empirical principle. For an important and relatively a priori argument for a language of thought drawing essentially on the resources developed in this book, see Davies 1991.

7. This passage need not be taken as Pears speaking for himself; it could be merely a statement of Wittgenstein's position.

8. There is a special problem in the early Wittgenstein's thought that makes my resolution unavailable to him. Since he recognized no level of sense, there is for him nothing for a theory of grasp to be a theory *of*. One cannot plausibly say it is a theory of the nature of the objects referred to. Though Wittgenstein shows signs of slipping into this, the issues here clearly concern grasp, rather than objects on the level of reference. If Wittgenstein were to introduce different relations to objects at the level of reference, he would be introduction senses by the rear door: different senses would correspond to different relations to a given object.

9. I am indebted to Martin Davies for drawing my attention to Fisher 1974. Fisher's main concern is knowledge of the rules of language. He develops the theory that knowing a rule of language is not propositional knowledge, by which he means that it does not consist in knowing any proposition about the rule. But he goes on to suggest that, more generally, such nonpropositional knowledge "seems to be essentially involved . . . in what it is to have a concept" (p. 254) and to suggest that this knowledge of rules must be nonpropositional, on pain of infinite regress (pp. 254–255). My work, if right, can be regarded as a vindication and theoretical elaboration of these points, with satisfaction of a possession condition playing the role of Fisher's "non-propositional rule knowledge."

10. "Sub-personal theories proceed by analyzing a person into an organization of subsystems . . . and attempting to explain the behavior of the whole person as the outcome of the interaction of these subsystems" (Dennett 1978, 153).

11. It may be tempting to add that while the semantic information is in the content of a subdoxastic state, a thinker's satisfaction of a possession condition is not a subdoxastic state. I think it is right to succumb to this temptation in the case of semantic information. But the contrast with satisfaction of the possession condition involves some delicate issues. As far as I know, current use of the label "subdoxastic" traces back to Stephen Stich, who picked out subdoxastic states as those that "play a role in the proximate causal history of beliefs, though they are not beliefs themselves" (1978, 499). On my account, satisfying a possession condition for a concept should not be regarded as standing in a propositional-attitude relation to a propositional content at all, and a fortiori it is not a case of having a belief. I have also said that a thinker's satisfaction of a possession condition does play a role in the proximate causal history of some beliefs. So, to take the quoted definition literally, satisfying a possession condition is a subdoxastic state after all, according to the account I am developing. There is, though, a strong and, I think, sound intuition that what this shows is that the definition does not capture fully certain intuitions that make us want to call some states subdoxastic. To draw all the distinctions needed here, we need to use a notion I introduce later, that of a *subrational* state (see section 7.1).

Chapter 3

1. On some construals, propositional content is given by a type of possible worlds, a *world type*. On these construals, correctness of attitudes with these contents is also a

matter of instantiation by the actual world of this world type. As the reader will surmise, my view, like those of any broadly neo-Fregean writer, is that the arguments against an instantiation model for the content of propositional attitudes are much stronger than any against such a treatment of a basic level of perceptual content.

2. However, the time at which the mental representation underlying the experience is computed may bear a complex relation to the time represented in the content of the experience. See Dennett 1991, chapters 5 and 6.

3. There are other theoretical decisions to be taken in developing this account of scenario content. One such decision is whether the positioned scenario should be a content that involves individual objects having surface properties, being in a certain direction from the subject's body, and so forth, or whether this content should not involve particular objects but should rather be taken as existentially quantified. Important issues in epistemology and the philosophy of mind are linked with this decision. For present purposes, I am concerned only with acknowledging the level of the scenario and a corresponding notion of correctness: both of these alternatives do so.

4. For further discussion of closely related issues, see Campbell 1987, esp. 281 ff.

5. Palmer points out to me that these two figures trace back to Kopfermann 1930 and that the right-hand figure is sometimes referred to as a "Kopfermann square."

6. "People perceive different geometrical properties of the figure when it is seen as a square rather than as a diamond" (Palmer 1983, 293). Palmer's paper contains further material of great relevance to a philosophical theory of these matters.

7. Points corresponding to those made in note 3 above about scenario content apply equally to protopropositional content. A theory of protopropositional content could be developed according to which the protopropositional content is existentially quantified, rather than involving particular objects; or again, and perhaps equivalently, the theory could be developed so that the content is given by a propositional function. What matters for present purposes is that all these choices involve the notion of a property, as well as something involving predicational structure, as a constituent of the relevant level of representational content.

8. Consider the difference between an experience in whose positioned scenario a region has a certain property and one that additionally has in its protopropositional content that the region has that property. In the latter case we seem to have the property that intuitively lies behind one case of what Dretske (1981) calls "digitalization." Further investigation of the case should lead to a better understanding of digitalization.

9. This discussion revises the treatment of this example given in *Sense and Content* (Peacocke 1983). DeBellis (forthcoming) and Tye (1985, 1991) also treat this example by using propositional contents. From the standpoint of my present approach, it has to be said that the treatment of *Sense and Content* involved an unholy alliance of the view that all representational content in perception is conceptual with a tendency in particular cases to suppose that nothing more is involved in perceptual-representational content than positioned scenario content.

10. Note also that a subject may have the capacity to perceive something as having the property STRAIGHT without having the ability to make a judgement with the conceptual content that an unperceived object is straight.

11. Protopropositional content also allows a satisfactory description of what is called "visual disorientation." Visually disoriented subjects are able to identify and apparently perceive the shape of objects in their environment without experiencing them as having any particular (egocentric) location. There is a readable case study in Godwin-Austen 1965. As Campbell (1989) notes, these cases show another respect in which we need to revise Evans's description (quoted in section 3.3) of perceiving something as square. For Evans's description apparently leaves no room for the possibility of experiencing

something as square without experiencing it as having a particular location. My account can accommodate the possibility at the level of protopropositional content. Even if edge e and edge e′ are not localized in the subject's perception, that perception can still have the protopropositional content that e IS PARALLEL TO e′. The same applies to protopropositional contents about the relations SYMMETRY and BEING AT A RIGHT ANGLE TO. But for something to be perceptibly square is to be defined in terms of these notions. I thus allow that something is perceived as square without being localized. This does not mean that scenario content drops out altogether from an account of what it is for an experience to have a protopropositional content containing a given property. Plausibly, such a subject must have some ability to use perceptual experiences in which instances of properties are localized to confirm or refute the represented instantiation that occurs without localization. (If this ability has disappeared altogether, attributions of perceptual identifications without localization will still be correct because there was once a connection with such abilities.)

12. Evans's position was that a perceptual-informational state with a nonconceptual content is an experience only if it serves as input to a "*thinking, concept-applying and reasoning system*" (1982, 158, Evans's italics). He regarded this as a "further link" of perceptual-informational states with nonconceptual content. He also said of the operation of the informational systems that include the perceptual systems that their operations are more primitive than those involving the "far more sophisticated cognitive state" of belief (p. 124), and he speculated that these more primitive operations may be carried out "in some phylogenetically more ancient part of the brain" (p. 158).

13. A question worth investigation is how the limb is given in this distinctive knowledge. It is certainly not descriptively conceptualized, as a particular finger might be conceptualized as the fourth finger on my left hand. On the way a particular finger is given in the content of the distinctive knowledge, it is potentially informative that it is the fourth on one's left hand. One supposition worth considering is that the way the finger is given in the distinctive knowledge is partially constituted by the fact that the intention (or subintention) to move the finger, thus given, from one place to another is one that, when things are working properly, results in that movement of that finger.

14. I should emphasize that subintentional states and acts in O'Shaughnessy's sense are not subpersonal in Dennett's sense. O'Shaughnessy's subintentional states are so characterized because their content is not fully conceptualized, but they occur at the personal level.

15. Perenin and Vighetto 1988, 661. See also p. 662: "None of the patients showed any significant motor, proprioceptive, visual field or visual space perception disturbances." My thanks to R. McCarthy for this reference.

16. McGinn indexes mental models with truth-evaluable propositions. If these propositions are built up from constituents solely at the level of reference, I would remarshal the arguments of section 3.2 to make a case that mental models deserve a more discriminating assignment of content. If the indexing propositions are at the level of sense, I would say that their constituents cannot be explained philosophically without mentioning scenario and protopropositional content. The assignment of these nonconceptual contents as contents of mental models is entirely within the spirit of McGinn's views.

17. The views expressed in this chapter have points of contact with other writings not already mentioned. In "Propositional Objects" (1969a, 147, 153–154), Quine emphasizes the need to provide some psychological states with contents that are neither conceptually nor linguistically individuated. More recently David Lewis states that the content of a visual experience is a set of possible individuals, "those possible individuals who, according to the content of his visual experience, he himself might be; they share just those properties he sees himself to have. These will mostly be relational properties:

properties of facing such-and-such an arrangement of nearby things" (1983b, 30). On Lewis's conception of possible individuals, a set of them is certainly not something linguistically or, in my sense, conceptually individuated. The relation of my own account to Lewis's merits extended discussion. Here I just note two major issues. First, Lewis attributes the same general kind of content (a set of possible individuals) to beliefs and desires as well as to perceptions. So one major issue is whether it is right to distinguish the kind of content enjoyed by perceptual states from those of the propositional attitudes. Second, while it is clear that every positioned scenario content is captured in Lewis's apparatus, that apparatus assigns no special status to the labeled axes and origins. I would argue that for an experience to have a correctness condition concerning, say, a particular direction in the real world, it is essential that it have a labeled origin and axes. It is, of course, open to Lewis to restrict the sets of possible individuals that may be contents of perception to take account of any such theses.

Chapter 4

1. To say that they cannot be fully expressed in language is not to say that they cannot be fully individuated by use of suitable language with the apparatus for making reference to the content of perceptual experience. They can be. But a statement of what fully individuates them does not, of course, have the same cognitive significance as the perceptual demonstratives themselves. Note also that the point in the text also rules out using the even simpler biconditional that the concept expressed by **A** = the concept expressed by **B** iff **A** and **B** are same-sensed.

2. Actually, on the positive account I offer in the text below, there will be true modalized biconditionals of the form "Necessarily, for any **M** and **M'**, the content of the belief **M** = the content of the belief **M'** iff ____ **M** ____ **M'** ____," where the blanks make no reference to concepts or thoughts. But the possibility of such modalized biconditionals is wholly parasitic on the account given below.

3. For an extremely clear description of this strategy, see Field 1989, 234. The strategy does not commit one to Field's more general views about truth in mathematics.

4. A corresponding proposal is available to those who, for various reasons, may prefer not to quantify over states. For them the proposal should be formulated thus: there is a relational property **R'** of the thinker, a relational property not involving relations to concepts or thoughts, such that (2) is equivalent to the conjunction that John has the relational property **R'** and the content that Lincoln Plaza is square is the unique content p such that necessarily, any thinker believes that p iff he has relational property **R'**.

5. Here I aim to give an individuating account of a recognitional way of thinking of an object by giving the condition for a thinker to possess it as a way of thinking of the object. The account is an account of the relation between the way of thinking and the object. This does not exclude the possibility of recognitionlike ways of thinking that fail to refer to anything. The possession condition for such a failing way of thinking will presumably be written by developing the point that for a thinker employing it, it is as if he were employing a mode of presentation that does refer. On this approach, though, the case in which the mode of presentation does refer is fundamental. The conditions of that case have to be used in elucidating the nonreferential case.

6. For a survey and extensive discussion of conceptual-role semantics, see Block 1986.

7. By way solely of clarifying the location of my position relative to others, I can say the following. The approach of this book does support, at the level of thought, a notion of "intersubjective synonymy." Quine's skepticism about synonymy is intimately related to his criticism of the analytic/synthetic distinction, the second dogma of empiricism

(1953). Fodor and LePore (1992) similarly argue that a notion of intersubjective synonymy must involve commitment to some form of the analytic/synthetic distinction. Acceptance of the theory of possession conditions as an account of concepts and content does indeed involve commitment to some analogue at the level of thought of the analytic/synthetic distinction. The fundamental commitment is to certain distinctive patterns of epistemic possibility and impossibility for someone who fully possesses a given set of concepts.

8. By the remarks early in section 3.4, the level at which no further conceptual elucidation is possible will itself be one involving a local holism.

9. The question arises of how the conditions for a belief to have a given content are related to the distinctive feature of belief that it aims at the truth. I have placed discussion of this in appendix A, as it involves terms of art, which would hold up the main discussion.

10. Field's postscript also reports David Lewis as discussing the comparison. Field's own favored solution involves taking "**x** believes that *p*" as equivalent to "There is a sentence or sentence analogue **s** such that **x** believes* **s** and **s** means that *p*." His solution does not involve positing propositions. Rather, he takes belief as a relation toward a meaningful sentence in a system of internal representation (1981, 98). Meaning for the sentential representations is given by a truth theory whose selection is sensitive only to the reference of the expressions in the sentences. This solution is unavailable to me. This is not because of a skepticism about systems of internal representation but because the approach will not capture differences of conceptual content unaccompanied by difference of reference. The above equivalence for "**x** believes that *p*" will serve my purposes only if "*p*" is taken as a variable over structured contents built up from concepts or modes of presentation, and then the equivalence will not address the metaphysical question with which this chapter opened. This is not meant as an argument against Field's stance—that would involve wider considerations about the notion of a concept and its role in explanation—but only a clarification of what is available to our respective positions.

11. "A fictionalist about mathematics-taken-at-face-value is someone who does not literally believe mathematical sentences, at least when they are taken at face value" (Field 1989, 2).

12. Schiffer's argument in the first four sections of "The Mode-of-Presentation Problem" (Schiffer 1990) is of this form.

13. It seems to me that the views developed so far in this book offer a blueprint for building an account of meaning and content that is a real alternative to the deflationary views developed, largely on ontological grounds, in Schiffer 1987. (Schiffer has other grounds too, of course.) Whether Schiffer's ontological physicalism is an obstacle to the claims of chapter 4 is a more complex issue. In *Remnants of Meaning* he does not consider whether the ontological physicalism he there endorses is consistent with the apparent reference made to abstract objects in discourse about the empirical world, including discourse in physics. If the thesis of ontological physicalism is held in full generality, so that it states that all things without exception are physical, then these references to abstract objects must be merely apparent. My account of the role of concepts and thoughts in empirical discourse could still be endorsed, but only in the context of a more general endorsement of fictionalism about abstract objects. A less stringent view would be that legitimation by application of a domain of abstract objects shows that discourse ontologically committed to these objects is no more problematic than purely physical discourse and is consistent with the original motivations for ontological physicalism. On this more relaxed view, my account of the empirical application of the apparatus of concepts and thoughts could be accepted without qualification.

Chapter 5

1. Though, of course, the normative character of concepts is likely to be the ultimate source of these problems, according to a theorist who believes in senses.

2. Compare the many subvarieties of causal explanation compatible with David Lewis's view (1986b) that to give a causal explanation of an event is to give some information about its causal history.

3. For emphasis on the nonnaturalistic character of this part of Descartes's thought, see Stroud 1977.

4. At a similar point in my exposition in Peacocke 1990a, p. 61, quotation marks came to be placed around a characterization of Millikan's position, even though the contained material is not from any of her texts. I apologize and hope that the characterization in the text here is more accurate.

5. Strictly, I should also take into account objects on which the thinker has a causal impact but that need not causally affect him. This addition is needed throughout the arguments below. I do not include it, because it complicates them but does not alter their conclusions.

6. See the later chapters of Millikan 1984. The problem of reduced content developed here for mental states can equally be developed for the theory of linguistic meaning that Millikan develops in that book.

7. In their formulations, neither Millikan nor Papineau is explicitly concerned with the level of sense. Indeed, Millikan is explicitly concerned with the level of reference (1986, 66). But the problem of reduced content still arises if we consider only the level of reference. In brief, the same arguments will show that "all" (for instance) will have a narrower semantic value on the teleological account than it intuitively possesses or has on a realist's account: it will not involve objects (or a condition on first-level functions or properties that concerns objects) outside those having a causal impact on the thinker.

8. Though I have this disagreement with Millikan, I should emphasize a major point of agreement with her. In recent developments of her position (1990), Millikan appeals to facts about historical explanation to exclude Kripkean "quus"-like descriptions of purpose and content. In the positive account I give below, causal explanation also plays a crucial role in excluding such unwanted contents, but it does so in the context of a nonteleological theory.

9. This claim about what is primitively compelling would need revision for a very sophisticated thinker (different from most of us) for whom (*n plus m*) *is k* is answerable to the truth of

If (there exist n x)Fx and (there exist m x)Gx and not (there exists x)(Fx and Gx), then (there exist k x)(Fx or Gx)

(or some modalization thereof). For such a thinker, the theory below should be modified as follows: all the points below in the text apply to her *pari passu*, but now they are applied to the form of the principle involving numerical quantifiers, rather than to the arithmetical principles and transitions discussed below.

10. Why haven't I developed the option of answering the question about semantic value by using the claim that the fact that, say,

(18 plus s(64)) is s(18 plus 64)

explains the subject's impression that these two quantities are equal? The point of this option would be to insist that what explains certain selected impressions involving the concept *plus* is a fact involving the function *addition*, and not any constructivist segment of it. I do not think it is incorrect to say this, but I do doubt that one can legitimately use the point at this stage in the argument. I take it that we are not accepting a Gödel-like account of a quasi-perceptual faculty whose states are caused by numbers. If we are not, then cases in which we say that an arithmetical fact explains an impression will be (among others) those in which the subject has a proof of the fact in question. But the proof will rely on some axioms, and we have to say in turn what is involved in the arithmetical facts explaining the subject's impression of the truth of these axioms. It seems that at this point we have to rely on an account like SV/*plus*.

11. The additional premise mentioned three paragraphs back is essential in arguing for these points. If someone could grasp the concept *plus* without finding the appropriate instances primitively compelling, then the considerations just canvassed would not establish that *plus* as used by him has a certain semantic value or has certain normative liaisons.

12. Here I prescind from indexicality; taking it into account affects only the formulation of the point, not its force.

13. Stephen Schiffer (1987, 178) raises a question essentially the same as that asked above about the putative concepts C and C'. Of the question whether someone could mean C rather that C' in the given circumstances, he writes that it is "just like" the problem of the empirical adequacy of these two theories about the explanation of sense experience: the theory that sense experience is caused by material objects of familiar sorts and the theory that sense experience is caused by an evil demon. From my standpoint the case of meaning is very different from Schiffer's case of the explanation of sense experience. What makes the difference is the principle that the nature of concepts is to be elucidated in terms of what it is to grasp them. This makes the failure of supervenience in the meaning case unacceptable. But presumably few today (and certainly not Schiffer) would say that the existence and nature of external physical objects is to be elucidated in terms of sense experiences of them. This difference between the cases raises the issue of how much room in logical space there is for Schiffer's favored combination of ontological physicalism and sentential dualism. The issue merits extended independent discussion. It is pressing for one, like Schiffer, who is skeptical of the possibility of supervenience without reduction.

14. At this point we have to consider a linguistic expression rather than a concept. If there really is a concept that the thinker is employing, it must be significant in the sense that there must be some condition for something to be its referent.

Chapter 6

1. See, for example, the interesting papers Goldman 1989 and Heal 1986. I think that this is one of several issues on which not enough theoretical options are acknowledged in the literature on belief.

2. Here I differ from Mellor (1977) and Rosenthal (1989, 1990). I am instead at one with the commitments of Williams (1977, 83), where he remarks that a proposition that is "evident" (i.e., believed if true) may nevertheless refer to an unconscious state, since the belief may be unconscious too.

3. The qualification is not explicit in Evans 1982, but he certainly allowed that I may sometimes ascribe a belief to myself on the same grounds that I ascribe it to others, and that this possibility is an essential component of the concept (1982, 226).

4. Some of Burge's points nevertheless apply beyond the self-verifying cases. This is true of his point that we discriminate our thoughts from others that we would have on, say, Twin Earth simply by thinking those thoughts (1988, 656).

5. For further discussion of the limits of the category of self-verifying attitudes, see Boghossian 1989, 20–22.

6. For other examples of the connection, see the discussion of knowledge of instances of logical principles in Peacocke 1987, 177–178, and the final chapter of Peacocke 1986b.

7. This is essentially part (b) of the second conjecture of Peacocke 1987, 178. That essay draws a distinction between "attributional" and "direct" accounts of concepts: the former give attribution conditions, the latter give normative properties of concepts. But by the claims of the preceding chapter, the possession condition determines the normative properties of a concept. This allows the reference to direct accounts in the second conjecture to be replaced with mention of a possession condition.

8. For an argument to the conclusion that knowledge of logical principles is an example of this general phenomenon, see Peacocke 1987. Another example of essentially the same phenomenon is a thinker's knowledge that an object falls under a shape concept, when (a) his judgement is suitably based on a perceptual experience with a nonconceptual representational content by which that concept is in part individuated (as in chapter 3), and (b) his perceptual mechanisms are functioning properly in actual and nearby possible circumstances. I say "essentially the same phenomenon" because in the perceptual case the necessary caveats in (b) go beyond what is present in the case of belief. But the reference to an experience of the sort mentioned in the possession condition for the shape concept is still crucial.

9. I should not leave the impression that Wright's account is without resources at this point. One possibility would be for him to develop the line that the contents of the first-order attitudes of language-using creatures are not the same as those of nonlinguistic creatures. If he also held an expression-based account of conscious belief, it would then be open to him to hold that the first-order beliefs about the world held by language-using creatures do have contents specific to language-using creatures who ascribe beliefs to themselves. This position might be, but need not be, combined with the view that there are no interesting possession conditions for the concepts of language-using creatures. The argument will then continue.

10. Stephen Schiffer (1987, 77) considers whether we can say that in asserting "Ralph believes that flounders snore," a speaker asserts that Ralph is in a belief state that has the same content as the belief state the speaker himself would be in if he were to utter "Flounders snore" sincerely and assertively. The proposal is adapted from a well-known suggestion developed by Stephen Stich (1983, chapter 5). As Stich notes, the germ of the proposal can be found in Quine (1960, section 45), who in turn acknowledges a debt to Davidson. Schiffer raises objections to the proposal, objections showing that it cannot work without explicit reference to the content of the sentence "Flounders snore." I agree with Schiffer's objections and his diagnosis. But if we have a working notion of conceptual content—a supposition that Schiffer and Stich would, of course, not accept— then Schiffer's objections would not apply to the more limited goal of using a similar proposal to build a bridge out from first-person ascriptions of belief with a given content to third-person ascriptions. The possibility of doing so seems to me to be the core of what is right in Stich's idea.

11. "Vico nowhere, so far as I know, fully or exactly explains the way in which men understand other men. . . . He does not account for our knowledge of other selves . . . by invoking the language of sympathy, or analogical reasoning. . . . That has been left to his interpreters. He rests his case on his conviction that what men have made, other men, because their minds are those of men, can always, in principle, 'enter into'" (Berlin 1976, 27).

12. Goldman (1989, 182) writes, "Simulation assumes a prior understanding of what state it is that the interpreter ascribes to [the ascribee]." On the formulation of the simulation account in the text, only understanding of first-person ascriptions is presup-

posed. There is no circularity in principle in using this understanding to elucidate third-person ascriptions. There is also a question about the use of the notion of a belief state employed by Goldman in this quotation. He may not intend it to be read in any theoretically committed fashion. But if we distinguish between the state and the concept, then the account of what belief *states* are is not something the simulation account should be providing. It is already provided by the kind of theory given in chapter 4. The simulation theory is aiming rather at an account of the concept when applied in the third person. However, it will be clear from what follows that I am in agreement with one of Goldman's conclusions, that "there is little hope of treating 'M is ascribed (or ascribable) to **S** on the basis of simulation' as constitutive of '**S** is in M'."

13. For an excellent exposition and critique of simulation accounts of folk psychology, see Stich and Nichols (1992). Their criticisms are complementary to those developed here. Their criticisms treat either cases in which the subject is wrong about his own beliefs in hypothetical circumstances or cases in which the subject, like a young child, has only a partial grasp of folk pyschology (however it is characterized). The criticisms developed here apply to cases in which a mature subject is right about his own beliefs in hypothetical cases. Though Stich and Nichols are naturally read as treating simulation accounts as theories of the state of belief, rather than as part of a theory of the concept, their points are still germane to the latter. For, as always, we have to provide a determination theory for any possession condition for belief that makes reference to simulation inferences, and the Stich and Nichols examples bear on the plausibility of the truth conditions for belief ascriptions that result from the natural determination theory for a simulation-based possession condition for the concept of belief.

14. Since the possession conditions for many basic concepts will make reference to perceptual experience, appreciating correctly the role of many beliefs will involve possessing some conception of others' experiences. This is another of the points at which consciousness is inextricably intertwined with these issues.

Chapter 7

1. For a classical statement of this conception, see Turing 1950. Turing there emphasizes those "functions of the mind" that are "operations which we can explain in purely mechanical terms," and he clearly held that "the whole mind is mechanical" (pp. 454–455). His conception of what mechanism has to involve is now superseded. He identified machines with digital computers. I take it as clear that there is a sense in which the explanations appropriate for a connectionist system are still mechanical.

2. There is more to be said about these cases. Although the form of the transition in the case of conjunction (and that of *plus*) is not conceptualized, arguably it is something of which the thinker is aware, and awareness of it is influential in causing him to find the relevant transition compelling. It is a good question whether this awareness of the form is possible without the thinker having the means for expressing the transition in an outer language. If it is not possible, the mental representations whose properties explain the thinker's meeting the possession condition must also stand in appropriate relations to these outer expressions.

3. In the case in which the personal-level state is itself a role state, the subrational realization will be a state that realizes that role. But this requirement applies even when a state is not wholly individuated by its role.

4. On the importance of counterfactuals to claims of causal relevance, see LePore and Loewer 1987.

5. A more general treatment should consider analogues of this requirement in the other special sciences.

6. There is here an obvious parallel, and a connection, with Dennett's (1978) discussion of the way in which artificial intelligence accounts can explain the presence of intelligence and comprehension by positing devices of lesser intelligence and lesser understanding.

7. If the possession condition for a concept gives the requirements for mastery of the concept, then we must acknowledge that often we attribute attitudes to others using a concept even though the other does not meet its possession condition. In a case of partial grasp of a concept, there is a further kind of norm to which the thinker is answerable: that he defer to the correct judgements of those with greater mastery of the concept. This phenomenon certainly undermines any identification of possession conditions with attribution conditions (see section 1.4). It also undermines the view that all norms characteristic of the attribution of concepts are somehow fixed directly just by the possession condition. But it does not undermine the core of the Simple Account. When a thinker has an incomplete or incorrect grasp of some concept, there will be a specification of what it is to have such an incomplete or incorrect grasp. A subpersonal psychology can still explain why the thinker makes the transitions involved in meeting that specification of an incomplete or incorrect grasp.

8. In formulating the Ratification Thesis, I have been much helped by the discussion in Wright 1980, chapter 11.

9. I do not mean that when the explaining conditions are met, the corresponding judgement will be made, without exception. Anything from sudden distraction to neural failures can produce a gap. I take it, though, that there are apparently explanatory principles in psychology. What matters here is that the explaining conditions obtained from a possession condition can function as the explaining conditions in such an explanatory principle. How such explanatory principles work, however, remains in need of a great deal of clarification. See Schiffer 1991 and Fodor 1991.

10. This applies to the account in Pettit 1990. What he there calls the "inclinations" of the thinker in response to a set of initial examples are treated case by case. Pettit could, though, easily modify the theory there to take into account the explanation of the inclinations without losing any of the desirable features of his discussion.

Chapter 8

1. Newton did suggest possible experiments for confirming hypotheses about the relations of objects to absolute space. But positive outcomes to these experiments support rather the postulation of a neo-Newtonian space-time (see Sklar 1974, 202–206). Sklar describes the objections to Newtonian space-time as "verificationist" (p. 206). If the arguments of this chapter are sound, one can make these objections without a commitment to verificationism. A theory of neo-Newtonian space-time also has features that may be questioned on content-theoretic grounds. In particular, it allows for the non-Leibnizian possibility that the entire material universe might have been differently located. Whether this too is excluded by the nonverificationist theory I will be developing depends on its consequences for the transworld identity of locations. It is certainly not immediately excluded by the arguments presented here.

2. I write "seemingly" because it is not at all clear that one who requires verification in principle can acknowledge the possibility of setups in which something is actually the case, but if he were to investigate, then the investigation itself would cause it not to be the case. I do not know an adequate verificationist solution to this problem.

3. Certainly the three-tier model I offered in chapter 5 of Peacocke 1986b and natural variants thereof do not make this requirement.

4. The Discrimination Principle is a less loaded label for what in *Thoughts* (1986b) I called "manifestationism."

5. Another application of the point is found in Evans 1985a. More applications and a general formulation are in Peacocke 1983, chapter 3, "The Tightness Constraint."

6. The three-tier model in Peacocke 1986b also purports to be a model of grasp of a content that respects the Discrimination Principle but is not verificationist.

7. See Peacocke 1986b, chapter 5.

8. "Noninferential" here requires at least that the subject is not discriminating what are in fact the light gray objects by experiencing them to have some property **P** other than a shade of gray and then inferring from the premise that an object has **P** to the conclusion that it has a certain shade of gray.

9. The "prima facie" is to cover inattentiveness, compartmentalization, and the host of other qualifications that must be present in any such constraint on radical interpretation.

10. Further below, I in effect address the position of an extreme theorist who (1) introduces a notion of "intentional" sameness of experience, as allegedly distinct from qualitative sameness of experience, and (2) acknowledges the constitutive anchor for intentional sameness but not for qualitative sameness.

11. I have described the constitutive point as showing how the Discrimination Principle is met for our actual concepts of color experience. But the argument so far could be accepted without accepting this principle. As an anonymous referee once pointed out, so far the argument relies only upon the incompatibility of the extreme position with the constitutive point. It is against the determined defender of the extreme position (see below) that the Discrimination Principle is indispensable.

12. To suppose that any outcome of the Michelson and Morley experiment could show anything about absolute location is analogous to making this supposition about extreme spectrum inversion: that we can discover whether another's spectrum is inverted, in the sense of the extreme theorist, relative to our own by investigating whether he is in the same brain states as us when looking at the same object. But such investigations can tell us nothing about inversion on the extreme conception, since on that conception, correlations of brain states and experiences may vary wildly from individual to individual.

13. For more details, see van Fraassen 1980, 49–50. As he notes, he there follows Poincaré.

14. The restriction to sentences free of logical constants is necessary. Take "Every material object has some absolute location." This comes out true outright under the conditions of the example, but it is not necessarily equivalent to a condition not mentioning absolute location.

15. I am presuming that the phenomenon of vague predicates is to be distinguished from that of indeterminacy.

16. The possibility of knowing what the other judges relies on the distinction between employing a mode of presentation and referring to it. Also see Peacocke 1981, 191.

17. Would Wittgenstein have accepted this reading of the private-language argument as relying on the Discrimination Principle? It seems certain that he would have disliked its whiff of systematic theory. Yet he himself seems to give arguments that veer close to, or even enter, the territory ruled by the Discrimination Principle. In section 271 of the *Investigations* he considers a spurious hypothesis: "'Imagine a person whose memory could not retain *what* the word "pain" meant—so that he constantly called different things by that name—but nevertheless used the word in a way fitting in with the usual symptoms and presuppositions of pain'—in short he uses it as we all do. Here I should like to say: a wheel that can be turned though nothing else moves with it, is not part of

the mechanism." What is a wheel that is not part of the mechanism? Presumably it is one that is not engaged with anything else that, for Wittgenstein, would be in a positive account, meeting the Discrimination Principle, of grasp of the predicate "is in pain." I conjecture that besides the private-language argument, many other arguments in the history of philosophy that have been taken as relying on verificationist assumptions can more fruitfully be construed as relying only on the Discrimination Principle. Kant's arguments against the illusions of rational psychology provide another example. A more recent case is provided by Dennett's felt need in *Consciousness Explained* to classify himself as a verificationist, albeit as an urbane verificationist (1991, 461). The techniques of this chapter allow Dennett to make his points without any commitment to verificationism. It is noteworthy that one of the examples Dennett gives in support of verificationism, the unintelligibility of a dispute over whether the universe is right side up or upside down, is equally classified as spurious by the Discrimination Principle.

18. It seems clear that the biconditional in Dummett's definition of reducibility is too weak to capture his intended notion. Finding an appropriate strengthening is a delicate matter. I have tried not to trade on this complication in these remarks.

Appendix A

1. I oversimplify. In Peacocke 1987, I emphasized that the fact that there are no *other* clauses in a possession condition may help to determine semantic value. The rest of the text should strictly be reformulated to accommodate this case.

2. A set of clauses will be selected when the relevant semantic value depends on all of them. An example would be the extension of a first-level concept in a thought in which a second-level concept is applied to it.

Appendix B

1. I take it that there is a "slight inaccuracy" because the thinker is not required, for possession of the concept *F*, to have fundamental Ideas of all the *G*s there are. Evans makes a point that entails that it is not required (pp. 108–109). I will not be trading on this marginal point.

2. I say "in the most basic case" because perceptual-demonstrative thought about an object seems to me to be possible even when the subject's experience misrepresents the location of the perceived object. I defend that view in Peacocke 1991c. For a statement of a contrary view, see McDowell 1990. If McDowell is right, the qualification "in the most basic case" can be removed. If, however, it is necessary, the sense in which experiences that give genuine perception of the location of their objects are more basic is as follows. Perceptual experiences that misrepresent the location of their objects are possible against a background of experiences for which this is not generally the case, but not conversely.

3. Kripke in lectures as yet unpublished; Johnston 1987.

References

Anderson, John. 1983. *The Architecture of Cognition.* Cambridge: Harvard University Press.

Anscombe, G. E. M. 1981. "On Sensations of Position." In her *Metaphysics and the Philosophy of Mind: Collected Papers,* vol. 2. Minneapolis: University of Minnesota Press.

Ayer, Alfred. 1946. *Language, Truth, and Logic.* 2nd ed. London: Gollancz.

Baker, Gordon, and Hacker, Peter. 1984. *Language, Sense, and Nonsense.* Oxford: Blackwell.

Barwise, Jon, and Perry, John. 1983. *Situations and Attitudes.* Cambridge: MIT Press.

Berlin, Isaiah. 1976. *Vico and Herder.* London: Hogarth Press.

Block, Ned. 1986. "Advertisement for a Semantics for Psychology." *Studies in the Philosophy of Mind.* Midwest Studies in Philosophy, vol. 10. Minneapolis: University of Minnesota Press.

Boghossian, Paul. 1989. "Content and Self-Knowledge." *Philosophical Topics* 17:5–26.

Burge, Tyler. 1974. "Demonstrative Constructions, Reference, and Truth." *Journal of Philosophy* 71:205–223.

Burge, Tyler. 1979. "Individualism and the Mental." *Studies in Metaphysics.* Midwest Studies in Philosophy, vol. 4. Minneapolis: University of Minnesota Press.

Burge, Tyler. 1988. "Individualism and Self-Knowledge." *Journal of Philosophy* 85:649–663.

Campbell, John. 1986. "Conceptual Structure." In *Meaning and Interpretation,* ed. C. Travis. Oxford: Blackwell.

Campbell, John. 1987. "Is Sense Transparent?" *Proceedings of the Aristotelian Society* 88:273–292.

Campbell, John. 1989. Review of Evans 1985. *Journal of Philosophy* 86:156–163.

Chisholm, Roderick. 1970. "Reply to Strawson's Comments." In *Language, Belief, and Metaphysics,* ed. H. Kiefer and M. Munitz. New York: SUNY Press.

Churchland, Patricia Smith, and Sejnowski, Terrence. 1989. "Neural Representation and Neural Computation." In *Neural Connections, Mental Computation,* ed. L. Nadel, L. Cooper, P. Culicover, and R. Harnish. Cambridge: MIT Press.

Churchland, Paul. 1979. *Scientific Realism and the Plasticity of Mind.* Cambridge: Cambridge University Press.

Craig, Edward. 1990. "Advice to Philosophers: Three New Leaves to Turn Over." *Proceedings of the British Academy* 76:265–281.

Crimmins, Mark, and Perry, John. 1989. "The Prince and the Phone Booth: Reporting Puzzling Beliefs." *Journal of Philosophy* 96:685–711.

Cussins, Adrian. 1990. "The Connectionist Construction of Concepts." In *The Philosophy of Artificial Intelligence,* ed. M. Boden. Oxford: Oxford University Press.

Davidson, Donald. 1984. "The Inscrutability of Reference." In *Inquiries into Truth and Interpretation.* Oxford: Oxford University Press.

Davies, Martin. 1986. "Tacit Knowledge, and the Structure of Thought and Language." In *Meaning and Interpretation,* ed. C. Travis. Oxford: Blackwell.

Davies, Martin. 1987. "Tacit Knowledge and Semantic Theory: Can a Five Per Cent Difference Matter?" *Mind* 96:441–462.

Davies, Martin. 1989. "Tacit Knowledge and Subdoxastic States." In *Reflections on Chomsky,* ed. A. George. Oxford: Blackwell.

Davies, Martin. 1991. "Concepts, Connectionism, and the Language of Thought." In *Philosophy and Connectionist Theory*, ed. D. Rumelhart, W. Ramsey, and S. Stich. Hillsdale, N.J.: Erlbaum.

DeBellis, Mark. Forthcoming. *Music and Conceptualization*. New York: Cambridge University Press.

Dennett, Daniel. 1969. *Content and Consciousness*. London: Routledge.

Dennett, Daniel. 1978. *Brainstorms*. Cambridge: MIT Press.

Dennett, Daniel. 1991. *Consciousness Explained*. Boston: Little, Brown and Co.

Diamond, Cora. 1976. *Wittgenstein's Lectures on the Foundations of Mathematics, Cambridge, 1939*. Sussex: Harvester.

Dretske, Fred. 1981. *Knowledge and the Flow of Information*. Cambridge: MIT Press.

Dummett, Michael. 1956. "Nominalism" *Philosophical Review* 65:491–505.

Dummett, Michael. 1973. *Frege: Philosophy of Language*. London: Duckworth.

Dummett, Michael. 1975. "What Is a Theory of Meaning?" In *Mind and Language*, ed. Samuel Guttenplan. Oxford: Oxford University Press.

Dummett, Michael, 1976. "What Is a Theory of Meaning? (II)." In *Truth and Meaning*, ed. G. Evans and J. McDowell. Oxford: Oxford University Press.

Dummett, Michael. 1978a. "What Do I Know When I Know a Language?" Stockholm: Universitas Regia Stockholmensis.

Dummett, Michael. 1978b. *Truth and Other Enigmas*. London: Duckworth.

Dummett, Michael. 1981. *The Interpretation of Frege's Philosophy*. London: Duckworth.

Dummett. 1987. "Reply to John McDowell." In *Michael Dummett: Contributions to Philosophy*, ed. B. Taylor. Dordrecht: Nijhoff.

Evans, Gareth. 1982. *The Varieties of Reference*. Oxford: Oxford University Press.

Evans, Gareth. 1985a. "Identity and Predication." In *Collected Papers*, ed. Antonia Phillips. Oxford: Oxford University Press.

Evans, Gareth. 1985b. "Molyneux's Question." In *Collected Papers*, ed. Antonia Phillips. Oxford: Oxford University Press.

Field, Hartry. 1974. "Quine and the Correspondence Theory." *Philosophical Review* 85:200–228.

Field, Hartry. 1981. "Mental Representation." In *Readings in Philosophy of Psychology*, vol 2, ed. N. Block. London: Methuen.

Field, Hartry. 1989. *Realism, Mathematics, and Modality*. Oxford: Blackwell.

Fisher, John. 1974. "Knowledge of Rules." *Review of Metaphysics* 28:237–260.

Fodor, Jerry. 1987. *Psychosemantics*. Cambridge: MIT Press.

Fodor, Jerry. 1991. "You Can Fool Some of the People All of the Time, Everything Else Being Equal: Hedged Laws and Psychological Explanations." *Mind* 100:19–34.

Fodor, Jerry, and LePore, Ernest. 1992. *Holism: A Shopper's Guide*. Oxford: Blackwell.

Frege, Gottlob. 1953. *The Foundations of Arithmetic*. Trans. J. L. Austin, 2nd ed. Oxford: Blackwell.

Frege, Gottlob. 1979. "Logic." In *Posthumous Writings*, ed. H. Hermes, F. Kambartel, and F. Kaulback, trans. P. Long and R. White. Oxford: Blackwell.

Godwin-Austen, R. 1965. "A Case of Visual Disorientation." *Journal of Neurology, Neurosurgery, and Psychiatry* 28:453–458.

Goldman, Alvin. 1989. "Interpretation Psychologized." *Mind and Language* 4:161–185.

Goodman, Nelson. 1977. *The Structure of Appearance*. 3rd ed. Dordrecht: Reidel.

Gregory, Richard. 1970. *The Intelligent Eye*. London: Weidenfeld and Nicolson.

Hayes, Patrick. 1979. "The Naive Physics Manifesto." In *Expert Systems in the Micro-electronic Age*, ed. D. Michie. Edinburgh: Edinburgh University Press. Reprinted in *The Philosophy of Artificial Intelligence*, ed. Margaret Boden (Oxford: Oxford University Press).

Heal, Jane. 1986. "Replication and Functionalism." In *Language, Mind, and Logic*, ed. J. Butterfield. Cambridge: Cambridge University Press.

Jackendoff, Ray. 1989. "What Is a Concept, That a Person May Grasp It?" *Mind and Language* 4:68–102.

Jackson, Frank, and Pettit, Philip. 1988. "Functionalism and Broad Content." *Mind* 97:381–400.

Johnston, Mark. 1987. "Is There a Problem about Persistence?" *Proceedings of the Aristotelian Society*, suppl. vol. 61: 107–135.

Keil, Frank. 1989. "Spiders in the Web of Belief: The Tangled Relations between Concepts and Theories." *Mind and Language* 4:43–50.

Kopfermann, H. 1930. "Psychologische Untersuchungen über die Wirkung zweidimensionaler köperlicher Gebilde." *Psychologische Forschung* 13:293–364.

Kripke, Saul. 1982. *Wittgenstein on Rules and Private Language*. Oxford: Blackwell.

LePore, Ernest, and Loewer, Barry. 1987. "Mind Matters." *Journal of Philosophy* 84:630–642.

Lewis, David. 1980. "Psychophysical and Theoretical Identifications." In *Readings in the Philosophy of Psychology*, vol. 1, ed. Ned Block. Cambridge: Harvard University Press.

Lewis, David. 1983a. "How to Define Theoretical Terms." In Lewis's *Philosophical Papers*, vol. 1. New York: Oxford University Press.

Lewis, David. 1983b. "Individuation by Acquaintance and by Stipulation." *Philosophical Review* 92:3–32.

Lewis, David. 1986a. *On the Plurality of Worlds*. Oxford: Blackwell.

Lewis, David. 1986b. "Casual Explanation." In his *Philosophical Papers*, vol. 2. New York: Oxford University Press.

Lieberman, A., and Studdert-Kennedy, M. 1978. "Phonetic Perception." In *Handbook of Sensory Physiology*, vol. 8, ed. R. Held, H. Leibowitz, and H.-L. Teuber. Berlin: Springer.

McDowell, John. 1986. "Functionalism and Anomalous Monism." In *Actions and Events: Essays on the Philosophy of Donald Davidson*, ed. E. LePore and B. McLaughlin. Oxford: Blackwell.

McDowell, John. 1987. "In Defense of Modesty." In *Michael Dummett: Contributions to Philosophy*, ed. B. Taylor. Dordrecht: Nijhoff.

McDowell, John. 1989. "One Strand in the Private Language Argument." *Grazer Philosophische Studien* 33–34:285–303.

McDowell, John. 1990. "Peacocke and Evans on Demonstrative Content." *Mind* 99:255–266.

McDowell, John. Forthcoming. *Mind and World*. The John Locke Lectures, delivered at Oxford University, 1991.

McGinn, Colin. 1989. *Mental Content*. Oxford: Blackwell.

McGinn, Colin. 1991. "Mental States, Natural Kinds, and Psychophysical Laws." In *The Problem of Consciousness: Essays Towards a Resolution.* Oxford: Blackwell.

Mach, Ernst. 1914. *The Analysis of Sensations* Chicago: Open Court.

Marr, David. 1982. *Vision.* San Francisco. Freeman.

Mellor, D. H. 1977. "Conscious Belief." *Proceedings of the Aristotelian Society* 78:87–101.

Millikan, Ruth. 1984. *Language, Thought, and Other Biological Categories.* Cambridge: MIT Press.

Millikan, Ruth. 1986. "Thoughts without Laws: Cognitive Science with Content." *Philosophical Review* 95:47–80.

Millikan, Ruth. 1990. "Truth Rules, Hoverflies, and the Kripke-Wittgenstein Paradox." *Philosophical Review* 99:323–353.

Nagel, Thomas. 1986. *The View from Nowhere.* New York: Oxford University Press.

O'Shaughnessy, Brian. 1980. *The Will.* Vol. 2. Cambridge: Cambridge University Press.

Palmer, Stephen. 1983. "The Psychology of Perceptual Organization: A Transformational Approach." In *Human and Machine Vision,* ed. J. Beck, B. Hope, and A. Rosenfeld. New York: Academic Press.

Papineau, David. 1987. *Reality and Representation.* Oxford: Blackwell.

Peacocke, Christopher. 1981. "Demonstrative Thought and Psychological Explanation." *Synthese* 49:187–217.

Peacocke, Christopher. 1983. *Sense and Content.* Oxford: Oxford University Press.

Peacocke, Christopher. 1986a. "Explanation in Computational Psychology: Language, Perception, and Level 1.5." *Mind and Language* 1:101–123.

Peacocke, Christopher. 1986b. *Thoughts: An Essay on Content.* Oxford: Blackwell.

Peacocke, Christopher. 1986c. "Analogue Content." *Proceedings of the Aristotelian Society,* suppl. vol. 60: 1–17.

Peacocke, Christopher. 1987. "Understanding Logical Constants: A Realist's Account." *Proceedings of the British Academy* 73:153–200.

Peacocke, Christopher. 1988. "The Limits of Intelligibility: A Post-verificationist Proposal." *Philosophical Review* 97:463–496.

Peacocke, Christopher. 1989a. "What Are Concepts?" In *Contemporary Perspectives in the Philosophy of Language,* vol. 2. Midwest Studies in Philosophy, vol. 14. Notre Dame, Ind.: University of Notre Dame Press.

Peacocke, Christopher. 1989b. "Possession Conditions: A Focal Point for Theories of Concepts." *Mind and Language* 4:51–56.

Peacocke, Christopher. 1989c. "Perceptual Content." In *Themes from Kaplan,* ed. J. Almog, J. Perry, and H. Wettstein. New York: Oxford University Press.

Peacocke, Christopher. 1989d. "When Is a Grammar Psychologically Real?" In *Reflections on Chomsky,* ed. A. George. Oxford: Blackwell, 1989.

Peacocke, Christopher. 1990a. "Content and Norms in a Natural World." In *Information, Semantics, and Epistemology,* ed. E. Villaneuva. Oxford: Blackwell.

Peacocke, Christopher. 1990b. "Philosophical and Psychological Theories of Concepts." Forthcoming in *Turing 1990,* ed. A. Clark and P. Millican.

Peacocke, Christopher. 1991a. "The Metaphysics of Concepts." In the centennial issue *Mind and Content,* ed. S. Blackburn and R. M. Sainsbury, of *Mind* 100:525–546.

Peacocke, Christopher. 1991b. "Proof and Truth." Forthcoming in *Realism and Reason*, ed. J. Haldane and C. Wright.

Peacocke, Christopher. 1991c. "Demonstrative Content: A Reply to John McDowell." *Mind* 100:123–133.

Peacocke, Christopher. 1992. "Scenarios, Concepts, and Perception." In *The Contents of Experience: Essays on Perception*, ed. T. Crane. Cambridge: Cambridge University Press.

Pears, David. 1987. *The False Prison*. Vol. 1. Oxford: Oxford University Press.

Pears, David. 1988. *The False Prison*. Vol. 2. Oxford: Oxford University Press.

Perenin, M.-T., and Vighetto, A. 1988. "Optic Ataxia: A Specific Disruption in Visuomotor Mechanisms."*Brain* 111:643–674.

Pettit, Philip. 1990. "The Reality of Rule-Following." *Mind* 99:1–22.

Pettit, Philip. 1991. "Realism and Response-Dependence." In the centennial issue *Mind and Content*, ed. S. Blackburn and R. M. Sainsbury, of *Mind* 100:587–623.

Prior, Arthur. 1967. "The Runabout Inference Ticket." In *Philosophical Logic*, ed. P. Strawson. Oxford: Oxford University Press.

Putnam, Hilary. 1970. "On Properties." In *Essays in Honor of Carl Hempel*, ed. N. Rescher. Dordrecht: Reidel.

Putnam, Hilary. 1974. "Comments on Wilfrid Sellars." *Synthese* 27:445–455.

Putnam, Hilary. 1988. *Representation and Reality*. Cambridge: MIT Press.

Putnam, Hilary. 1990. *Realism with a Human Face*. Cambridge: Harvard University Press.

Quine, Willard. 1953. "Two Dogmas of Empiricism." Reprinted in *From a Logical Point of View*. Cambridge: Harvard University Press.

Quine, Willard. 1960. *Word and Object*. Cambridge: MIT Press.

Quine, Willard. 1969a. "Propositional Objects." In *Ontological Relativity and Other Essays*. New York: Columbia University Press.

Quine, Willard. 1969b. "Ontological Relativity." In *Ontological Relativity and Other Essays*. New York: Columbia University Press.

Rorty, Richard. 1980. *Philosophy and the Mirror of Nature*. Oxford: Blackwell.

Rosenthal, David. 1989. *Thinking That One Thinks*. Report no. 11 of the Research Group on Mind and Brain. Zentrum für interdisziplinäre Forschung, University of Bielefeld, Bielefeld Germany.

Rosenthal, David. 1990. *Why Are Verbally Expressed Thoughts Conscious?* Report no. 32 of the Research Group on Mind and Brain. Zentrum für interdisziplinäre Forschung, University of Bielefeld, Bielefeld Germany.

Sainsbury, Mark. 1990. "Concepts without Boundaries." Department of Philosophy, King's College, London.

Schiffer, Stephen. 1987. *Remnants of Meaning*. Cambridge: MIT Press.

Schiffer, Stephen. 1990. "The Mode-of-Presentation Problem." In *Propositional Attitudes: The Role of Content in Logic, Language, and Mind*, ed. C. Anthony Anderson and J. Owens. CSLI Lecture Notes No. 20. Chicago: University of Chicago Press.

Schiffer, Stephen. 1991. "Ceteris Paribus Laws." *Mind* 100:1–17.

Sedivy, Sonia. 1991. *The Determinate Character of Perceptual Experience*. Ph.D. thesis, University of Pittsburgh.

Sellars, Wilfrid. 1968. *Science and Metaphysics: Variations on Kantian Themes.* London: Routledge.

Sellars, Wilfrid. 1974. "Meaning as Functional Classification." *Synthese* 27:417–437.

Shepard, Roger. 1981. "Psychophysical Complementarity." In *Perceptual Organization,* ed. M. Kubovy and J. Pomerantz. Hillsdale, N. J.: Lawrence Erlbaum Associates.

Shoemaker, Sydney. 1968. "Self-Reference and Self-Awareness." *Journal of Philosophy* 65:555–567.

Shoemaker, Sydney. 1970. "Persons and Their Pasts." *American Philosophical Quarterly* 7:269–285.

Shoemaker, Sydney. 1984. "The Inverted Spectrum." In *Identity, Cause, and Mind: Philosophical Essays.* Cambridge: Cambridge University Press.

Sklar, Lawrence. 1974. *Space, Time and Space-Time.* Berkeley: University of California Press.

Smolensky, Paul. 1986. "Neural and Conceptual Interpretation of PDP Models." In *Parallel Distributed Processing,* vol. 2, ed. J. McClelland, D. Rumelhart, and the PDP Research Group. Cambridge: MIT Press.

Stich, Stephen. 1978. "Beliefs and Subdoxastic States." *Philosophy of Science* 45:499–518.

Stich, Stephen. 1983. *From Folk Psychology to Cognitive Science.* Cambridge: MIT Press.

Stich, Stephen. 1990. *The Fragmentation of Reason.* Cambridge: MIT Press.

Stich, Stephen, and Nichols, Shaun. 1992. "Folk Psychology: Simulation or Tacit Theory?" Forthcoming in *Mind and Language.*

Stroud, Barry. 1977. *Hume.* London: Routledge.

Treisman, Anne, and Gelade, G. 1980. "A Feature-Integration Theory of Attention." *Cognitive Psychology* 12:97–136.

Treisman, Anne, and Schmidt, H. 1982. "Illusory Conjunctions in the Perception of Objects." *Cognitive Psychology* 14:107–141.

Turing, Alan. 1950. "Computing Machinery and Intelligence." *Mind* 59:433–460.

Tye, Michael. 1985. Review of Peacocke 1983. *Canadian Philosophical Reviews* 5:173–175.

Tye, Michael. 1991. *The Imagery Debate.* Cambridge: MIT Press.

Van Fraassen, Bas. 1980. *The Scientific Image.* Oxford: Oxford University Press.

Wellman, Henry. 1990. *The Child's Theory of Mind.* Cambridge: MIT Press.

Wiggins, David. 1968. "On Being in the Same Place at the Same Time." *Philosophical Review* 77:90–95.

Wiggins, David. 1980. *Sameness and Substance.* Oxford: Blackwell.

Wiggins, David. 1984. "The Sense and Reference of Predicates: A Running Repair to Frege's Doctrine and a Plea for the Copula." In *Frege: Tradition and Influence,* ed. C. Wright. Oxford: Blackwell.

Williams, Bernard. 1977. *Descartes: The Project of Pure Enquiry.* Harmondsworth: Penguin.

Wittgenstein, Ludwig. 1958. *Philosophical Investigations.* 3rd ed. Oxford: Blackwell.

Wittgenstein, Ludwig. 1961a. *Notebooks, 1914–1916.* Ed. G. von Wright and G. E. M. Anscombe. Trans. G. E. M. Anscombe. Oxford: Blackwell.

Wittgenstein, Ludwig. 1961b. *Tractatus Logico-philsophicus*. Trans. D. Pears and B. McGuinness. London: Routledge.

Wittgenstein, Ludwig. 1978. *Remarks on the Foundations of Mathematics*. 3rd ed. Ed. G. von Wright, R. Rhees, and G. E. M. Anscombe. Trans. G. E. M. Anscombe. Oxford: Blackwell.

Wittgenstein, Ludwig. 1980. *Philosophy of Psychology*. Vol. 1. Ed. G. E. M. Anscombe and G. von Wright. Trans. G. E. M. Anscombe. Oxford: Blackwell.

Wright, Crispin, 1980. *Wittgenstein on the Foundations of Mathematics*. London: Duckworth.

Wright, Crispin. 1983. *Frege's Conception of Numbers as Objects*. Aberdeen: Aberdeen University Press.

Wright, Crispin. 1988. "Why Numbers Can Believably Be: A Reply to Hartry Field." *Revue Internationale de Philosophie* 42:425–473.

Wright, Crispin. 1989a. "Wittgenstein's Later Philosophy of Mind: Sensation, Privacy, and Intention." *Journal of Philosophy* 86:622–634.

Wright, Crispin. 1989b. "Wittgenstein's Rule-Following Considerations and the Central Project of Theoretical Linguistics." In *Reflections on Chomsky*, ed. A. George. Oxford: Blackwell.

Wright, Larry. 1976. *Teleological Explanation*. Berkeley: University of California Press.

Index

Absolute space, 21, 200, 214–215, 217, 219
Access, epistemic, 159
𝒜(C) form
  and the concept of reference, 239 (n. 1)
  and the doctrine of showing, 52
  for indexicals, 11
  introduced, 6–9
  for local holisms, 10
  and modesty, 34–36
  for perceptual concepts, 89
  for perceptual demonstratives, 11
  and the Principle of Dependence, 6, 71
Actions, 91–97, 113
  basic, 94
  expectations about, 170
  success and failure of, 93
Acuity, perceptual, 63
Allen, Woody, 1–2
Anderson, John, 129
Anscombe, G. E. M., 92
Antirealism, 19, 36, 238 (n. 16). *See also* Constructivism; Verificationism
Artificial intelligence, 249 (n. 6)
Assertibility, 18–19
Ataxia, optic, 95
Attribution conditions, 27–33
Ayer, Alfred Jules, 201

Baker, Gordon, 191
Bare truth (Dummett), 49
  defined, 225, 239 (n. 4)
Barwise, Jon, 23, 238 (n. 13)
Behaviorism, 34–35, 143
Belief
  ascription of, 147, 155–164
  concept of, xii, 27, 147–176
  conscious, 152–154, 167, 175, 247 (n. 9)
  datum on conscious, 154–155
  first-person character of concept of, 164–165
  first-person knowledge of, 156–158
  functionalist theories of, 151
  hypothetical, 168
  illusions of, 158
  interaction with desire, 113
  putative, 114
  states, theory of, 148–149, 162, 166
  and truth, 25
  unconscious, 153–156, 175, 246 (n. 2)
  unintelligible, 165
Berlin, Isaiah, 247 (n. 11)
Bivalence, 18
Block, Ned, 243 (n. 6)

Blunt, Anthony, 153
Boghossian, Paul, 247 (n. 5)
Burge, Tyler, 29, 31, 64, 156, 238 (n. 17), 246 (n. 4)

Cambell, John, 239 (n. 2), 241 (nn. 4, 11)
Carnap, R., 229
Causal efficacy, 189–190
Causal explanation, 45, 56–57, 89, 127, 143, 145, 187, 245 (n. 2)
Chisholm, Roderick, 199, 215–216
Churchland, Patricia, 179
Churchland, Paul, 117
Cognitive maps, 78, 87, 90
Cognitive psychology, 128–129
Cognitive science, 3
Cognitive significance, 3, 30, 243 (n. 1)
Collingwood, R. G., 169
Computational psychology, 55, 180
Concept(s)
  acquisition of, 4, 178
  amodal, 86
  complex, 21–22
  of conjunction, 6–9, 12–14, 24, 35, 45, 47, 80, 107, 158–159, 183–184, 228
  demonstrative, 1, 10–12, 72, 83–85, 94, 97, 109, 126, 173–174
  distinctness of, 2
  as essentially concepts, 122
  first-person, 71–74, 85, 88
  hierarchy of, 139, 237 (n. 7)
  indexical, 1, 10–11, 73
  individuation of, simple account, 6
  intuitive identity conditions for, 2, 15
  and language dependence, 31
  Lincoln Plaza, 105, 108–112, 150, 185, 229
  as modes of presentation, 2
  natural-kind, 144
  not mental representations, 3
  not prototypes, 3
  observational, 14, 20, 61, 81, 107, 148, 164, 174, 183, 197, 233
  ontology of, xii, 5, 15, 40, 99–124 passim, 125–126
  open-endedness of, 39
  partial, 21
  partial grasp of, 41
  perceptual, xii, 61, 94, 97, 102, 109, 173–174
  philosophical and psychological theories of, xii, 177–197
  plus, 134–139, 183
  psychological, 20